THE DRIVE TO SUCCEED

Role Models of Motivation

Emerson Klees

Emerson Klees

Cameo Press, Rochester, New York

The Role Models of Human Values Series
*One Plus One Equals Three—Pairing Man / Woman Strengths:
Role Models of Teamwork* (1998)
*Entrepreneurs in History—Success vs. Failure: Entrepreneurial
Role Models* (1999)
Miniseries
Staying With It: Role Models of Perseverance (1999)
The Drive to Succeed: Role Models of Motivation (2002)
The Will to Stay With It: Role Models of Determination (2002)

Cameo Press
P. O. Box 18131
Rochester, New York 14618

Library of Congress Control Number 2002090008

ISBN 1-891046-02-0

Printed in the United States of America
9 8 7 6 5 4 3 2 1

Cover Design by Dunn and Rice Design, Inc., Rochester, NY

The images used herein, except for one on page 69 from
Crescent Books' *The Clip Art Book*, were obtained from IMSI's
MasterClips Collection, 1895 Francisco Blvd. East, San Rafael,
CA 94901-5506, USA.

THE ROLE MODELS OF HUMAN VALUES SERIES

"Example teaches better than precept. It is the best modeler of the character of men and women. To set a lofty example is the richest bequest a man [or woman] can leave behind."

Samuel Smiles

The Role Models of Human Values Series provides examples of role models and of lives worthy of emulation. The human values depicted in this series include teamwork, entrepreneurial ability, perseverance, motivation, and determination. Role models are presented in biographical sketches that describe the environment within which these individuals lived and worked and that delineate their personal characteristics.

These profiles illustrate how certain human values helped achievers reach their goals in life. We can learn from their lives to strengthen our own human values that are so important to our success and happiness. Each book in the series includes a prologue and / or introduction that highlights the factors contributing to these achievers' success.

The Drive to Succeed: Role Models of Motivation is the fourth book in the Role Models of Human Values Series. The first three books in the series are *One Plus One Equals Three— Pairing Man / Woman Strengths: Role Models of Teamwork, Entrepreneurs in History—Success vs. Failure: Entrepreneurial Role Models*, and *Staying With It: Role Models of Perseverance*.

PREFACE

"Every great example takes hold of us with the authority of a miracle and says to us, 'If ye had but faith, ye, also, could do the same things.'"

Abraham Jacobi

The Drive to Succeed: Role Models of Motivation is the overarching book in a three-book miniseries within the Role Models of Human Value Series. The other two books in the miniseries are *Staying With It: Role Models of Perseverance* and *The Will to Stay With It: Role Models of Determination*. The miniseries contains ninety-five biographical sketches.

This book provides role models of motivation worthy of emulation through profiles of twenty-five highly motivated men and women. The biographical sketches represent five categories of motivation:

- **D**ual careers—individuals who had sufficient motivation to have two careers in parallel
- **R**esilience—people who rebounded from serious handicaps or setbacks
- **I**nevitable winners—men and women whose cause was so just that ultimate victory was inevitable
- **V**alue unappreciated—achievers whose worth was recognized late in life or posthumously
- **E**nergetic endurers—those who overcame substantial physical limitations to succeed

These achievers inspire us by their example.

Profiles of Emmeline and Christabel Pankhurst, Carrie Chapman Catt, and Alice Paul are reprinted from *The Women's Rights Movement and the Finger Lakes Region;* those of Gail Borden and Al Neuharth are reprinted from *Entrepreneurs In History—Success vs. Failure: Entrepreneurial Role Models.*

4

TABLE OF CONTENTS

Page No.

Table of Contents

Page No.

NOTES	290
BIBLIOGRAPHY	305
INDEX	312

PROLOGUE

"Talent isn't enough. You need motivation—and persistence, too: what Steinbeck called a blend of faith and arrogance."

Leon Uris

Most of us do not achieve our potential in life. Many factors prevent us from making optimal use of our abilities. Lack of motivation is one factor, insufficient determination is another, and not persevering conscientiously toward our goals is a third. Many of our achievements in life go unrecognized. A number of factors contribute to this; lack of talent is not necessarily one of them. Nine-year-old Victoria Harris of Rochester, New York asked her grandmother how talent is recognized:

> When I was a young girl, I asked my grandmother, a concert pianist, "How are artists discovered?"

> "Most aren't, Vicki dear," was her surprising reply. "Talent is everywhere. And discovery is part talent, part whom you know, and part being at the right place at the right time. The greatest voices remain unlistened to, the greatest books lie in attics gathering dust, the greatest film scripts never reach the screen."[1]

Obviously, the talented people referred to by Victoria Harris's grandmother had the motivation and the discipline to become talented singers, authors, and scriptwriters. Her grandmother identified three factors involved in the discovery of talent:
- Existence of talent in the first place
- Whom you know
- Being at the right place at the right time

Other factors are important as well. Marketing is another element of success. We should all do some self-marketing. We feel more strongly about our personal achievements than anyone else does, even a parent, teacher, or mentor. However, we should be careful not to become obnoxiously self-serving.

Obviously, to be motivated toward a goal, a goal must exist. Understanding the importance of goals and goal-setting is a prerequisite to comprehending the quality of motivation, as well as determination and perseverance, in moving toward a particular goal.

The establishment of attainable goals is critical to the success of any endeavor; however, its importance is not universally understood, perhaps because we have an inherent fear of failure to reach our goals or because we don't know how to establish reasonable goals. Some people think that the more that they want something, the greater the disappointment if they don't get it. They are afraid to risk failure and the accompanying anguish.

Another fear in setting goals is fear of success. Lack of self-confidence and self-esteem are usually factors in this case. Individuals may feel, subconsciously, that they don't deserve the success for which their conscious self is striving. These individuals tend to magnify the difficulty of attaining a particular goal and may become discouraged from setting a goal.

Also, some people subscribe to the philosophy of "whatever will be, will be." These individuals think that everything is preordained. The viewpoint that fate dictates the outcome of everything that they do is a demotivating influence in setting goals.

Their fatalistic outlook prevents them from extending themselves in setting goals and from expending effort in the attainment of those goals. Setting an attainable goal is the first step in achieving success. The goal may be a "reach" goal or a "stretch" goal, but it must be attainable.

In the opinion of William James:

> Man alone, of all the creatures on earth, can change his own pattern; man alone is the architect of his own destiny ... men can alter their lives by altering their minds.... I have no doubt whatever that most people live whether physically, intellectually, or morally, in a very restricted circle of their potential being ... the so-called "normal man" of commerce, so to speak, the healthy Philistine, is a mere extract from the potentially recognizable individual he [or she] represents, and we all have resources to draw upon of which we do not dream.... Compared to what we ought to be, we are only half awake. Our fires are dampened, our drafts checked. We are making use of only a small part of our mental and physical resources.[2]

James thought that the average person used approximately ten percent of his or her potential.

According to Ivan Trefremov, Russian author and scholar:

> As soon as modern science gave us some understanding of the structure and work of the human brain we were struck by its enormous reserve capacity. Man, under average conditions of work and life, uses only a small part of his thinking equipment.... If we were able to force our brain to work only half its capacity we could, without any difficulty whatever, learn forty languages, memorize the large *Soviet Encyclopedia* from cover to cover, and complete the required courses of dozens of colleges.[3]

Trefremov seems overly optimistic; however, his estimate is not orders of magnitude different from that of William James. Hopefully, the profiles of achievers in this book will motivate us to use more than ten percent of our capabilities.

INTRODUCTION

"Motivation is the word used to describe those processes that can (a) arouse and instigate behavior, (b) give direction or purpose to behavior, (c) continue to allow behavior to persist, and (d) lead to choosing or preferring a particular behavior. A motive is any condition within a person that affect his / her readiness to initiate or continue any activity or sequence of activities."[4]

Raymond J. Wlodkowski

Abraham Maslow, who describes his theory of motivation in *Motivation and Personality,* outlines a hierarchy of needs in which people are concerned with needs at a higher level only when those at a lower level have been satisfied. The lowest level is the fulfillment of physiological needs, such as those for physical survival—food, drink, and shelter. The second level comprises safety needs, such as security, stability, protection, and freedom from anxiety and fear. Next are belongingness and love needs, topped by esteem needs.

Esteem needs, including those for self-esteem, self-respect, and the esteem of others, are divided into two categories. The first category involves the way that we see ourselves, e.g., the desire for strength, achievement, mastery, independence, and freedom. The second category concerns the way others see us, e.g., status, fame, dominance, recognition, and appreciation.

Maslow describes the need for self-actualization when all of the lower level needs are met:

> Even if all these needs are satisfied, we may still often (if not always) expect that a new discontent and restlessness will soon develop, unless the individual is doing what he, individually, is fitted for. A musician must make music, an artist must paint, a poet must write,

if he is to be ultimately at peace with himself. What a man can be, he must be. He must be true to his own nature. This need we may call self-actualization....

It refers to a man's desire for self-fulfillment, namely, the tendency for him to become actualized in what he is potentially. This tendency might be phrased as the desire to become more and more what one idiosyncratically is, to become everything that one is capable of becoming.

The specific form that these needs will take of course varies greatly from person to person. In one person it may take the form of the desire to be an ideal mother, in another it may be expressed athletically, and in still another it may be expressed in painting pictures or in inventions.[5]

The twenty-five achievers described in this book were successful individuals. In the words of Maslow, they were self-actualized people who found their niches in life and excelled in their endeavors. We can learn from them. We will know that we have arrived, in driving toward success, from Mrs. A. J. Stanley's description:

He has achieved success who has lived well, laughed often, and loved much; who has gained the respect of intelligent men and the love of little children; who has filled his niche and accomplished his task; who has left the world better than he found it, whether by an improved poppy, a perfect poem, or a rescued soul; who has never lacked the appreciation of the earth's beauty or failed to express it; who has looked for the best in others and given the best he had; whose life was an inspiration; whose memory is a benediction.[6]

CHAPTER 1

DUAL CAREERS

"To find a career [or endeavor] to which you are adapted by nature, and then to work hard at it, is about as near to a formula for success and happiness as the world provides. One of the fortunate aspects of this formula is that, granted that the right career has been found, the hard work takes care of itself. Then hard work is not hard at all."

Mark Sullivan

Chapter 1 provides examples of achievers who had sufficient motivation to have two parallel careers. One career was not enough for them. In some cases, the second career began as a hobby and then grew into a full-fledged second line of work.

William Herschel, discoverer of the planet Uranus, is an example of this. He began as an accomplished musician who stargazed in his off hours. He became more serious about astronomy when he realized that lenses and telescopes of the quality he needed could not be purchased. He had to make his own.

Oliver Wendell Holmes was a medical doctor who achieved overnight success as a young man with his poem *Old Ironsides,* which he wrote in one evening in 1830. The *USS Constitution* (*Old Ironsides*), a fixture in Boston harbor, was scheduled to be scrapped. His poem saved the historic vessel from destruction. Later, he became a popular literary figure with his *Autocrat of the Breakfast Table* series.

Alexander Borodin was a medical doctor who dropped the practice of medicine to become a research chemist and medical administrator. He composed music in his spare time. However, the demands of his position as an administrator severely restricted his time to compose. His masterpiece, *Prince Igor*, was incomplete at the time of his death. It was finished by his colleagues, Alexander Glazunov and Nikolai Rimsky-Korsakov.

Anton Chekhov, a practicing medical doctor who struggled with tuberculosis for much of his adult life, was also a highly regarded playwright. He found time to plan and pay for three schools and to provide books for other schools, including one in his hometown of Taganrog, Russia.

Louis Auchincloss was a prolific author of fiction while working full time for a high-powered Manhattan law firm. He left the practice of law to write full time; however, his productivity in writing novels was the same as when he worked in a law practice. He missed the law and returned to it after a two-year break.

Most of us are sufficiently challenged by one career. These individuals were motivated to work at two endeavors and were successful at it.

WILLIAM HERSCHEL (1738-1822) Musician and Astronomer

"If a man has a talent and cannot use it, he has failed. If he has a talent and uses only half of it, he has partly failed. If he has a talent and learns somehow to use the whole of it, he has gloriously succeeded and won a satisfaction and a triumph few men ever know."

Thomas Wolfe, *The Web and the Rock*

In April 1781, news circulated around the world that a new planet had been discovered. People had difficulty comprehending the idea of a seventh planet in our solar system. Until that time, Mercury, Venus, Earth, Mars, Jupiter, and Saturn were perceived to be the only planets in our galaxy. Verification by other astronomers was required before the new planet could be accepted by the scientific community. First, they had to ascertain that it was not a star or comet. A star remains fixed in the heavens, and a comet is usually distinguished by a tail.

A planet moves in an orbit around the sun. In order to verify that the sighting was a planet, readings were taken over a short period of time to confirm its solar orbit, and the planet that became known as Uranus was entered into science books. This discovery was made by a musician whose avocation was astronomy, not by an astronomer.

William Friedrich Herschel was born on November 15, 1738 in Hanover, Germany, one of four sons in a family of ten children. William's father, Isaac Herschel, was a professional musician who played oboe in the royal band and later was the bandmaster. Young William went to school at the military fort in Hanover where his studies included English, French, mathematics, and philosophy. He became an accomplished musician proficient on the oboe and violin as well as the harpsichord and organ.

Astronomy was Isaac Herschel's hobby, but he could not

afford a telescope; most of his stargazing was done with the naked eye. For his sons, he identified constellations: Draco, the Dragon; Gemini, the Twins; Orion, the Hunter; and Ursa Minor, the Little Bear. William became familiar with the rudiments of astronomy at an early age through this interest of his father.

The Seven Years' War began in 1775. The King of England and Ireland, King George II, was also the Elector of Hanover. William was assigned to a regimental band in Hanover as the German state mobilized. In the spring of 1756, the Hanover Guards with their regimental band were ordered to England to bolster the defense of the British Isles. William made friends in Kent and improved his fluency in English. He returned to Hanover with the Foot Guards in late 1756.

During the following years, the Guards saw action defending Hanover against the French. William returned home to find Hanover overrun by the French army and French soldiers quartered in their house. His mother gave him enough money to escape to England. When he ran out of money, he found a job as a music copyist. He moved to Durham to teach militiamen to become members of a military band and then became a concertmaster in Leeds, where he taught, conducted, and composed.

Herschel maintained his interest in astronomy even though music occupied his long workdays. In 1758, he observed Halley's comet. He was impressed that this comet, identified by Sir Edmund Halley, was the same comet that appeared over England in 1066, the year of the Norman conquest, and that this was its eighth appearance since then. Upon completion of his workday, he read books on astronomy, mathematics, and optics. A career in music was not enough for him; he was motivated to do more. He needed additional challenges like those provided by astronomy.

Herschel first became an organist in Halifax and then at the Octagon Chapel in Bath, which had become a fashionable resort after the reconstruction of the old Roman baths. He gave music lessons to supplement his income and still had time to compose.

In 1762, Isaac Herschel died. William Herschel invited his sister, Caroline, to come to England and live with him in Bath. Caroline had always wanted to take singing lessons, but her father would not permit it. Her brother promised that she could take singing lessons if she joined him in Bath, which she did in 1772.

Until this time, Herschel had not been able to afford to buy telescopes; however, he had found a two and one-half-foot telescope that he could rent. When he reached the point in his career that he could afford to buy telescopes, the sizes he wanted were not always available. He made his own. At an early stage, he realized that his manual dexterity as a musician was invaluable in lens grinding and telescope construction.

Herschel learned how to grind and polish a speculum, a metal reflecting surface made out of a copper-tin alloy. It was the precursor of the glass mirror used today. Caroline took singing lessons, as planned, and had many opportunities to perform; nevertheless, she was pressed into service assisting her brother with his astronomy projects. Herschel found a shopkeeper who sold him the necessary tools for his work as well as some partially finished reflectors. Herschel had to make some of the tools, including a lathe for turning eyepieces.

Herschel was aware that there were two types of telescopes: refracting, those used by Galileo and other early astronomers, and the reflector, the type used by Newton, sometimes called a Newtonian telescope. In the refracting telescope, an objective lens collects the light and forms the image while an eyepiece at the other end magnifies the image. The eye of the observer is in line with the telescope and the object, such as a comet, planet, or star. In the reflecting telescope, light is collected by a concave collecting surface (mirror), reflected onto another mirror, and then reflected onto the eyepiece. The eye of the observer is perpendicular to the line between the telescope and the object.

One of the first telescopes constructed by Herschel was a five and one-half-foot refracting telescope. An early reflecting telescope had an aperture of four and one-half inches and provided a magnification of 222 times. Although he experimented with ten-foot and twenty-foot telescopes, most of his early success was with a seven-foot telescope of Newtonian design. He had difficulty maintaining the rigidity of the cylinder over the length of the twenty-foot telescope.

One evening in December 1779, Herschel was outside of his house using his seven-foot telescope when Dr. William Watson, Fellow of the Royal Society of London, stopped by and expressed an interest in the telescope. The next morning, Dr. Watson visited Herschel again, this time in the company of Dr. Wevil Maskelyne, the Royal Astronomer. This was the beginning of a lifetime friendship between Watson and Herschel. Watson's principal scientific interest was marine biology; astronomy was his hobby.

Herschel's work began to attract attention. Two of his papers were read at a meeting of the Royal Society. Measurement of the elevations of the moon was the subject of one paper; the periodical star in Collo Ceti was the subject of the other. He began to study "double stars" and submitted a catalog of 229 stellar "pairs" to the Royal Society.

Herschel spent many hours outside viewing the heavens. Cold weather did not bother him; haziness that obscured his view did. He began a disciplined, systematic approach to sky-watching. He recorded the position of the stars down to the fourth magnitude each night using a lens that magnified 222 times.

On Tuesday evening, March 13, 1781, Herschel was following this organized approach when he made the discovery of a lifetime. Of that experience, he wrote, "In examining the small stars in the neighborhood of H Geminorium, I perceived one that looked visibly larger than the rest; being struck with its uncommon appearance, I compared it to H Geminorium and the small star in the quarter between Auriga and Gemini, and finding it so much larger than either of them, I suspected it to be a comet."[7]

Herschel replaced the 222-power eyepiece with a 460-power eyepiece and then with a 932-power eyepiece, which caused the object to go out of focus. He looked for a tail on the object to see if it were a comet; however, if it were a comet coming toward him, he would not be able to see the tail. He continued his nightly viewings and recorded its position each night. Four days later, he verified that the object had moved west to east in almost circular orbit and was acting like a planet.

Herschel sent a preliminary report entitled "Account of a Comet" to the Royal Society. Dr. Watson replied that Lexell at St. Petersburg and Laplace in France were following its path across the sky. Herschel calculated that the new planet, if it were a planet, must be about four times the size of Earth. While he waited for further verification, he compiled a second catalog of double stars.

In a second letter, Watson told Herschel that, although evidence was still far from complete, it appeared that he had discovered a planet. Watson invited him to Greenwich along with his "famous" seven-foot telescope and eyepieces.

The Royal Society was impressed that one of Herschel's sets of lenses had a magnification of 5400 times. Dr. Watson observed that the new planet had been discovered many times before, but viewers did not realize what they were seeing. Herschel's determined, systematic approach allowed him to identify the new planet. The discovery of Uranus could not be considered an "accident."

In Herschel's words:

> In the regular manner I examined every star in the heavens, not only of that magnitude but many far inferior, it was that night its turn to

be discovered.... Had business prevented me that evening, I must have found it the next, and the goodness of my telescope was such that I perceived its visible planetary disc as soon as I looked at it.[8]

Previously, Sir John Flamstead, the famous English astronomer, had recorded it as a star of the sixth magnitude. Herschel noted that Flamstead did not have the high-magnification eyepieces that he had.

Dr. Watson told Herschel that Lemonnier was the unhappiest astronomer alive. He had observed Uranus thirteen times and had thought it was a fixed star, despite the fact that four of his observations were on consecutive nights. He did not detect the change in position.

In December 1781, Herschel was invited to join the Royal Society of London by Dr. Maskelyne. Also that year, he was awarded the Copley gold medal for his "discovery of a new and singular star." In presenting the award, Sir Joseph Banks said:

In the name of the Royal Society I present to you this gold medal, the reward which they have assigned to your successful labors, and I exhort you to continue diligently to cultivate those fields of science which have produced to you a harvest of so much honor. Your attention to the improvement of telescopes has already amply repaid the labor which you have bestowed upon them; but the treasures of the heavens are well known to be inexhaustible.... Who knows what new rings, new satellites, or what nameless and numberless phenomena remain behind, waiting to reward future industry and improvement?[9]

Herschel was invited to an audience with King George III at Buckingham Palace. The interview went well; the King granted him a stipend of two hundred pounds a year to continue his efforts in astronomy. The newly discovered planet was named Uranus for Urania, the goddess of astronomy. Years later, Herschel discovered the moons of Uranus: Titania and Oberon.

Herschel was offered an additional annual stipend of fifty pounds for the assistance of his sister, Caroline, who was spending more time stargazing than singing. She was successful with her career in music; she performed as soloist at the Octagon Chapel singing works by Handel and Purcell.

These stipends required Herschel and Caroline to move to Datchet, near Windsor Castle, to be near the King. Work on a new twenty-foot reflecting telescope, which required scaffolding to support it, began immediately upon their arrival in Datchet. Herschel stood on the scaffolding, looked through the eyepiece, and called down readings for Caroline to record. He attacked his astronomy challenge with greater enthusiasm now that he was a full-time astronomer and no longer had to support himself as a musician.

The house in Datchet was in a swampy area that was damp and unhealthy for Herschel and Caroline, who spent hours every night out of doors peering at the sky. They moved to Slough, which was even closer to Windsor Castle. Mary Pitt, the landlady's daughter and the widow of John Pitt, was one of their first friends in Slough. Herschel and Mary established a close relationship and were married on May 8, 1783.

In 1785, Herschel began to build a forty-foot telescope at Slough that took two years to construct and employed forty workmen during the peak period. He used his twenty-foot telescope until the larger one was completed and lent his seven-foot telescope to Caroline. While Herschel was in Göttingen, Germany installing a telescope that he had helped to build, Caroline discovered a comet. Her brother was proud of her; she was the first woman in history to discover one.

Herschel continued to receive honors, including a letter from Benjamin Franklin informing him that he had been elected a member of the American Philosophical Society for his discovery of Uranus. Also, Oxford University awarded him an honorary degree, and the University of Glasgow honored him with a Doctor of Laws degree. In addition, he was elected a member of the Imperial Leopold Academy of Science.

On March 7, 1792, a son, John, was born to Mary Pitt Herschel. John Herschel attended Cambridge University, became an astronomer, and, like his father before him, was elected President of the Astronomical Society. He expanded his father's study of double stars, including writing a paper, "On the Investigation of the Orbits of Revolving Double Stars." In 1831, he was knighted by King William IV.

William Herschel also added to the knowledge of nebulae and star clusters. He documented his findings on 2,500 nebulae over a four-year period, producing catalogs for the Royal Society. He proved that the brightness of a star was not directly proportional to its distance from the earth, as had been assumed.

In 1811 Herschel presented to the Royal Society his comprehensive paper, "A Construction of Heavens," based on thousands of viewings. In 1816, he was made a Knight of the Royal Hanoverian Guelphic Order by the Prince of Wales, later to become King George IV. In 1820, Herschel was elected the first President of the Astronomical Society, later renamed the Royal Astronomical Society.

Herschel died in his sleep on August 25, 1822 at the age of eighty-three. He had distinguished himself in two careers. Caroline, who was credited with having discovered eight comets, returned to Hanover after the death of her brother. Her arrangement of Herschel's discoveries of nebulae and star clusters into a single catalog earned her the Gold Medal of the Astronomical Society. Caroline Herschel, who always credited her brother for her honors, died in Hanover in 1848.

OLIVER WENDELL HOLMES (1809-1894) Professor of Medicine, Essayist, and Poet

"Holmes knows more about my courses this winter than any-one—he spent three or four months in the hospital as apothe-cary.... He can tell you much that is interesting. Do not mind his apparent frivolity, and you will find that he is intelligent and well informed. He has the true zeal."[10]

Dr. James Jackson, Harvard Medical School professor

Dr. Oliver Wendell Holmes, Professor of Anatomy and Physiology at the Harvard Medical School, was sufficiently motivated to be an essayist and poet as well as a medical doc-tor. He was the father of Oliver Wendell Holmes, Jr., Associate Justice of the U.S. Supreme Court and author of *The Common Law*.

In his medical career, Oliver Wendell Holmes helped to found a small medical college in Boston and was the author of two dissertations that won Boyleston Prizes. As a poet, he achieved overnight celebrity status at the age of twenty-one with his poem *Old Ironsides*. He was also known for his poems *The Wonderful One-Hoss Shay* and *The Chambered Nautilus*.

In addition, Holmes was the author of a series of articles in the *Atlantic Monthly* magazine entitled *The Autocrat of the Breakfast Table*, followed by *The Professor at the Breakfast Table* and *The Poet at the Breakfast Table*, all of which had wide readership on both sides of the Atlantic Ocean. After his death, a writer for *Punch* magazine described him as "a fin-ished scholar, poet, wit, and good fellow." One career was not enough to consume all of his energy.

Oliver Wendell Holmes, the oldest son of Dr. Abiel Holmes and Sally Wendell Holmes, was born on August 29, 1809 in Cambridge, Massachusetts. Sally Wendell was the daughter of Judge Oliver Wendell, member of the Council and the Senate of the Commonwealth of Massachusetts. The Wendells were related to most of the movers and shakers in Boston: the Cabots, Eliots, Jacksons, Olivers, Phillipses, and Quinceys.

Abiel Holmes, a graduate of Yale College, was a Calvinist minister who took life very seriously. Sally tried to make him a less serious person. She asked, "Abiel, why are you afraid to be happy? Surely the Lord loves a cheerful heart! ... People don't have to be dreary to be good."[11] Abiel was a poet and author of four books, including *American Annals: A Chronological History of America,* for which he received acclaim in the *London Quarterly Review*. He was awarded an honorary degree from Edinburgh University for his literary endeavors.

Young Holmes, who grew up across the street from the red brick "Harvard Colleges," began his schooling at the Dame Prentiss School in Cambridge in 1815. In September 1819, Holmes entered Mr. Bigelow's School in Cambridgeport, a mile from his home. Reformer Margaret Fuller was in his class, and Richard Dana, author of *Two Years Before the Mast,* attended the Bigelow School while Holmes was there.

In 1824, Holmes enrolled at the Phillips Academy at Andover. He was small for his age and was the target of bullies; one bully in particular used to kick him repeatedly under the desk. Holmes told him that he was a bully and that when he was a man, he would be a murderer. Sadly, his prophecy was accurate.

In 1825, Holmes entered Harvard College. Samuel Francis Smith, who later composed "My Country, 'Tis of Thee," was a classmate, and future U.S. Senator Charles Sumner was in the class behind him. At the time, Harvard was incorporating the system of elective studies used in German universities, where philosophy and science were taught by men like Hegel and Schelling. He took courses in French and Italian and signed a petition to add science courses, such as chemistry and mineralogy, instead of additional courses in Greek.

Holmes wrote poetry at Harvard; he improved his writing skills under the tutelage of Edward Tyrrel Channing, who had taught Ralph Waldo Emerson and Henry David Thoreau. Channing's influence motivated Holmes to write:

> Channing, with his bland, superior look,
> Cold as a moonbeam on a frozen brook,
> While the pale student, shivering in his shoes,
> Sees from his theme the turgid rhetoric ooze.[12]

Holmes was elected to the Hasty Pudding Club and became the club's poet. His cousin, Wendell Phillips, who later became a staunch abolitionist, was president of the club. Holmes wrote poetry for an annual and became the class poet. When he graduated, he was still unsure about what to do with his life; however, he thought that writing might not be an appropriate career for him. He graduated seventeenth in a class of fifty-nine, which was good enough to be elected to Phi Beta Kappa.

Holmes knew what he did not want to be—a minister like his father. Abiel was going through a difficult phase. He stayed with his strict Congregationalist ways at a time when Unitarianism was becoming popular. Holmes said, with his father in mind, "I might have been a minister myself for aught I know if (a certain) clergyman had not looked and talked so like an undertaker."[13]

Holmes chose the law as a profession and enrolled at the new Harvard Law School to study under Judge Story. He found it rough going from the first and struggled for four months. It was too impersonal a subject for him. In a letter to a friend, he wrote: "I am sick at heart of this place and almost everything connected with it. I know not what the temple may be to those who have entered it, but to me it seems very cold and cheerless about the threshold."[14]

In September 1830, Holmes became an overnight celebrity. The frigate *USS Constitution* (*Old Ironsides*), with her record of victories, was about to be scrapped. The federal government declared that she was taking up valuable space in Boston harbor, and, furthermore, the cost of her maintenance was too high. The people of Boston, in fact the whole county, wanted to save the historic vessel. Holmes went up to his room and wrote a poem that came very easy to him:

> Ay, tear her tattered ensign down!
> Long has it waved on high,
> And many an eye has danced to see
> That banner in the sky....
> Oh, better that her shattered hulk
> Should sink beneath the wave;
> Her thunders shook the mighty deep,
> And there should be her grave;
> Nail to the mast her holy flag,
> Set every threadbare sail,
> And give her to the god of storms,
> The lightning and the gale![15]

. . . .

Holmes's poem was printed the next day in the Boston *Daily Advertiser* and was distributed in Boston, Washington, D.C., and around the country. The *Constitution* was saved, and Oliver Wendell Holmes became a household name.

Holmes knew that he could not earn a living by writing; he had to make a career decision. He considered studying medicine, and he discussed this choice with his brother-in-law, Dr. Parsons. Holmes was seeing a young lady, Amelia Jackson of Bedford Place, Boston. Not only was he attracted to her, but she liked his poetry. He discussed his career decision with Amelia's uncle, Dr. James Jackson, a Harvard Medical School professor, who convinced him to study medicine.

Holmes wrote a letter to a friend describing his activities: "I have been quietly occupying a room in Boston, attending medical lectures, going to the Massachusetts Hospital, and slicing and slivering the carcasses of better men and women than I ever myself am or likely to be. It is a sin for a puny little fellow like me to mutilate one of your six-foot men as if he were a sheep, but Vive le Science!"[16]

Holmes decided to broaden his medical education by studying in Europe. Paris, with the foremost physicians in the world, was the place to go at the time. He studied abroad for two and a half years with the great physicians of Europe. He learned three principles in Paris: "Not to take authority when I can have facts; not to guess when I can know; and not to think a man must take physic [medication] because he is sick."[17] He also visited England, Germany, Holland, Italy, and Scotland. Chevalier's microscope was just coming into use; Holmes brought one home as a gift for Dr. Jackson.

In December 1835, Holmes returned to Cambridge. He received his M.D. degree in 1836. The new Dr. Holmes established his medical practice in Boston; it grew very slowly, partly because he did not aggressively seek patients and also because his reputation as a poet did not add to his standing as a physician. In addition, his youthful appearance did not inspire confidence.

In 1836, Holmes won the Boyleston prize for his paper, "Intermittent Fever in New England." The following year, he followed that recognition with a first prize for his paper on neuralgia and a second prize for his paper, "Direct Exploration in Medical Practice." He became a popular physician because of his cheerfulness and his bedside manner as well as his practice of prescribing a minimum of medication.

In late 1836, Holmes published a small book of his poems that included *Old Ironsides*. Also in the volume was his best-known poem, *The Last Leaf*, which was inspired by Herman Melville's grandfather, a participant in the Boston Tea Party and a veteran of the Revolutionary War. The poem described Major Melville in his old age, when he was barely able to move about:

> ... a crook is in his back
> And a melancholy crack
> In his laugh.
>
> I know it is a sin
> For me to sit and grin
> At him here;
> But the old three-cornered hat,
> And the breeches, and all that,
> Are so queer!
>
> And if I should live to be
> The last leaf upon the tree
> In the spring,
> Let them smile, as I do now,
> At the old forsaken bough
> Where I cling.[18]

In later years, Abraham Lincoln, born in the same year as Holmes, memorized the poem.

Holmes's younger brother, John, who attended Harvard Law School, was as quiet as Oliver was talkative. John's advice to his brother was that if he could find a girl who could shut him up, he should marry her without hesitating. Holmes knew just the girl to shut him up, Amelia Jackson. They were married on June 15, 1840 in King's Chapel in Boston and moved into their own home near Boston Commons.

On August 29, 1841, their first son, Oliver Wendell Holmes, Jr., was born. He was to become Chief Justice of Massachusetts, author of *The Common Law*, and Associate Justice of the U.S. Supreme Court. He lived a long and productive life and became better-known than his father. He was known for his strong determination to follow his own judge-

31

ment no matter how strong an opposition was pitted against him.

In 1838, Dr. Holmes accepted a position as Professor of Anatomy at Dartmouth College, requiring him to be in residence from August through October each year. Also, with three other physicians, he established a medical school on Tremont Street in Boston. He continued to write about medical subjects. He was concerned with the high fatality rate due to childbed fever. Approximately half the young women who entered the hospital in good health were dying in childbirth.

In 1843, Dr. Holmes delivered his paper, "The Contagiousness of Puerperal Fever," before the Boston Society for Medical Improvement. He believed that childbirth fever was a uterine infection carried from patient to patient by doctors and their assistants. His paper was controversial, but he persisted and had it reprinted in 1855. Dr. Ignaz Semmelweiss, who was on the same track in Vienna, became interested in the subject in 1844-46.

Dr. Holmes taught at the Harvard Medical School for thirty years as Professor of Anatomy and Physiology. He suggested the name "anaesthetic" for the first use of sulphuric ether at the Massachusetts General Hospital in 1846. In his later years, he was one of the founders of the American Medical Association. His classes were popular because he interspersed humor with his presentation of the subject matter. He once pointed to the underside of a cadaver and said, "These, gentlemen, are the tubersities of the ischia, on which man was designed to sit and survey the works of creation."[19]

In parallel with his medical career, Dr. Holmes wrote on other than medical subjects, including contributions to the *Atlantic Monthly*, which was edited by his friend, James Russell Lowell. Lowell asked Holmes to contribute a humorous article each month. Holmes reached back to his experiences at a boarding house when he was in medical school, and the result was the popular *Autocrat of the Breakfast Table*.

At about this time, Holmes's poem *The Chambered*

Nautilus was published, including the verses:

> Thanks for the heavenly message brought by thee,
>> Child of the wandering sea,
>> Cast from the lap, forlorn!
> From thy dead lips a clearer note was born
> Than ever Triton blew from wreathed horn!
>> While on mine ear it rings,
>> Through the deep caves of thought
> I hear a voice that sings.
> Build thee more stately mansions, O my soul,
>> As the swift seasons roll!
>> Leave thy low-vaulted past!
> Let each new temple, nobler than the last,
> Shut thee from heaven with a dome more vast,
>> Till though at length art free,
> Leaving thine outgrown shell by life's unresting sea![20]

Holmes's poem, *The Deacon's Masterpiece, or the Wonderful 'One-Hoss-Shay,'* was a celebration of the fall of Calvinism. The deacon's shay, or two-wheeled carriage, analogous to the beliefs of Calvinism, was well-constructed, supposedly durable, and not in need of maintenance. However, when its useful life was over, it fell apart all at once, as Calvinism did when new knowledge caused its beliefs to be questioned. Later in life, when he received honorary doctorates from Cambridge University and Edinburgh University, Holmes was asked by cheering students if he had come in his "one-hoss-shay."

Holmes's *Autocrat* series was followed by *The Professor at the Breakfast Table* in 1860 and *The Poet at the Breakfast Table* in 1872. Also, he wrote three novels: *Elsie Venner, The Guardian Angel,* and *A Mortal Antipathy;* they were not critical or popular successes. He was a humorist who always had a ready quip, such as "I was always patient with those who thought well of me."[21] He viewed himself as a dilettante, a literary amateur. A critic said of him: "Life was too agreeable for him to take the trouble to become an artist."[22]

Dr. Oliver Wendell Holmes died on October 7, 1894 at the age of eighty-five, in the company of his daughter, Fanny, who was very attentive to him in his later years. As he had requested, a memorial tablet in King's Chapel lists his achievements: "Teacher of Anatomy, Essayist, and Poet," along with an inscription from Horace's *Ars Poetica: Miscuit Utile Dulci* (He mingled the useful with the pleasant).

ALEXANDER BORODIN (1834-1887) Medical Doctor and Composer

"So far as the traditional symphonic form is concerned, the master craftsman of the last quarter of the nineteenth century was not Brahms but Borodin."

Philip Heseltine, *Daily Telegraph*, October 13, 1923

Any discussion of the music of Alexander Borodin includes a description of the music of the "Kuchka" (the mighty handful), also called the "circle of five" and the "invincible band," successors to Michael Glinka and Alexander Dargomijsky in moving Russian composers away from European forms of music, particularly German and Italian styles. They encouraged Russian composers to base their work on Russian music, folk songs, and Slavonic folklore.

The "mighty handful" included:
- Mili Balakirev, piano virtuoso, leader, organizer, and mentor of the group
- Alexander Borodin, scientist and composer known for the opera, *Prince Igor; Symphony No. 1 in E flat major;* and many pieces of chamber music
- César Cui, publicist of the group and composer of *Andante and Scherzo for violin and piano, Tarantella,* and the operas, *Ratcliffe* and *The Caucasian Prisoner*
- Modest Mussorgsky, musical innovator and giant of Russian opera, known for *Boris Godunov*
- Nikolai Rimsky-Korsakov, master of orchestration and composer of *Scheherazade*

Alexander Borodin, the illegitimate son of Luka Gedianov, a Georgian prince, was born in St. Petersburg on October 31, 1834. His mother was Avdotya Konstantinovna Antonova, the "daughter of a soldier," an understanding and liberal-minded woman; she loved her son and spoiled him but ensured that he received a good education.

Borodin displayed a talent for music at an early age; at the age of nine, he composed *Polka in D minor*. He took flute lessons as well as piano lessons and played piano duets with a friend while being introduced to the symphonies of Haydn, Mendelssohn, and Beethoven. He attended symphony concerts regularly. Borodin taught himself how to play the cello. In 1847, he composed *Trio in G major for two violins and a cello* in addition to *Concerto for flute and piano*. Two years later, he composed two piano pieces that were reviewed in the local newspaper and subsequently published.

In parallel with his interest in music, Borodin developed a fascination for chemistry that started by making fireworks and doing small chemical experiments. By the age of thirteen, he had built a chemical laboratory in his home where he conducted electrotype experiments and made his own watercolors. He read many scientific journals and textbooks and became absorbed in the subject of chemistry.

In 1850, Borodin passed his entrance examination to the college in St. Petersburg with high marks and became an external student at the Academy of Physicians. He studied with Nikolai Zinin, the "grandfather of Russian chemistry," who became his mentor. Borodin took courses in anatomy, botany, crystallography, and zoology; his interest in botany lasted a lifetime. He was near the top of his class in every subject and graduated "cum laude" in 1855.

Borodin's musical activities paralleled his efforts in chemistry. He attended many concerts and played in many quartets and chamber ensembles. Also, he continued to compose, including *String Trio*, *String Quintet in F minor with two cellos*, and *Scherzo in B flat minor for piano*. The academic community questioned his interest in music. Professor Zinin told him: "Mr. Borodin, it would be better if you gave less attention to writing songs. I have placed all my hopes in you, and want you to be my successor some day. You waste too much time thinking about music. A man cannot serve two masters."[23]

In 1856, Borodin was appointed medical practitioner at the Second Military Hospital. While serving at the hospital, he completed his first piece of scientific research, a paper on hydrobenzamide, and worked on his dissertation, "On the Like Action of Arsenic and Phosphoric Acids on the Human Organism." In 1858, he graduated from the Academy of Physicians as a Doctor of Medicine.

Borodin met Modest Mussorgsky one evening in the orderly room while working at the military hospital. Mussorgsky, the duty officer, and Borodin, the duty doctor, struck up an easy conversation and became friends. They met subsequently at parties at the home of Dr. Popov, the senior doctor at the hospital. Mussorgsky, a ladies man, impressed the young women by sitting down at the piano and playing selections from *La Traviata* and *Il Trovatore*.

In 1857, Borodin went abroad for the first time; he attended an international ophthalmological congress in Brussels and traveled to France, Germany, and Italy. In 1859 in St. Petersburg, Borodin again met Mussorgsky, who had resigned from the army because "his special interest was music, and it was somewhat complicated to combine a military career with music." Mussorgsky knew Balakirev, the leader of the "circle of five," and was familiar with the new developments in the world of music, including the work of Schumann.

Mussorgsky played his *B flat major Scherzo* for Borodin. When Mussorgsky played the Trio, he said: "'Look, this is oriental,' and I [Borodin] was astonished by this strange kind of music, which was like nothing I had ever heard before. I won't pretend that I was very much taken with it; I was a little perplexed by the novelty of it at first. But when I had heard a little more of it, I soon developed a taste for it."[24]

Borodin's musical development was spurred by "the strange new elements" introduced to him by Mussorgsky. This development was made easier because Michael Glinka, the model for the circle of five, was Borodin's favorite composer.

Glinka, known for his essays on Russian nationalism, wrote the operas, *A Life for the Czar* and *Russlan and Ludmilla*, in which he moved away from the influence of Italian operas, including weak plots, set numbers (stand-alone solos, duets, and chorus pieces), and prima-donna divas. Dargomijsky, the other predecessor of the circle of five, followed Glinka's lead in his opera, *Russalka*, in departing from Italian and German styles. Dargomijsky, an experimenter with the opera form, took this approach even further with his opera, *L'Hôte de Pierre*, based on Alexander Pushkin's play.

In October 1859, Borodin was sent to Europe as a delegate of the Academy of Physicians to gain experience before taking up the position of Professor of Chemistry upon his return. Borodin was moving on from his medical career to become a scientific researcher and teacher in the field of chemistry. He traveled to Heidelberg, where he was scheduled to work in Bunsen's laboratory; it didn't work out, and he did his research in the laboratory of Emil Erlenmeyer.

In 1860, he published a paper, "The Investigation of Certain Derivatives of Benzine." He toured Switzerland with Zinin and fellow chemist Dmitri Mendeleev. Later, the three chemists attended an international congress of chemists in Karlsruhe, where Borodin, despite his youth, was elected a member of the congressional committee. Later, he traveled to Italy and then resided in Paris, where he attended lectures by Claude Bernard and Louis Pasteur and joined the Chemical Society of Paris.

Borodin kept up his musical activities in Germany. He played the flute and the cello, as well as quintets, string quartets, and piano duets. Also, while in Heidelberg, he composed the *B minor cello Sonata*, the *G minor string Trio,* the *D major piano Trio*, and the *D minor string Sextet*.

In May 1861, Borodin met his future wife, the accomplished pianist Catherine Protopopova, who had come to Heidelberg for treatment of tuberculosis. Their mutual love of music cemented their relationship. Catherine remembered this early relationship: "We were often together. His day was usually arranged as follows: From five in the morning till five in the afternoon he was in his laboratory; from five till eight we went for a stroll in the hills. What pleasant walks these were; we must have talked about every subject under the sun. From eight or nine in the evening till midnight, we had music in the pension."[25]

Borodin realized that Catherine was the woman for him when he found out that she had perfect pitch. They were listening to an orchestra in Baden-Baden when Catherine observed to Borodin: "What a fine modulation there." He said, "What! You mean to say that you have absolute pitch? But that's quite unusual!"[26]

Catherine said that he seemed happy and that his eyes were bright, but she didn't know what he was thinking. He had just realized that he was in love with her. They became engaged in August during a walk in the hills. They socialized with the famous violinist, Ferdinand Laub, who predicted that Borodin would be a great musician some day.

As autumn approached, Catherine developed a cough and pain in her lungs; her Heidelberg doctor prescribed a warm climate. They spent the winter in Pisa, Italy where two Italian chemists made a laboratory available to Borodin. His work in the laboratory was documented in three papers published in 1862 in the journal *Il Nuovo Cimento*. Borodin and Catherine played in amateur chamber ensembles, and he played cello in the local opera orchestra. He composed *Tarantella in D major* and *C minor Quintet* in Pisa.

When they returned to St. Petersburg, Borodin undertook his responsibilities as Professor of Chemistry teaching organic chemistry and as Zinin's assistant in the Academy of Physicians. In late autumn of 1862, Borodin finally met Balakirev at a professor's house. Mussorgsky and Balakirev sat down at the piano and played the Finale of the *First Symphony* of Rimsky-Korsakov, who was on an extended voyage. Borodin was impressed by Rimsky-Korsakov's work and by the enthusiasm of his friends' playing; he realized how much he had in common with the circle of five, and what they were trying to accomplish.

Balakirev counseled Borodin to take himself more seriously, to be less self-deprecating, and to concentrate on composing. Balakirev stimulated a creative rush in Borodin, motivating him to write his own first symphony. By the end of December, Borodin had completed the first Allegro of the symphony that he reviewed with Balakirev. All members of the circle of five reviewed one another's work, to their mutual benefit.

In *Borodin*, Serge Dianin comments on Borodin's becoming a member of the circle of five:

> It was not for nothing that Borodin became a member of the Balakirev circle; for he became aware of his own potentialities as a result, and saw clearly from then on that it was his task to help create a Russian musical idiom, and to overcome Western influences. This event in Borodin's life is not so much a turning point as the natural outcome of earlier stages in his musical development. As a composer, he was now sufficiently mature to retain his individuality in the face of the powerful influence of Balakirev.[27]

Gerald E. H. Abraham provides an excellent overview of Borodin's compositions in *Borodin: The Composer and His Music*:

> In considering Borodin's compositions as a whole one naturally turns first to those for orchestra, for in them we find every characteristic quality one associates with his name—nationalism, orientalism, lyric beauty, massive structural strength, and wealth of color—each

at its best.... In the matter of "color" ... which is produced by orchestral combinations he has few superiors.... Borodin's orchestration, at its best, reminds one frequently of a brilliant pattern in mosaic, in which the brightest elementary colors are placed in immediate juxtaposition.[28]

On April 17, 1863, Borodin and Catherine were married in St. Petersburg. They stayed there that summer because of his duties as Zinin's assistant during the completion of construction of a new chemistry laboratory. That fall they moved into a first-floor apartment in the new building, where Borodin was to live for the remainder of his life. He had a laboratory adjacent to their apartment, but he really had no quiet place at home to work, particularly during Catherine's relatives' frequent visits.

Borodin completed the Scherzo of his *First Symphony* during the summer of 1864. The following summer, they went to Graz, Austria, where Borodin composed the middle section of the Andante to his *First Symphony* while on a walk in the mountains. Catherine commented upon her husband's creative process: "Alexander returned from an excursion in the mountains around Graz. He was walking by some arbor in the grounds of an old castle when the D flat major middle section of the Andante came into his head, especially those rising and falling sighs in the accompaniment which go so well there. I can see him now, sitting at the piano."[29]

In December 1865, Borodin attended the première performance of his *First Symphony* at the Free School of Music in St. Petersburg. He continued to work on the *First Symphony* until its completion in May 1866 after five years of effort.

Borodin's next project was the music for an operatic farce by V. A. Krylov, *The Valiant Knights*. The original plan was to write all original music for the parody, but there wasn't sufficient time. The compromise was for Borodin to write some new pieces and combine them with music "from the existing theatrical repertoire." The result was a pastiche of original music and carefully chosen extracts from popular operas.

The operatic parody was produced at the Bolshoi Theater on October 13, 1867; it was not a success. Critics didn't realize that it was intended as a farce. Theatergoers saw it as a warming over of familiar songs with some new songs by a unknown composer. *The Valiant Knights* closed after one performance. The opera's only redeeming quality was that Borodin learned from it and applied that knowledge to his later work, *Prince Igor.*

In December 1868, Borodin participated in founding the Chemical Society. His research at the time included work on the condensation of valerian aldehyde; the evaporation of water-based solutions, the attraction of water by substances that dissolve and become liquid by absorbing moisture from the air; and various experiments in physical chemistry.

Borodin continued to revise his *First Symphony* and to correct many errors that had been made in preparing the score for orchestra. On January 4, 1869, it was conducted by Balakirev at the Musical Society. Sparse applause greeted the first part, the Scherzo was awarded a long applause, and the Finale generated thunderous applause.

The composer was called back to the stage many times. Borodin was uplifted; he began to work immediately on his *B minor Symphony*. The success of his *First Symphony* and of his songs, "The Sleeping Princess" and "The Song of the Dark Forest" motivated him to work on his *Second (Heroic) Symphony*. However, what he really wanted to do was an opera.

One of Borodin's friends suggested that he write the score for *The Lay of Igor's Campaign*, an epic in three acts based on history. He studied historical resource material, folk tales, and ballads from Russian narrative poems. "Yaroslavna's Dream" was the first piece that he completed while heavily occupied with laboratory work. He also worked on the first Allegro of the *B minor Symphony* at this time.

Borodin had heard that the German chemist Kekulé was also working on the condensation of valerian aldehyde, so he hurried to complete his work and to publish first. Also, he was burdened with tutorial work and administrative tasks, such as writing memoranda and doing the laboratory accounts. His musician friends criticized him for his meager composition output. He commented: "Our musicians never stop abusing me. They say I never do anything and won't drop my idiotic activities, that is to say, my work at the laboratory."[30]

In early 1872, Borodin was expected to contribute to the composition of a fairy opera about the Baltic Slavs, *Mlada*, a joint "circle of five" project whose libretto had been written by V. A. Krylov. The first act was to be written by Cui, the second and third acts were the joint responsibility of Mussorgsky and Borodin, and the fourth act was assigned to Borodin.

Borodin's creative juices were flowing as he worked on the fourth act. A friend observed his efforts:

> At the time ... I was seeing a good deal of him, and I frequently found him of a morning standing in front of his high-writing table actually engaged in composition. He looked inspired; his eyes were on fire, and he looked transformed. One occasion I remember in particular. He had not been very well and had been staying at home for the past two weeks; but during the whole of that time, he had scarcely left the piano. It was then that he was composing the most monumental and amazing moments of *Mlada*. Whenever I turned up, he immediately played and sang everything he had just written with most extraordinary fire and enthusiasm.[31]

Borodin quickly produced a majestic fourth act. Unfortunately, funding for the opera fell through, and it was never produced.

Catherine's sleep habits made it difficult for the rest of the household. In *Borodin*, Serge Dianin describes them:

> Catherine was in the habit of going to bed about three or four o'clock in the morning; up to that hour neither she or anyone else in the house could get any sleep, including her husband. She usually got up very late, around three or four o'clock in the afternoon. As a result of such an existence, Borodin began to suffer from lack of sleep. This disruption of his life made him unsystematic and slack in other matters as well. Quite frequently, the Borodins did not have their dinner before midnight. The harmful effects of this routine were cumulative and were one of the factors affecting his health; they undoubtedly hastened the onset of the heart disease which led to his death.[32]

After an interval of four years, Borodin was encouraged by friends to continue with his work on *Prince Igor*. He rewrote some of the music he had created for *Mlada, The Tsar's Bride,* and other works for incorporation into *Prince Igor*. He also worked on his *First String Quartet* and a piano-duet version of his *First Symphony*. This didn't prevent him from publishing a paper, "On Nitrosoamarine."

In early 1875, Zinin retired, and Borodin had to do all of the administrative work. He was now responsible for the laboratory, which he expanded. He worked on a program for women's medical courses, and he assisted in organizing charity concerts to earn tuition money for poor students.

During the summer of 1875, Borodin finished the *B minor Symphony*, worked on the *A major Quartet*, and completed significant portions of *Prince Igor*. Pieces of the opera were performed as they were completed; his friends were very enthusiastic. He emphasized the vocal part of an opera; to him, the orchestra was secondary. In January 1876, his *B minor Symphony* was performed for the first time to an audience that did not particularly like the music of the circle of five. The *B minor Symphony* was a failure, and the sensitive composer was upset by the audience's reaction. He turned his efforts to composing the *A major Quartet*.

During the winter of 1878-79, Borodin devised a method for determining the nitrogen content of urea. His individual research was now rare; most of his laboratory work involved supervising the work of students. He was active in the Chemical Society and spent most of his time lecturing, attending meetings, and performing administrative tasks.

Scheduling a musical piece to be performed at the Free School concerts motivated all of the circle of five, including Borodin, to compose. Borodin had to revise his *B minor Symphony* for a February 1879 concert. In early 1880, he completed *In the Steppes of Central Asia*. Its popularity spread from Russia to Europe. In the spring of 1882, Borodin met the gifted, young composer, Alexander Glazunov, whose *E major Symphony* was performed at a Free School concert. Borodin's work on *Prince Igor* was ongoing.

The pace of Borodin's life was catching up with him. The usually amiable composer experienced bouts of irritability. He reacted:

> God knows, I am expected to be Glinka and
> Semyon Petrovich [a government official],
> scientist and committee-man, artist, official,
> benefactor, father of adopted children, doctor,
> and invalid, all rolled into one.... But it won't
> be long before I am nothing more than the last
> of these, to the exclusion of all the other roles.
> I would go anywhere just to get away from

here, to the country, anywhere, to the devil
even.[33]

Glazunov copied parts of Borodin's completed works as a
favor to him to prepare for concerts.

In the fall of 1886, Borodin began to have chest pains.
The diagnosis was serious heart disease; however, the patient
was not told of his condition. Rimsky-Korsakov and
Glazunov were aware that their friend's health was slipping.
They kept a close watch on his output on *Prince Igor*.
Borodin knew that his work on the opera was lagging. He did-
n't even like to talk about *Prince Igor*.

Borodin worked with creative fervor on the Finale for the
opera. A student in the laboratory next door to the room in
which Borodin composed was moved by the music he heard:

> He thundered away for quite a long time play-
> ing this tremendous music of his, and then he
> stopped. A few minutes later he came into the
> laboratory in a state of excitement and joy;
> there were tears in his eyes.... He said, "I know
> that some of the things that I have written are
> not bad. But this finale! ... What a finale!" As
> he said this, Borodin covered his eyes with one
> hand and gesticulated with the other.... But not
> a single bar of this finale has survived; unfor-
> tunately, he never got as far as writing it
> down.[34]

After his death, Borodin's music manuscripts were given by
Glazunov to the St. Petersburg conservatory. Included were
short sketches for the Andante but none for the Finale.

Borodin planned a costume ball to be held at the Academy
on February 15, 1887. He dressed as a Russian peasant with
a dark red wool shirt and baggy dark blue trousers. The hall
was packed; everyone was in high spirits.

Borodin stood in a group of his friends. As he spoke; his words became indistinct, and he began to sway on his feet. He looked frightened and appeared not to be in control. He fell forward onto the floor heavily. A friend standing next to him did not react fast enough to break his fall. Doctors from the Academy attended to him and tried to revive him. The autopsy showed that an artery in his heart had burst. When he fell, his temple struck a corner of the stove next to where he was standing, causing a brain hemorrhage.

Borodin's funeral was well attended by relatives, friends, and those whom he had helped along the way. He was buried in the cemetery adjacent to the Alexander Nevsky Monastery, next to Mussorgsky's grave and in the vicinity of Dargomijsky's grave.

Rimsky-Korsakov and Glazunov edited and published Borodin's uncompleted compositions. Glazunov edited two movements of Borodin's *Third Symphony*, one of which he wrote from memory. Glazunov had a phenomenal memory; he could write a score from memory after hearing it once. He added a Trio to the Scherzo based on the *Merchant's Tale,* as Borodin had planned.

Glazunov completed the Third Act of *Prince Igor* and then edited it as well as the Overture. Rimsky-Korsakov completed the orchestration of the other parts of the opera. Catherine was unhappy when she heard about this. She was seriously ill, and this news weakened her. Dropsy worsened her condition. She died on June 28, 1887.

In 1888, the complete score and piano arrangement for *Prince Igor* were published. By 1897, accumulated royalties from *Prince Igor* alone were 50,000 rubles, which was donated to the St. Petersburg Conservatory to establish a Borodin Scholarship for young composers. The melody for the popular song, "Stranger in Paradise," is from *Prince Igor*.

In *Borodin: The Composer and His Music*, Gerald E. H. Abraham summarized Borodin's life:

If, as Carlyle said, the only true happiness of a man is that of "clear, decided activity in the sphere for which, by nature and circumstances, he has been fitted and appointed," Alexander Borodin must have been a supremely happy man.... Of a sympathetic and affectionate disposition, his love was extended not merely to individuals but to his fellow-man in the mass, and his one object in life was to show sympathy in practical forms. It was his special good fortune to be able to do this in two ways—by medical and sociological work during his life and by the creation of immortal beauty for all time—a combination of gifts which is practically unique in the history of art.[35]

ANTON CHEKHOV (1860-1904) Medical Doctor and Playwright

"Medicine is my lawful wife, and literature is my mistress. When I tire of the one, I spend the night with the other. As long as it does not become a regular habit, it is not humdrum and neither of them suffers from my infidelity. If I did not have my medical pursuits, I should find it difficult to devote my random thoughts and spare time to literature."[36]

Anton Chekhov

Anton Chekhov, who created a new style of literature, was the first in a series of talented writers who flourished in Russia late in the nineteenth century and early in the twentieth. Tolstoy observed:

> One cannot compare Chekhov as an artist with any of the previous writers, Turgenev, Dostoevsky, or myself. Like the impressionists, Chekhov possesses his own peculiar style. One watches him daub on such colors as he has by him with apparent carelessness, and one imagines that all of these splashes of paint have nothing in common between them. But as soon as one stands back and looks from a distance, the effect is extraordinary. Before one, there emerges a picture that is striking and irresistible.[37]

Chekhov's early works in the 1880s were mainly humorous short stories. Although his work became increasingly more mature and complex, his early writing indicated his superior talent and his regard for his fellow man. In *Makers of the Modern World*, Louis Untermeyer comments:

> It is one of literature's paradoxes that Anton
> Pavlovich Chekhov, who loved the comic ele-
> ment in life and who was known to most of his
> countrymen as the author of countless humor-
> ous short stories, is celebrated today as a
> writer who founded a new literature of unre-
> solved suspensions, subdued in tone and minor
> in key, expressive of man's sense of unhappy
> isolation and his failure to understand his fel-
> low man.[38]

Chekhov, whose goal was "making the reader think," said, "When I write, I stake everything on the reader and count on him to supply for himself whatever elements may be lacking from my story." His writing always reflected his inner lights. He believed "that one should never listen to anyone's advice. One should work, and, in this work, be bold. There are big dogs and little dogs, but the little ones should not allow themselves to be intimidated by the presence of the big ones; it is the duty of them all to bark, and bark with the voice that God has given them."[39] His life and his illness, tuberculosis, are reflected in many of his works, particularly in the plays that he wrote later in his life.

Anton Chekhov was born on January 17, 1860 in Taganrog, a port on the Sea of Azov. His artistic father, Pavel, was a marginally successful shopkeeper, religious zealot, and strict disciplinarian who beat his five sons regularly. Pavel's father had been born a slave but had worked hard to purchase his freedom. Chekhov's mother, Evgenia, was a warm person with a happy disposition whose father, a cloth merchant, had ensured that she received some education. She and the Chekhov children's nurse were accomplished storytellers.

Chekhov's older brothers, Alexander and Nicholas, drank and generally avoided obligations of any kind. Young Chekhov, who from the age of eight worked in the family store, became the one who assumed family responsibilities as he grew older. He was a "nice, easy-going fellow," a handsome youth with a way with women. From an early age, he was a great storyteller and mimic; also, he was accomplished in improvisation. His teachers liked him, but he wasn't an exceptional student. He and his classmates started a magazine, and his first literary efforts, a drama and a vaudeville sketch, were done while he attended school in Taganrog.

When Chekhov was sixteen, his father's business failed and he left Taganrog to avoid his creditors. The family joined Pavel in Moscow, except for Anton, who remained in Taganrog to finish his schooling. He lived with friends of the family and earned his keep by tutoring. As a youth, Chekhov loved the theater and went to plays whenever he could. He was strongly impressed by the landscape of the steppe north of his home town, which he and his family crossed on their way to visit his grandfather.

Chekhov became seriously ill by taking an ice-cold bath after a long, hot walk. This illness permanently weakened him and probably increased his susceptibility to the tuberculosis that would haunt him as a adult. The young man living away from his family was treated by a kind German physician, Dr. Strümpf. This illness and the care provided by Dr. Strümpf were factors in his deciding to become a doctor himself.

In August 1879, Chekhov joined his family in Moscow. Although he loved Moscow in his adult years, his first impressions weren't favorable. The poverty in which he found his family probably contributed to his early impressions. His father worked six long days a week in a store. Chekhov's two older brothers had moved out of the family apartment. He became the economic and disciplinary support for his two younger brothers and his sister. His younger brother, Michael, said, "His will became the dominant one."

Over the next seven years, Chekhov earned money to help support the family by writing for humor magazines. He used a pseudonym, Antoshe Chekhonte, when writing potboilers, principally parodies and satires, to earn money for the family.

At the age of nineteen, he passed the examination for medical school on his second attempt and won a scholarship.

He never regretted his career choice of medicine. He felt that his knowledge of science made him question the unknown and helped to give him a real direction in life. His colleagues believed that his ability to make scientific observations was a major influence on his literary works.

Chekhov applied himself to medical school, which was very demanding, and to writing. He was a prolific writer whose stories became more critical and satiric as he grew older. By the age of twenty-seven, concurrently with medical school, internship, and three years of private practice, he had written 600 short stories. The stressful life that he lived contributed to his contracting tuberculosis in his mid-twenties, however. He recognized the symptoms but downplayed its seriousness to his family and to himself. He could not afford the time or the cost of extended treatment.

Chekhov's medical practice grew slowly, and occasionally he was bored. His close friend and mentor, Suvorin, gave him valuable advice about his writing that helped him change his style. His friend, a self-made man who was twenty-five years his senior, impressed upon him his responsibility as a literary artist. He advised Chekhov "to respect his talent, and to publish only truly finished stories."

Chekhov enjoyed pursuing two careers. Suvorin encouraged him to give up his medical practice to write full time. He responded in a letter to Suvorin: "You advise me not to hunt two hares at once, and not even to think about my medical profession. Why not? I feel more cheerful and satisfied when I realize that I have two things to do instead of one."[40]

Chekhov wrote an unsuccessful novel, in which he attempted to enlighten rather than to entertain. His next effort was a play about a man of the 1880s, *Ivanov*, which received both critical and popular acclaim. Also, he was awarded a Pushkin prize for a collection of short stories. Although he was now a successful writer, he had difficulty believing that the popularity of his literary works would last. He continued to drive himself, partly because he still bore the financial responsibility for his family.

Chekhov's drive to write may be explained in the words of the character Trigorin in his play, *The Sea Gull*:

> Day and night I am in the grip of one besetting need to write, write, write. Hardly have I finished one book than something urges me to write another, and then a third, and then a fourth! I write ceaselessly.... I cannot escape myself, though I feel that I am consuming my life ... no sooner does one book leave the press than it becomes odious to me; it is not what I meant it to be; I made a mistake to write it at all; I am provoked and discouraged.... Then the public reads it and says: "Yes, it is very clever, very pretty, but it is not nearly as good as Tolstoy." ... I too, love my country and her people. I feel that, as a writer, it is my duty to speak of their sorrows, of their future, of science, and the rights of man. So I write on every subject, and the public hounds me on all sides, sometimes in anger, and I race and dodge like a fox with a pack of hounds on his trail.[41]

In 1888, Chekhov wrote a second play, *The Wood Spirit*, which was unsuccessful. This failure reinforced his belief that he was not a playwright; he did not attempt another play for seven years.

Chekhov, who felt that he needed a change of pace and a change of scenery, decided to visit the Russian penal colony on the island of Saghalien. He had heard that state criminals were virtually ignored after their trials. He wasn't sure that his trip would make a contribution either to science or to his literature; nevertheless, despite warnings from his friends who were concerned for his health, he was determined to gather information about the state criminals at Saghalien. He interviewed every convict and prepared the only census that had ever been done at the penal colony.

Exhausted by his efforts, Chekhov returned to Moscow in December 1890. He published a series of humanitarian articles about his experiences. When he returned home, he sent large quantities of books to the island's schools. Upon leaving for Saghalien, he had given up his medical practice. From this time onward, he wrote full time and had only one income.

Chekhov was also a humanitarian in his home region. He donated 10,000 rubles for the construction of model schools at Melikhovo, Novoselki, and Talezh. He contributed many books to the school in his hometown, Taganrog—eight large consignments in one two-year period. One year, he sent 319 books by French authors to Taganrog from Nice. He really couldn't afford to do this, but he did it anyway because he was aware of the critical need.

During the summer of 1892, Chekhov was unable to pursue his literary work. As a medical doctor, he was asked to prepare for an expected cholera epidemic. The Melikhovo district had experienced a severe epidemic in 1848, and the anticipated one was expected to be at least as serious. Medical facilities in the region were limited, and it was difficult to transport patients elsewhere because of the poor roads.

In 1895, Chekhov wrote his third play, *The Sea Gull*. His friends didn't like it, and the patrons at the Alexandrinski Theater in St. Petersburg, who had expected a comedy, booed loudly at the première and called it "decadent." It was a dismal failure, partly because the producer had not understood Chekhov's intentions for the play.

Two years later, Vladimir Nemirovich-Danchenko and Konstantin Stanislavski, co-founders of the Moscow Art Theater, resurrected the play. A reviewer described the audience's reaction:

The curtain fell and what happened then was something that only happens in the theater once in ten or twenty years: a silence, a deep silence, both in the audience and on the stage; those in the audience remained frozen in their seats, those on the stage had not yet grasped what had happened.... This lasted for a long time. The cast jumped to the conclusion that the first act had flopped, flopped so badly that there was not even a single friend who could bring himself to applaud, and they were reduced to a state of nerves bordering on hysteria. Then suddenly, it was as though a dam had broken, as though a bomb had burst: a deafening explosion of applause. Everybody applauded, friends and foes alike.[42]

Drama critic Brooks Atkinson of the New York *Times* wrote a perceptive review of *The Sea Gull:* "Beyond and behind the surface, Chekhov has caught the great truths of life—the carelessness, selfishness, and weariness of civilized existence—the candid truth of human society, comic in its inadequate grasp of the fundamentals of social living, tragic in its consequences."[43]

Chekhov rewrote his play, *The Wood Spirit*, and renamed it *Uncle Vanya*. The Moscow Art Theater produced it; it was a resounding success. In the play, Chekhov describes a "slice of life," leaving the audience to imagine what had preceded those events and what followed them. In *The Personal Papers of Anton Chekhov*, he wrote, "The artist should be not the judge of his characters, but only an unbiased witness.... My business is merely to report ... to be able to distinguish important and unimportant statements, to be able to illuminate the characters and speak their language ... to transmit the conversation exactly as I hear it and let the jury—that is, the readers—estimate its value."[44]

Chekhov's views were echoed by Maurice Maeterlinck, the Belgian dramatist and poet, who said, "It is in a small room, round the table, close to the fire, that the joys and sorrows of mankind are decided. We suffer, or make others suffer, we love, we die, there in our corner."[45]

Chekhov spent most of his time in Yalta, where the climate was more favorable for his health than Moscow. However, he came to love Moscow and the Moscow Art Theater that produced his plays. Olga Knipper, one of the leading actresses of the Moscow Art Theater, had been romantically interested in Chekhov for several years. In October 1898, Chekhov wrote to Suvorin from Yalta:

> Before my departure I attended the rehearsals of *Tsar Fedor Ioannovich*. I was moved by the intelligence which marked the performance. Real art was on the stage.... Irena [Olga Knipper] I think excellent. Her voice, the elevation of her character, her sincerity are so wonderful that I enjoy the mere recollection of it.... Best of all is Irena! If I had stayed in Moscow I should have fallen in love with that Irena.[46]

Olga pursued him for two years and, finally, proposed to him. On April 18, 1901, he wrote to her: "If you promise to me that not a soul in Moscow shall know about our wedding before it has taken place, I will marry you on the very day of my arrival. Somehow I dread the ceremony, the congratulations, the champagne glass in my hand, and a vague smile on my face."[47]

On May 25, 1901, Chekhov and Olga Knipper were married. No wedding announcements were sent out, and he told neither his mother nor his sister, with whom he was close, prior to the wedding. In fact, he had talked with his brother,

Ivan, on the morning of the wedding and didn't tell him either.

In 1900, Chekhov was elected to the belles-lettres division of the Russian Academy. His good friend and fellow author, Maxim Gorki, was expelled from the Academy in 1902 for his political beliefs. Chekhov resigned from the Academy that year to protest his friend's expulsion.

In 1900-01, Chekhov wrote *The Three Sisters*, considered the gloomiest of his plays. He conceived this play and his last play, *The Cherry Orchard*, as comedies; however, audiences looked upon them as bleak plays depicting Russian life. Upon reading *The Three Sisters* for the first time, the actors and actresses were confused by it. They viewed it as a scheme, not a completed play. To them, it was composed of hints and intimations, not well-delineated roles.

Olga played the second of the sisters, Masha. The *Three Sisters* is intended as a dialog between the author and Masha in the distance. This play, perhaps his most nostalgic, is a drama of restlessness and strain in the provinces; however, it also provides glimpses into the future. Although initially less successful than *The Sea gull* and *Uncle Vanya,* it had more performances than his earlier plays.

In 1903-04, Chekhov wrote *The Cherry Orchard*, subtitled *A Comedy*. His health was declining rapidly; in considerable physical pain, he could write only a few lines a day. He intended the play to be a comedy using irony, but the producer portrayed it as the tense drama of the replacement of old criteria by new standards as a fading upper class gave way to increasing materialism. The advertising referred to it as a drama. The première performance, an overwhelming success, was on January 17, 1904.

In early 1904, Chekhov's condition became acute. His wife, the joy of his later years, was always at his bedside. She observed, "Growing weaker in body but stronger in spirit, he took a perfectly simple, wise, and beautiful attitude to his bodily dissolution, because he said, 'God has put a bacillus in me.'"[48] In June, Chekhov and his wife traveled to a sanatorium at Badenweiler in the Black Forest of Germany. He told his friends that he was going away to "peg out."

On July 2, Chekhov awakened in the middle of the night with difficulty breathing. He became delirious and talked about Russia and her people. He regained consciousness and was given a glass of champagne to stimulate his heart. He said, "Ich sterbe" (I am dying) and died. He was buried in Moscow alongside his father. Chekhov said, "Everything I have written will be forgotten in a few years. But the paths I have traced will remain intact and secure, and there lies my only merit."[49] As usual, he underestimated himself. His works are performed, and he is remembered.

After Chekhov's death, Maxim Gorki wrote a moving memoir about his friend:

> I have never known a man feel the importance of work as a foundation of civilization as profoundly and completely as Anton Chekhov. It was apparent in the everyday details of his personal life, in his choice of themes, and in that noble love of things which, free from any desire to acquire them, never tires of admiring in them the creations of the human mind. He loved to build, to plant gardens, to embellish the world; he felt the poetry of work. With what touching solicitude he watched the growth of the fruit trees and ornamental shrubs that he had planted! While his house on Yalta was being built, he used to say: "If everyone, on his little patch of ground, did what he might, how beautiful our land would be."[50]

LOUIS AUCHINCLOSS (1917-   ) Lawyer and Author

"Although recognized as a 'significant' American novelist well before 1960, the year that *The House of Five Talents* would propel him toward the front rank, Louis Auchincloss did not begin to receive serious critical attention until the seventh decade of his life. Clearly the peer, quite possibly the superior of such older writers as John P. Marquand, John O'Hara, and James Gould Cozzens, all now deceased, for reasons that remain obscure, he has only recently [1988]—having lived longer than the first two authors named—begun to receive the recognition that has long been his due."

David B. Parcell, Preface, *Louis Auchincloss*

Louis Auchincloss, who wrote about the New York establishment, was a rarity—an author positioned as an insider among the businessmen and lawyers of Manhattan. He has been accused of writing about a narrow range of white, Anglo-Saxon Protestants. His response to that was: "When I am told that I have confined my fiction to too small a world, I find it difficult to comprehend. For it seems to me as if I should never come to the end of the variety of types represented by my relatives alone. Auchinclosses, Russells, Dixons, Stantons, how could anyone lump such people into one mold?"[51]

Auchincloss has written over twenty-three novels, seven collections of short fiction, and thirteen collections of essays, criticisms, and belles-lettres. He was a prolific writer who, except for two years, worked full time as a lawyer in Manhattan. From 1956 to 1966, his most productive decade, he wrote *The Great World and Timothy Colt* (1956), *Venus in Sparta* (1958), *Pursuit of the Prodigal* (1959), *The House of Five Talents* (1960), *Portrait in Brownstone* (1962), *The Rector of Justin* (1964), and *The Embezzler* (1966), as well as short fiction and essays.

Auchincloss was considered a writer of novels of manners in the tradition of James Fenimore Cooper, William Dean Howells, Henry James, Edith Wharton, Sinclair Lewis, F. Scott Fitzgerald, James Gould Cozzens, John P. Marquand, and John O'Hara. Lionel Trilling explained "manners" in an essay:

> What I understand by manners, then, is a culture's hum and buzz of implication. I mean the whole evanescent context in which its explicit statements are made. It is that part of a culture which is made up of half-uttered or unutterable expressions of value. They are hinted at by small actions. Sometimes by the arts of dress or decoration, sometimes by tone, gesture, emphasis, or rhythm, sometimes by the words that are used with a special frequency or a special meaning.

> They are the things that separate them from people of another culture. They make the part of a culture which is not art, or religion, or morals, or politics and yet it relates to all these highly formulated departments of culture. It is modified by them; it modifies them; it is generated by them; it generates them. In this part of culture assumption rules, which is often so much stronger than reason.[52]

Auchincloss's immediate predecessors in writing novels about manners were John P. Marquand, author of *H. M. Pulham, Esquire* and *The Late George Apley*, and John O'Hara, who wrote *Appointment in Samarra*. Auchincloss came from a different background than theirs. He claimed that there never was an Auchincloss fortune; nevertheless, he was a member of one of New York's leading white, Anglo-Saxon Protestant families, whose male members either earned substantial incomes or married into money.

The families of Marquand and O'Hara were not as affluent as the Auchincloss family. Marquand was descended from the aristocratic New England Fullers and O'Hara's family was known for its industry. Both families experienced financial setbacks, which prevented Marquand from attending private preparatory school and O'Hara from attending college.

Louis Auchincloss was born to Howland and Priscilla Auchincloss in Lawrence, Long Island on September 27, 1917. Howland Auchincloss was a partner in the New York law firm, Davis, Polk, Wardwell, Gardiner, and Reed. Senior partner John Davis ran against Calvin Coolidge as the Democratic Party's candidate for President in 1924. Priscilla was a strict parent who believed strongly in duty.

Auchincloss attended the private Bovee school. Bovee students were a mix of New York children from the great Jewish families, offsprings of the Astors, and the sons of performing artists. Mel Ferrer and Efrem Zimbalist, Jr., the son of a renowned violinist, were peers of Auchincloss at Bovee.

After Bovee, Auchincloss enrolled at Groton, the private boarding school in New England that Franklin Roosevelt had attended. Auchincloss went to Groton "to begin the dusty task of being a man" and, along the way, "learned a great deal about the arrogance and insularity of the business and banking class."[53]

Dr. Endicott Peabody, the headmaster of Groton, was thought by many to be the model for Francis Prescott, the headmaster in Auchincloss's *Rector of Justin*. Auchincloss claimed that the headmaster in his popular book was based on Judge Learned Hand. Auchincloss considered Hand the greatest human being he had ever met.

Dr. Peabody had "command presence." Auchincloss had never met a man with such an aura of authority. Endicott Peabody was in a class with the great headmasters: Frank Boyden of Deerfield, Mather Abbot of Lawrenceville, William Thayer of St. Mark's, and Samuel Drury of St. Paul's.

Malcolm Strachan, who taught English at Groton, was a strong influence on young Auchincloss. Strachan moved around a subject casually, but he lived the piece of literature that he was teaching. He taught Auchincloss about the equal partnership that exists between the writer and the reader.

In 1935, Auchincloss entered Yale University, which many of his relatives had attended. His brother was in his second year at the Yale Law School. Auchincloss did not participate in many campus activities in his three years at Yale; however, he wrote four stories for the *Yale Literary Magazine* and played two parts in Dramatic Society plays.

William Scranton, William Bundy, Richard Ellman, and Cyrus Vance were in his class in New Haven. Auchincloss had definite opinions about Yale: "You couldn't go through any place as amiably Philistine as Yale in my day without realizing that what Gore Vidal calls 'the real world' has nothing to do with the world of letters."[54]

In his sophomore year, Auchincloss began writing a novel, *A World of Profit,* which he finished early in his junior year. When he showed the completed 424-page manuscript to his parents, they advised against publishing it. His mother didn't like "the vulgarity of the society parts," and his father told him that it wouldn't help him to get started in a law career. It was, to a large extent, an autobiographical novel, like so many first novels.

Auchincloss claimed that this was the point at which he learned that all of a novelist's characters are himself. He submitted the manuscript for publication to Scribner's, who rejected it, but asked to see his "next." He completed half of a second manuscript during the summer after his junior year but threw it out without letting anyone read it.

Auchincloss decided to leave Yale after three years if he could find a good law school that admitted applicants without a degree. His father advised him against leaving college without his BA degree. He told his son that he would go through life explaining why he left Yale early. His father was right.

Auchincloss was accepted at the law school of the University of Virginia. He was pleased with the quality of the professors and was enchanted with Charlottesville. He claimed that he never relaxed and enjoyed myself until he arrived in Virginia.

Auchincloss completed his third attempt at a novel during the summer after his first year of law school. After rereading the finished manuscript, he threw it in the trash can and went out. Later, he had second thoughts and decided to retrieve it. However, the garbage truck had picked it up; it was irretrievable. In his second year of law school, he and nine other scholars were chosen for the University of Virginia's Law Review. For the remainder of his time in law school, he wrote only legal notes and decisions.

During the summer before his last year of law school, Auchincloss worked for Sullivan & Cromwell, the prestigious New York Law firm. He graduated from law school in 1941 and returned to New York to prepare for the bar exam. In July 1941, he started his job at Sullivan & Cromwell, which later became known as the firm of the Dulles brothers, John, Secretary of State, and Allen, Director of the Central Intelligence Agency, in President Eisenhower's administrations.

During the "phony war" in 1941, leading up to the bombing of Pearl Harbor, Auchincloss knew that he would have to either enlist or be drafted. He admitted to himself that: "There had always lurked in the back of my mind an uneasy sense that over and above the test of manhood that school and Wall Street were bound to provide, there might lie in wait an even rougher and more elementary one: that of war."[55] He applied for a commission in Naval Intelligence and was criticized by his mother and his friends for signing up for a desk job.

Auchincloss attempted to change his designator from intelligence officer to deck officer and to become a ship driver. He applied for midshipmen's school and took a night course in trigonometry to qualify for it. However, the attack on Pearl Harbor occurred before he began midshipmen's school, and he was ordered to duty as an intelligence officer. For the next fifteen months, he was assigned to Fifteenth Naval District Headquarters in Balboa, Panama Canal Zone, doing his best to deal with what he viewed as appalling bureaucracy. At least he had the opportunity to read the classics that he had missed.

Auchincloss finally received orders for sea duty and completed amphibious training before being assigned as executive officer aboard the tank landing ship LST 980, a lumbering, awkward amphibious warfare ship designed to open her doors on a beach to offload tanks and other vehicles. The crew practiced landings in Chesapeake Bay. LSTs were considered second-class vessels in the Navy, as indicated by a message LST 980 received in Chesapeake Bay from the *USS New York*, "Get your trash out of my way."[56]

After the completion of training in late 1944, LST 980 steamed to Plymouth, England. On D-Day, June 6, 1945, the ship loaded British and Canadian troops in Southampton and delivered them to beaches in France. The Luftwaffe wasn't a factor during the first few days of the invasion; nevertheless, one night while moored off Gold Beach, LST 980 was hit by three bombs from a German aircraft. Two of the bombs went through bulkheads into the water; the third bomb lodged in an ammunition truck. A British demolition team successfully removed the third bomb, or Lieutenant Auchincloss's writing career would have been abbreviated.

LST 980 made many trips between England and France; the young author found plenty of time to read Shakespeare and Marlowe. The ship sustained hull damage on a rocky beach near Le Havre and was ordered to return to the United States. Auchincloss applied for command of an LST in the Pacific Theater. He was assigned as skipper of LST 130, a worn-out veteran of the war in the Pacific. The ship had returned to California for repairs when V-J Day was announced. When repairs were completed, LST 130 was sent to Sasebo, Japan. Lieutenant Auchincloss steamed into Sasebo harbor without a harbor pilot; he now considered himself a member of "the real world."

Auchincloss had begun to write another novel late in his tour of duty in the Navy; he worked furiously to complete it before rejoining Sullivan & Cromwell. When he submitted the manuscript to Little, Brown and Company, it was rejected. He tried again with Prentice-Hall, and it was accepted. His parents were so strongly against his publishing *The Indifferent Children* that he used a pseudonym, Andrew Lee, an ancestor from his mother's branch of the family.

William McFee reviewed Auchincloss's book in the New York *Sun*: "Here is a novelist of the caliber of the Henry James who wrote *Washington Square* and *The Portrait of a Lady* rather than the author of *The Ambassadors*. It is James alive to our times, aware of things and people James himself never even sensed, but with the psychological alertness and a mastery of English the master would have enjoyed very much indeed."[57]

Resuming his law career after an absence of over four years was difficult; Auchincloss attended lectures at the Practicing Law Institute to remove the cobwebs from his law school education. When he began to publish under his own name, people who knew of Sullivan & Cromwell's reputation for working their law clerks hard were surprised that he found time to write. When senior partner John Foster Dulles was accused of overworking his associates, he replied that, to the contrary, they had to write novels to keep busy.

Auchincloss wrote evenings and weekends and wondered if he were slighting his writing by working full time for a law firm. However, he liked his job at Sullivan & Cromwell, and, furthermore, he did not want to be financially dependent on his parents. He had no ambition to be a partner in the firm; he was happy being a lawyer and an observer.

One evening at a cocktail party, Auchincloss mentioned to the wife of one of the associates that he might eventually leave Sullivan & Cromwell to write full time. She goaded him by pointing out that he was a big boy now, and that he should be able to make up his mind. The struggle between wanting to be considered for partner but not wanting to be a partner eventually took its toll. His father told him that he would provide financial support if he chose to write full time. Late in 1951, with considerable anguish and misgiving, Auchincloss left Sullivan & Cromwell.

During 1952 and 1953, Auchincloss wrote full time. He completed a novel, *A Law for the Lion,* and a collection of stories, *The Romantic Egoist.* He wrote mornings and afternoons but not evenings. On Sunday afternoons, he met at the White Horse Tavern in Greenwich Village with other young authors, including Norman Mailer, William Styron, Herman Wouk, and Gore Vidal.

Auchincloss realized that two years of writing full time added nothing to his recognition as a writer. Although his writing time increased, in his opinion, the quantity and quality of his writing did not change. He decided to return to the practice of law.

When Auchincloss returned to Wall Street in the spring of 1954, he felt that he had returned home. Sullivan & Cromwell couldn't take him back because they had a policy against it; however, a Sullivan & Cromwell lawyer found him a position at Hawkins, Delafield, and Wood in the Trust and Estates Department. Auchincloss observed:

> I was sure that I would not give up the law again, and indeed, I have not. People ask me how I manage to write and practice. Sometimes I think it is the only thing about me that interests them. All I can say is that a great step was taken when I ceased to think of myself as a "lawyer" or a "writer." I was simply doing what I did when I did it....

So often men are born with all the tools they
need, but are blocked by the simple fear of
using them. Yet I suppose that the very act of
overcoming that fear may in itself be an indis-
pensible educative process toward using those
tools.[58]

In his next book, *The Great World and Timothy Holt,* published in 1956, Auchincloss tried to capture the atmosphere of
a Wall Street law firm during the years 1946-51. 1957 was an
eventful year for him; he married Adele Lawrence and
became a partner in Hawkins, Delafield, and Wood. Adele,
the friend of a friend, had asked him to a dinner party as a fill-
in, and he had declined. He called back and accepted at the
last minute and met the woman he was to marry after a
courtship of less than a year.

Adele Lawrence was related to the Vanderbilts, Sloanes,
and Burdens. Her education at Milton Academy and Bryn
Mawr was on a par with Auchincloss's education at Groton
and Yale. However, her two years at the Potter School in
Tucson, her year at the University of Florence studying
Italian, and her Master's degree in industrial design from the
Parsons School made her more well-rounded.

Auchincloss published *Venus in Sparta* and *Pursuit of the
Prodigal* in 1958 and 1959. *The House of Five Talents*, published in 1960, was a novel written as a memoir told by an
older woman, the granddaughter of the man who had earned
the family's wealth. Considered his best novel so far, it was
his seventh and the first not written as a third-person narrative. This first best seller was part history, part sociology.

Auchincloss's next book, *Portrait in Brownstone*, set in
the first half of the twentieth century, depicts the waning of
family loyalty and the decline of common values and the
resultant impact on society. In 1964, he published *The Rector
of Justin* about the headmaster of Justin Martyr Academy, a
fictitious Episcopal church school in New England. The story

of the headmaster's influence on those around him is told by six people. In this book, he addresses the contradiction of an elitist educational system based on the British model of Eton and Harrow in democratic America.

In 1966, *The Embezzler* was published to critical and popular acclaim. Auchincloss told a story loosely based on the life of Richard Whitney, president of the New York Stock Exchange in the 1930s, who embezzled to cover up personal financial losses. Although Auchincloss changed many of the facts in the Whitney case, his parents and the Whitney family opposed publication of the novel.

Also in 1966, Auchincloss became the partner in charge of the Trust and Estates Department at Hawkins, Delafield and Wood, when Lawrence Morris, the partner who had succeeded Dexter Hawkins as managing partner, died. Auchincloss managed the department for the next twenty years. Although he had carried the workload of the department during the reigns of his two predecessors, the firm's clients were not aware of this, and business fell off when he took over. He and one associate could handle the workload. One client went to another law firm, reasoning that an author as prolific as Auchincloss must be slighting his legal responsibilities.

Auchincloss admitted that: "I never recovered from the general belief that Dexter Hawkins and Lawrence Morris did everything, and I don't think people like their lawyers writing novels. Many people think that you can't do two things at one time. I think it's hurt me, has impeded my career. That doesn't mean it wiped me out. I produced clients, but not substantially. We lived on Larry's clients."[59]

Louis Auchincloss was successful in two endeavors. His energy level was well above average; he definitely had the drive to have two concurrent careers.

CHAPTER 2

RESILIENCE

"Life affords no higher pleasure than that of surmounting difficulties, passing from one step of success to another, forming new wishes and seeing them gratified. He that labors in any great or laudable undertaking has his fatigues first supported by hope and then by joy."

Samuel Johnson

Chapter 2 provides examples of men and women who overcame major obstacles to meet their goals in life and to continue to be productive. Many of us would have wavered when confronted with the challenges they faced. They did not give up, nor did they scale back on their objectives.

Frederick Delius continued to compose after becoming virtually blind and having severe restrictions placed on his movements by paralysis. He was a strong-willed individual who had to compose, regardless of the obstacles in his path. The lightness of his music belied the strength of his character.

Franklin Delano Roosevelt overcame polio to become Governor of New York State and the only four-term President of the United States. After contracting polio, his mother thought that he should retire to Hyde Park and become a country gentleman. Most people were aware of his physical disabilities but did not know the details of his struggle to rehabilitate himself. He did everything possible to improve his physical condition and to prepare himself for public office.

Helen Keller's story is well-known because of William Gibson's play, *The Miracle Worker.* Helen was only nineteen-months old when an illness left her blind, deaf, and mute. Overcoming her handicaps to learn how to communicate and to earn a college degree were monumental accomplishments. Her notable drive helped her to become a successful author, feminist, humanitarian, and advocate for the handicapped. She accomplished considerably more in her lifetime than most of us who have no handicaps.

Gail Borden, developer of evaporated milk, was a highly motivated inventor during his lifetime. He had several inventions that were failures and was almost fifty-six before he obtained a patent for his first successful development, evaporated milk. He encountered many disappointments along the way; however, he didn't give up. He drove himself until he finally was successful.

Al Neuharth was the highly regarded Chief Executive

Officer of the Gannett Corporation when he created a national newspaper, *USA Today*. He could have just maintained the status quo, but he was a man of vision. He knew that, with the advances in communications technology, a national newspaper was feasible. However, pioneers on the cutting edge usually suffer, and Neuharth was no exception. In August 1984, *USA Today* was losing $10 million a month with forecasted losses of $400 million before the paper was profitable. This was "as close as we ever came to folding;" Neuharth knew that painful cuts and changes were required to turn the paper around. He was driven to succeed. He made the necessary changes, and finances of the new venture improved.

Many of us could not have overcome the obstacles that confronted these individuals. They inspire us.

FREDERICK DELIUS (1862-1934) Rebounded from Serious Illnesses to Compose

"I think that the most stupid thing one can do is to spend one's life doing something one hates, or in which he has no interest; in other words, it is a wasted life. I do not believe in sacrificing the big things in life to anyone or anything.... Everything depends on your perseverance. One never knows how far one can go.... Emerson says in one of his essays ... something to this purpose, 'A man who works with his whole soul at anything whatever will make it a success before he is fifty,' and I believe this to be perfectly true. One's talent develops like muscles that you are constantly training. Trust more in hard work than inspiration."[60]

Frederick Delius

The music of English composer Frederick Delius is delicate and reserved, perhaps too delicate to be widely appreciated; nevertheless, he is considered one of the masters of music of his time. He composed over ninety works, including six operas, four concertos, five pieces of chamber music, and a number of songs.

At its première in the fall of 1935, George Gershwin's popular *Porgy and Bess* was hailed as the first Negro opera. Delius's *Koanga*, a Negro opera in three acts with unforgettable melodies, had its première at the Stadttheater in Eberfield, Germany over thirty years earlier, in 1904. In 1935, it was revived in London by Sir Thomas Beecham at Covent Garden and then taken on tour.

Delius's choral works include *A Mass of Life, Sea Drift, A Song of the High Hills,* and *Requiem.* Examples of orchestral works are *Over the Hills and Far Away, Paris: The Song of a Great City, Life's Dance, Brigg Fair,* and two exquisite pieces for small orchestra, *Summer Night on the River* and *On Hearing the First Cuckoo in Spring.*

In his Introduction to *Frederick Delius* by Peter Warlock

(Philip Heseltine), Hubert Foss compares the man, who continued to compose after going blind and becoming paralyzed, with his music:

> Out of all of this ... will emerge, I deeply hope, some sense of that curiously complicated, yet oddly simple character, Frederick Delius. To those who know the sounds, bathe in the beautiful warm, sunlit sea of harmony in his music ... to those people it may come as a surprise to discover a character of immense virility and even obstinacy. "Delius's music is so tender," said [composer] Norman O'Neill. The man Delius was not tender but purposeful and projective. The legend that has grown out of his paralyzed blindness ... is entirely at variance with the trapper of dreams himself.... The man Delius was totally unlike his music, the one displaying a most purposeful character, the other a vivid nebulosity of dreams.[61]

Frederick Delius, the second son of Julius and Elise Krönig Delius, was born on January 29, 1862 in Bradford, England. Julius Delius was a successful wool merchant with an international business. He took his children to Manchester to hear the Hallé Orchestra and to the Theatre Royal in Leeds to see the opera. He appreciated music and was a patron of the Hallé Orchestra and willingly paid for music lessons for his children. Young Frederick chose the violin as his first instrument and also played the piano. His mother encouraged him to improvise when he played.

Delius was educated at the Bradford Grammar School and the International School, Isleworth, London. He studied Latin, Greek, geography, mathematics, natural history, physics, and social science. He wasn't much of a scholar, but he excelled at cricket. Going to school in London gave him access to concerts at Covent Garden and St. James Hall, where he discovered Wagner, Grieg, and Berlioz. Delius's father expected him to go into the family business after his graduation from the International School.

Delius went to work for Delius and Company in Bradford but spent all of his spare hours on music and traveled to London to hear Chopin, Grieg, and Wagner. He was sent to Chemnitz, Germany and to Norrköpping, Sweden as an unpaid apprentice to learn all aspects of the wool industry. While in Sweden, he took hiking trips to Norway where he learned Norwegian and was introduced to Ibsen's plays.

Delius was particularly impressed by the lines of Ibsen's clergyman hero in *Brand:*

> One thing a man cannot give: his soul.
> He cannot deny his calling.
> He dare not block that river's course;
> It forces its way to the ocean....
> A place on earth where one can be wholly oneself:
> That is Man's right, and I ask no more.

Delius was doing what his father wanted him to do; however, he was not doing it well, and he certainly was not enjoying it.

Julius was disappointed with reports about his son's performance as an unpaid apprentice. Young Frederick had wandered off from the workplace and had attended concerts in Germany and in Sweden. Next, Julius sent his son to St. Etienne, France with little money to spend on concerts. Frederick failed there and again as an assistant office manager in Bradford. He wanted to attend the Leipzig Music Conservatory, but his father refused to pay his tuition.

Delius saw a poster in Bradford advertising farmland planted in orange groves in Florida. He told his father that he would like to become an orange grower. His father reluctantly agreed to lease an orange and grapefruit plantation with an option to buy for Delius to manage. Delius and a friend traveled to Solano Grove, forty miles south of Jacksonville. The rundown plantation was cared for by the Anderson family, African Americans who had worked for the previous owner.

Delius was more fascinated by Negro music, including hymns and spirituals, than by the challenge of growing oranges and grapefruit. The instruments used were banjos, cowbells, log drums, and seed pods. He was moved by the music, which was about slavery and separation; he entered into, in his words, "a state of illumination" and realized that the only future for him was music. He began to compose music in his head similar to what he had heard at the Anderson home.

On a trip to Jacksonville, Delius met Thomas Ward, organist at the Catholic cathedral in St. Augustine, who gave music lessons in Jacksonville. Ward offered to teach him the basics of harmony and counterpoint and lent him Hector Berlioz's book on orchestration. Ward moved to Solano Grove to give music lessons to Delius on a rented piano. Delius wanted to capture the Negro music. The only other composer to attempt this was Louis Gottschalk, who had written pieces based on the music of New Orleans.

When his father found out that Delius was concentrating on music and paying no attention to orange-growing, he cut off his allowance. His older brother, Ernest, who had failed at sheep farming in New Zealand, arrived unexpectedly at Solano Grove, and Delius turned over the plantation to him. Delius moved to Jacksonville and gave music lessons. He had many eager students, but he heard of a better opportunity teaching music at Roanoke Female College in Danville, Virginia.

One of his sponsors at the Roanoke Female College wrote to Delius's father about his success in teaching music and asked him to reconsider sending his son to a music conservatory. Julius Delius gave in and agreed to pay for an eighteen-month course in music theory at the Leipzig Conservatory. Delius received instruction in performing with musical instruments, but he did not receive substantial instruction on composing.

Delius composed *Florida*, which was based on the music he had heard there. His professors were not comfortable with his unconventional passages and did not encourage him. However, he had met Edvard Grieg on a hiking trip to Norway; Grieg was very supportive and encouraged him to compose according to his own lights.

Delius moved to Paris to compose while living on a miniscule allowance from his father. He worked on *Magic Fountain,* a opera about the search for the fountain of youth in Florida by a Spaniard named Solano with the help of a Seminole Indian princess, Watawa. It was not successful, but an earlier work, *On the Heights*, about the composer's memories of Norway's mountains, enjoyed a limited success. He worked to improve *Magic Fountain* as well as *On the Heights*.

In 1896, Delius composed an African-American folk opera, *Koanga*, about an African prince captured by slave traders. The storyline was about planters and overseers on plantations and in the fields, a subject Delius knew from his time in Florida. The instruments used were banjos, bones, and fiddles.

While working on *Koanga,* he met a young artist, Helen Sophie Emilie Rosen, who went by her childhood name, Jelka. She loved his music and encouraged him to continue his work on *Koanga*. She fell in love with him; it took him a long time to realize that he was in love with her as well.

Jelka painted in the garden of an old rundown house in Grez, a hamlet forty miles south of Paris. Eventually, she bought the house. Delius found it a peaceful place in which to compose. His compositions did not sell well, however. His New York agent told him that his harmonies were too complicated, his melodies were not memorable, and the discords were not appreciated.

Delius finally realized that he was in love with Jelka. He

missed her when she left Grez; he realized that he couldn't live without her. They were married on September 23, 1903. He was forty-one; she was thirty-five. Jelka gave up her career in art and devoted the rest of her life to Delius. She did everything that she could, including financial and administrative tasks, so that her husband could concentrate on composing.

A reporter described Delius at this time:

> He is a pale man, ascetic and monkish; a man with a waspish wit, a man who allows his wit to run away with him so far that he is tempted to express opinions that he does not really hold. He is a man who pursues a path of his own, indifferent to criticism, and perhaps indifferent to indifference. Decidedly a man of most distinguished intellect, and a quick, eager, but not responsive personality.... He is about forty years of age, taller than one at first thinks, lean, wiry, strenuous in every movement, a fine face with piercing eyes. Every movement he makes is rapid, decisive; he is a prodigious walker, bicyclist, and swimmer.[62]

A Norwegian playwright, Gunnar Heiberg, wrote a political satire, *The Council of the People*, and asked Delius to write the accompanying music. Since it was mocking and satirical, Delius wrote the background music, *Norwegian Suite*, in the same tone. Delius conducted its première in Christiana, now Oslo. The audience booed, hissed, and eventually cursed at Heiberg's mockery of the Norwegian parliament.

When they heard Delius's parody of the Norwegian anthem in a minor key, the audience gasped, stomped their feet, and rushed the conductor and the orchestra. A pistol was waved, and a shot rang out. The conductor and playwright ran out of the theater's rear exit to the Grand Hotel next door, while the police dealt with the crowd outside.

An elderly gentleman with white sideburns looked at them quizzically until Delius explained what had happened. The gentleman said, "I am sorry for the affront Norway has offered a distinguished visitor, Herr Delius. You must remember we are barbarians up here. Allow me to apologize. I am Henrik Ibsen."[63] When the crowd had settled down, Delius returned to his own hotel, only to be told that he could not stay there.

In 1913, the première of Igor Stravinsky's *Le Sacre du Printemps* at the Théâtre des Champs-Elysées in Paris caused a near riot. The audience hissed, shouted, and whistled at what they viewed as an affront to traditional music. Pandemonium reigned, but nobody shot at the conductor. Fortunately for Delius, the pistol used to shoot at him was loaded with blanks.

A young German conductor, Fritz Cassirer, offered to conduct Delius's symphony, *Appalachia,* in London. Delius, who had just met Sir Thomas Beecham, asked if Cassirer could use his orchestra. Beecham agreed and then sat in the audience. He was captivated by Delius's compositions. Beecham became the most active promoter in England of Delius's music, which was popular in Germany but not in England. The famous conductor included at least one Delius work every year in his programs and occasionally used his own money to pay for performances. Beecham's father had made his fortune making and selling Beecham's Little Liver Pills.

Beecham liked Delius personally in addition to liking his music. He commented on Delius's strengths: "Delius in his own way was a complete man, carved by nature in a clear and definable piece out of the rough and shapeless stone of her raw material; a signpost to others on the way of life, a light to those in darkness; and an unfailing reassurance to all those who strive to preserve their faith in those two supreme virtues, honesty and independence."[64]

Beecham was known for his conducting ability, his memory, and his sense of humor. One evening he was conducting an opera in which everything that could go wrong, did. Musicians missed their cues, singers sang off key, and props fell onto the stage. Finally, a young elephant that was part of the opera story defecated on the stage. Beecham looked at the odoriferous pile, halted the orchestra, turned around to face the audience and said: "The critics have spoken." He resumed conducting the opera after the stage was cleaned.

Delius worked so hard that he was exhausted and did not feel well. In the fall of 1910, Jelka took him to a sanitarium in Germany. Slowly, he began to regain his health. Percy Grainger visited him and suggested that he write music for smaller orchestras that would be less expensive to produce. The results of this suggestion were *On Hearing the First Cuckoo in Spring* and *Summer Night on the River.*

In the spring of 1915, Delius had problems with his eyesight and began to wear thick glasses. The fingers on his right hand had stiffened. One morning while at the piano composing *Hassan*, an Arabian Nights type of story about the Near East, the pen fell out of his hand. With difficulty, he picked up the pen with his left hand, but his right hand could not grip the pen. He was listless, and his legs were weak. A homeopathic doctor in the area told him that it was a "lameness that would pass off."

By the summer of 1922, Delius needed two canes to walk. On some days, he could only see large objects that were close to him. Two years later, he began to use a wheelchair. He tried hydrotherapy, electric shock treatments, and hypnotism, but no treatment improved his condition for long. Eventually, he had to be carried everywhere by a male nurse, and he virtually lost his sight. His condition slowed his composing, but it did not stop it.

Jelka helped Delius to finish *Hassan*; however, she was a painter, not a musician. She was not familiar with orchestration; she made many mistakes, and the score had many erasures. Finishing the work was painful both for Jelka and for Delius. Obviously, he could not continue to compose music in this fashion. In between working on his own compositions, Percy Grainger helped Delius when he could.

In May 1928, Delius received a letter from a young Yorkshireman, Eric Fenby, who offered to come to Grez to take dictation from Delius to help him in composing his music. Fenby was willing to give up several years of his life and to delay his career to perform what he considered his self-imposed duty. Fenby was a hard-working, shy, religious person who wanted Delius's composing to continue; also, he realized that he would receive valuable training that he could not get elsewhere.

Initially, Fenby struggled, and Delius became impatient. Fenby was not fast enough for him. After several months, they evolved a productive way of working together. Delius became a news item. He was referred to as the "blind composer" and the "crippled genius." Newspaper journalists frequently described his working relationship with Fenby, who described life at Grez:

> There was nothing of the sickly, morbid, blind composer as known by popular fiction here, but a man with a heart like a lion, and a spirit that was as untamable as it was stern ... once you had crossed the threshold of that great door to the street you found yourself in another world—a world, peaceful and self-sufficient, which centered around the figure of Delius. It was a world with its own laws, its own standards of right and wrong, in all things, its own particular sense of beauty and its own music. It had been created for music-making.[65]

In January 1929, King George presented Delius with the Order of the Companion of Honor. Delius was pleased and proud of the recognition. In the fall of 1929, Sir Thomas Beecham convinced Delius to come to London to hear his music performed in a series of six concerts. Delius was overwhelmed by the enthusiasm of his fans in England. Beecham had prepared well, and the concerts were standing room only. Delius was asked to speak after one of the concerts: "Ladies and gentlemen. Thank you for the very fine reception you have given me. It was wholly unexpected. I also wish to thank Sir Thomas Beecham for the inspired manner in which he played my music. This festival has been the time of my life. Again I thank you."[66]

Delius, Jelka, and Fenby returned to Grez, where Delius worked on a sonata. The pressure of working with an elderly person who was ill was taking a toll on Fenby. He was on the verge of a nervous breakdown. He told Delius that he had to go home to England, at least briefly. Fenby returned to Grez early in 1931 to help Delius with his work on *Irmelin*, an opera about a princess who fell in love with a wandering troubadour and a prince who searched for a magic river.

Fenby again was weighed down by his role and had to return to England, where he collapsed from the strain late in 1931. In August 1932, he returned again to Grez to help Delius with *Fantastic Dance*, based on Negro blues music. In the summer of 1933, Fenby left Grez a third time. It was a solitary existence for a young man, and Delius's irritability was difficult to handle. Delius's niece, Margaret, his sister Clare's daughter, came to Grez to help. Margaret read to her uncle daily until she had to return to her job in London.

In January 1934, Delius began to sleep during much of the day. In May 1934, Jelka had an operation for cancer, and Fenby returned to help the nurse care for Delius. Jelka returned from the hospital the following month and was home in Grez on June 10, 1934, when Delius died. The British Broadcasting Corporation released a news bulletin: "We regret to announce the passing of Mr. Frederick Delius, Companion of Honor." The bulletin was accompanied by the playing of "The Walk to a Paradise Garden" from *A Village Romeo and Juliet*. A newspaper headline announced: "MUSIC'S BLIND HERO IS DEAD; HIS SOUL GOES MARCHING ON."

The place of Delius's music is described in a postscript by Hubert Foss to *Frederick Delius* by Peter Warlock (Philip Heseltine):

> Delius's music, it seems to me, is of the eternal kind that appeals to the young. At the hopeful stage, the sounds sweep beautifully over one's soul; and the secret which Delius himself had and kept and gave to us is the saving, the preservation in beauty, of those early memories.... Let us thank God for the possession of Delius's music—for its sheer beauty, for its sound, for its dreams, for its emotion, for its intensity, for its power to continue in its purposes.[67]

Jelka and Fenby took Delius's body to England for burial in Limpsfield Churchyard, Surrey. Jelka died on May 28, 1935 after contracting pneumonia on the ship crossing the channel. Jelka had given given up a promising career as a artist to support her husband's career as a composer. In Fenby's opinion, "One thing was uppermost in my mind at Grez, and that was that only there, and with such constant care as his wife lavished upon him, could he [Delius] go on living. Her name deserves a very prominent place on the scroll of those who have given themselves unstintingly for others."[68]

FRANKLIN DELANO ROOSEVELT (1882-1945)
Conquered Polio and Led the U.S. Out of the Depression

"No matter whether Governor Smith wins or loses, Franklin D. Roosevelt stands out as the real hero of the Democratic Convention of 1924. Adversity has lifted him above the bickering, the religious bigotry, conflicting personal ambitions and petty sectional prejudices. It has made him the one leader commanding the respect and admiration from all sections of the land.... Roosevelt might be a pathetic, tragic figure but for the fine courage that flashes in his smile. It holds observers enchained."[69]

New York *Evening World*

In July 1921, Franklin Delano Roosevelt was an ambitious young man attempting to defend his position as Assistant Secretary of the Navy during World War I. He worked long days to respond to fifteen volumes of testimony of a Senate subcommittee investigating the administration of naval affairs during the war. He and his aide, Steve Early, were given very little time to respond to the 6,000-page testimony, so they worked around the clock in the hot, humid Washington weather. He successfully defended his role and the Navy Department's performance during the war.

Roosevelt had been looking forward to spending the month of August vacationing with his family on the island of Campobello in the Bay of Fundy, as he did every year. When he got off the boat at Campobello, he was surrounded by his five children: Anna, fifteen; James, fourteen; Elliot, eleven; Franklin, Jr., seven; and John, five. Eleanor Roosevelt, Mrs. Louis Howe, the wife of his political advisor and good friend, and Hartley Howe, the Howes' five-year-old son, also greeted him.

Roosevelt spent the next few days deep-sea fishing in the Bay of Fundy. On the last day of fishing, he fell overboard into the ice-cold water of the bay. He was chilled to the bone.

He was used to swimming in the cold water of the bay, but he had never experienced the paralyzing cold of the water that day. Perhaps he was affected by the contrast of the water with the hot, humid weather in addition to the heat of the engine near where he had been fishing on the deck.

During the next day, Roosevelt was tired, and his golf game was off. After assembling gear for a camping trip with the children planned for the following day, he took them for a sail in the family sailboat, *Vireo*. As they sailed, they saw a fire on one of the islands. They landed, and Roosevelt cut evergreen branches for everyone to use in beating the flames from a grove of spruce trees that was on fire. When the fire was under control, the exhausted firefighters sailed for home.

Roosevelt suggested that the sweaty, bedraggled group go for a swim in Glen Severn, a small lake on the other side of the island. After jogging back to the cottage after the swim, he couldn't resist another swim in the Bay of Fundy; he didn't even consider his chill of the previous day. The swim was exhilarating, but his tiredness persisted. He had several chills and decided to go to bed, to bundle up, and to have supper in his bedroom. The chill stayed with him and the following morning, when he got out of bed, he noticed that his left leg ached and was sluggish. He had a temperature of 102. Eleanor called the family doctor, Dr. Bennett, who examined Roosevelt and diagnosed an ordinary cold, but a severe one. He prescribed bed rest.

The next morning, Roosevelt experienced tenderness in the front of his thighs; even the weight of the covers caused him pain. When he got out of bed, his right knee buckled. His temperature remained at 102. His muscles became more sensitive, and he could barely move his legs. The following day, his legs were completely paralyzed, and his back ached. Louis Howe arrived at Campobello that afternoon and acted immediately. He took the launch to Bar Harbor, Maine to bring back Dr. W. W. Keen, a well-known diagnostician who was vacationing there.

Dr. Keen found that Roosevelt was completely paralyzed below the waist, and his arms were heavy. His diagnosis was a blood clot in the lower spinal cord. He thought that Roosevelt would recover, but that it would take many months. He prescribed rigorous massaging of Roosevelt's thighs and lower legs, beginning immediately. Until a masseuse could get to Campobello from New York, Eleanor and Howe massaged his legs, causing him considerable pain. His condition worsened; he was helpless. Dr. Keen changed his diagnosis from a clot on the lower spinal cord to a lesion on the lower spinal cord.

Eleanor wrote to Roosevelt's uncle, Frederic Roosevelt, describing the illness. Uncle Frederic was not satisfied with the diagnosis and immediately contacted Dr. Robert W. Lovett, a prominent Boston specialist. Dr. Lovett was out of town, so uncle Frederic described the symptoms to Dr. Lovett's colleague, Dr. Samuel A. Levine, who immediately diagnosed the ailment as poliomyelitis. He suggested discontinuing the massages; they were doing more harm than good. Roosevelt's temperature continued to fluctuate; however, his temperament was better than everyone expected it would be.

Dr. Lovett came to Campobello to examine Roosevelt. He agreed with Dr. Levine's diagnosis and his suggestion to stop the massages. Dr. Lovett recommended warm saline baths and suggested that Roosevelt spend some time in the hospital to help speed his recovery. He was admitted to Presbyterian Hospital in New York under the care of his old Groton classmate, Dr. George Draper, who struck a balance between encouragement and realism. Dr. Draper made a statement about his patient's condition to the newspapers. Louis Howe, always alert to public relations, added the following statement to that of Dr. Draper: "He will not be crippled. No one need have any fear of permanent injury from this attack."

Dr. Draper recommended that straps be installed in the ceiling over Roosevelt's bed, so he could pull himself up to a sitting position and turn in bed. Later, straps were also installed over his bed at Hyde Park. Dr. Draper forwarded a progress report on his classmate to Dr. Lovett in Boston:

> I am much concerned at the slow recovery both as regards the disappearance of pain, which is generally present, and as to the recovery of even slight power to twitch the muscles. There is marked falling away of the muscle masses on either side of the spine in the lower lumbar region.... The lower extremities present a most depressing picture. There is a little motion in the long extensors of the toes of each foot....

> I feel so strongly ... that the psychological factor in his management is paramount. He has such courage, such ambition, and yet at the same time an extraordinarily sensitive emotional mechanism that it will take all the skill which we can muster to lead him to the recognition of what he really faces without crushing him.[70]

Roosevelt kept his spirits up and greeted all visitors heartily. He didn't complain or seek pity for his bad luck. He joked and laughed with his visitors; if they weren't in a happy frame of mind when they arrived, they were when they left his room. He referred to his paralyzed lower extremities as "my somewhat rebellious legs." After six weeks in the hospital, he was allowed to go home even though he was still weak, and the fever kept returning. Dr. Draper was concerned with the slow progress. He entered the evaluation "not improving" on Roosevelt's chart.

Upon his release from the hospital, Roosevelt moved into one of the twin houses on East Sixty-fifth Street owned by his Mother, Sara Roosevelt. He was confident that he would recover and would walk again. However, early in the following year, his right knee buckled followed by his left knee; his tendons were tightening. Dr. Draper had both legs encased in plaster casts, causing considerable pain. Every day, part of the cast was chipped away at the back of the cast to allow a wedge to be driven in to stretch the muscles. After two weeks, the muscles in the legs were loosened and straightened.

Roosevelt displayed enormous endurance. After his legs were straightened, he was fitted for braces. Because he was tall, he had a high center of gravity, which made it more difficult to maintain balance. The braces were heavy and had to be sent back for adjustment several times. Using crutches caused sores in his armpits unless he distributed his weight evenly to his shoulders, wrists, and hands. He gradually extended the distance that he walked on crutches.

In May 1922, Roosevelt moved to Hyde Park on the Hudson River for the summer. He had a set of parallel bars constructed on the south lawn of his home, Springwood. They were ten-feet long on a circular base with waist-high lower bars and shoulder-high upper bars. He used the parallel bars daily until he slipped one day and tore some ligaments. Also, he swam in neighbor Vincent Astor's heated pool until he could have one built at his home. He enjoyed swimming and was a strong believer in water therapy. He said that water had gotten him into this predicament, and that he was counting on water to get him out of it.

Roosevelt taught himself to crawl to increase his ability to move around the house. He placed his weight on his wrists and hands and dragged his legs behind him. He was fitted for a lighter pair of braces and a corset to help hold him erect. He wrote an article about the relations between the United States and Japan that was published in *Asia* and talked about writing a history of the U.S. Navy, but he didn't seriously pursue it. In September, he moved back to New York City.

Dr. Draper had advised Roosevelt to become active in business or politics instead of concentrating exclusively on physical fitness. Roosevelt went to his insurance office at 120 Broadway, which was easily accessible for him, for a few hours each day. His old law office, Marvin, Emmett, and Roosevelt, that he had formed with two friends after his vice presidential campaign in 1920, was only accessible by a flight of stone stairs.

At Hyde Park, Roosevelt had practiced getting out of a car—a laborious process involving many steps. He had to:

- Ensure that his braces were locked.
- Grip the back of the "jump-seat," and pull himself forward.
- Move his inflexible legs out of the car.
- Push his legs in front of him.
- Grip the "jump-seat," place his weight on the armrest, and hoist himself up and out of the car.
- Shift his weight to the driver, who handed his crutches to him.
- Place the crutches under his arms, move forward, and smile all the time.

One day Roosevelt fell going to work at his insurance office, and his driver wasn't strong enough to pick him up by himself. Roosevelt had to ask a young onlooker for a hand. Another onlooker, a lawyer with an office in the building adjacent to Roosevelt's office, was impressed with the spirit his neighbor had shown in recovering from the fall. Basil O'Connor later became a partner and a lifelong friend.

Roosevelt enjoyed going to the office, but he missed the sunshine and the swimming therapy. He decided to rent a houseboat and to spend at least part of the winter in Florida. Sunshine and swimming would help him to improve, and he enjoyed fishing. His upper body muscles gained strength to compensate for the weakness in his lower limbs. After he returned to Hyde Park, he tried horseback riding. Initially, his daughter Anna led him around the estate on a docile pony.

Roosevelt experimented with a new means of locomotion using a crutch under his right arm and a strong arm to grip with his left hand. With his braces locked into position, he could swing on his arms and shoulders and force his body forward by brute strength. Initially, his chauffeur, James Depew, and then his son, James, supported him. They had to learn to synchronize their steps with his and, above all, to smile and not look strained.

Roosevelt rejoined the political scene by accepting the position of pre-convention campaign manager for Governor Al Smith for President. He was asked to make the nominating speech for Al Smith at the Democratic National Convention at Madison Square Garden in New York. As Roosevelt approached the podium, he realized that no one had checked to see if it was sturdy enough to hold him. He asked a national committeeman to test the podium, and it was strong enough. Since he had to hold onto the podium and couldn't lift his arms, he smiled and lifted his head. He was greeted by loud applause and many cheers.

Roosevelt became more confident the longer that he spoke. He described Al Smith: "He has a power to strike at error and wrongdoing that makes his adversaries quail before him. He has a personality that carries to every hearer not only the sincerity but the righteousness of what he says. He is the 'Happy Warrior' of the political battlefield."[71] Delegates responded noisily in one of the most tumultuous demonstrations ever seen in Madison Square Garden. However, Smith didn't win the nomination; John W. Davis did.

Roosevelt returned to Hyde Park to continue his physical therapy. One of his visitors was New York banker George Foster Peabody, who told him of a mineral spring at Warm Springs, Georgia that had virtually cured a young boy of infantile paralysis. Roosevelt decided to check out Warm Springs on his next trip to Florida. It had been an "in" resort before the Civil War but had encountered hard times. Its main building, Meriwether Inn, had fallen into disrepair, and the grounds had become overgrown. The 50 by 150 feet pool was the principal attraction of the place.

Geologists explained that the source of the water was rain that fell on Pine Mountain, five miles away, and "runs down 3,800 feet to a deep pocket of rock, where it is warmed by the inner earth, and then returned to the surface at a temperature of 88 degrees Fahrenheit at a rate of 800 gallons a minute."[72] The mineral content of the water provided its buoyancy. Roosevelt dipped his feet into the water and immediately had a tingling sensation in his toes. He called the water "marvelous," and said that he had "more life [in his toes] than he'd felt in them since August 1921."

Roosevelt wrote to his mother: "When I get back, I am going to have a long talk with Mr. George Foster Peabody, who is really the controlling interest in the property. I feel that a great 'cure' for infantile paralysis and kindred diseases could well be established here."[73] He envisioned a prosperous resort for all victims of paralysis. When Roosevelt returned to New York, he became a partner of Basil O'Connor in the practice of law. He persuaded his new partner to evaluate the property in Warm Springs and later to become one of its organizers.

Roosevelt went to Florida for the winter. On returning from a fishing trip, he fell on the launch and tore some knee ligaments, setting back his rehabilitation program. He returned to Warm Springs to find that publicity had attracted additional sufferers of paralysis to the spa. Roosevelt worked with the newcomers, always radiating hope and enthusiasm. He stressed that they had to have confidence that they were going to improve. Roosevelt began to lay out plans for a beautiful resort. He decided to forego his houseboat trips and fishing expeditions in Florida and to visit Warm Springs every winter.

About this time, Roosevelt traveled to Marion, Massachusetts to receive treatment from Dr. William McDonald. McDonald advocated less time in braces to strengthen the muscles and exercise on a "walking board." The walking board was a rectangular wooden platform surrounded by wooden railings. The patient, without leg braces, pulled himself or herself around the platform with a hand-over-hand motion. One day, Roosevelt exercised too long, and one of his knees locked.

Roosevelt described the exercises to Dr. Draper: "Where Lovett gave a single direct pulling exercise for the quadriceps in the direction of gravity, McDonald exercises the quadriceps with and against gravity, direct motion singly, in pairs, alternately, reciprocally and also with a rotary motion, singly, in pairs, alternately and reciprocally."[74] Late in his stay in Marion, he was able to walk a block wearing only one brace and using a cane. He was willing to try any treatment in the chance of improving, and it paid off. "I'll walk without crutches, I'll walk into a room without scaring everyone half to death. I'll stand easily in front of people so that they'll forget that I'm a cripple."[75]

Roosevelt continued his efforts as consultant and "architect" in improving Warm Springs. A table was installed twelve inches below the surface of the water to help patients with their exercises and ramps were installed at all buildings to improve access for the handicapped. He ensured that an active social life was provided, including bridge and poker parties and picnics. He decided to buy the property and to run it as a nonprofit organization. Eventually, the spa received recognition as a "hydrotherapeutic center" from the American Orthopedic Association.

In September 1926, Al Smith asked Roosevelt to be temporary chairman of the New York State Democratic Convention and to make the keynote speech. Louis Howe advised him not to be drawn into any run for public office. Even though Roosevelt radiated health because of his exercise and his life outdoors, Howe knew that his candidate was at least two years away from public office.

Governor Smith asked him again in 1928 to give the keynote speech at the Democratic National Convention. Will Durant, who covered the convention in Houston for the New

York *World-Telegram* wrote:

> Here on the stage is Franklin Roosevelt,
> beyond comparison the finest man that has
> appeared at either convention.... A figure tall
> and proud even in suffering; a face of classic
> profile; pale with years of struggle against
> paralysis; a frame nervous yet self-controlled
> with that tense, taut unity of spirit which lifts
> the complex soul above those whose calmness
> is only a solidity; most obviously a gentleman
> and a scholar. A man softened and cleansed
> and illumined with pain....
>
> Hear the nominating speech; it is not a battery
> of rockets, bombs, and tear-drawing gas—it is
> not shouted, it is quietly read; there is hardly a
> gesture, hardly a raising of the voice. This is a
> civilized man; he could look Balfour and
> Poincaré in the face. For the moment, we are
> lifted up.[76]

Al Smith was nominated on the first ballot.

Al Smith asked Roosevelt to run for Governor. He declined; Howe was relieved that his man wasn't going to run in 1928. Smith continued to pursue him. He arranged for Herbert Lehman, the Democratic candidate for Lieutenant Governor, to offer to stand in for him when he went to Warm Springs.

Finally, Smith called Roosevelt to ask him if he were nominated by the delegates at the convention, would he refuse the nomination? Roosevelt hesitated, and Smith knew that he had the answer that he wanted. Roosevelt realized that public office would probably limit improvement of his physical condition.

The press was critical of Governor Smith for talking

Roosevelt into running for Governor, so that he could improve his own chances for the Presidency. Journalists concentrated on Roosevelt's handicap. Smith responded, "A Governor does not have to be an acrobat. We do not elect him for his ability to do a double back-flip or a handspring."[77] Roosevelt promised to go more places and make more speeches than any office seeker in New York State.

In one sense, Roosevelt's illness improved him as a candidate. Jean Gould comments upon this in *A Good Fight*:

> Here the habit of listening that he formed during the last six years stood him in good stead. People whom he once would have considered bores, back in the days when he was a State Senator, when he could (an often did) turn and walk away from them, he now found himself listening to, not only because he couldn't help himself, but because he was interested in their project, in finding out what what Mr. Average Man thought, felt, and did.[78]

When Roosevelt went to vote at the Hyde Park town hall, newspaper journalists and photographers were gathered at the entrance. He looked at the photographers, smiled, and asked them to take no photographs of his getting out of the car; they complied. From then on in his public career, he was photographed only from the waist up or after posing for a standing shot.

Governor Smith lost the election overwhelmingly to Herbert Hoover. Roosevelt became Governor of New York State by just 25,000 votes. This margin was improved to 725,000 votes when he ran for reelection in 1930. When he became a serious candidate for President of the United States, a national magazine suggested that a report of his daily routine and of his state of health be made by a panel of doctors. He agreed immediately.

Three doctors: a diagnostician, an orthopedist, and a neurologist examined him and reported:

> We have today examined Franklin D. Roosevelt. We find that his organs and functions are sound in all respects. There is no anemia. The chest is exceptionally well developed, and the spinal column is perfectly normal; all of its segments are in alignment, and free from disease. He has neither pain nor ache at any time.
>
> Ten years ago, Governor Roosevelt suffered an attack of acute infantile paralysis, the entire effect of which was expended on the muscles of his lower extremities. There has been progressive recovery of power in the legs since that date; this restoration continues and will continue.... We believe that his powers of endurance are such to allow him to meet all the demands of private or public life.[79]

In January 1932, Roosevelt announced his candidacy for the office of President of the United States. In November, he won the election with almost 23,000,000 votes, fifty-seven percent of the popular vote. The "brain trust" that he had assembled in Albany followed him to Washington, including Adolf A. Berle, Jr., James Farley, Frances Perkins, Samuel Rosenman, and Rexford Tugwell. Many programs that they had tried at the state level were polished and expanded for the federal level. Because of his reduced mobility, people came to him instead of his going to them. Eleanor Roosevelt became his traveling eyes, even to the extent of descending into a mine to inspect the working conditions of miners.

When historians are polled, Franklin Delano Roosevelt is always listed as one of the five "great" presidents. Early surveys ranked him third behind Lincoln and Washington. A later survey ranked him second after Lincoln and before Washington. Eleanor Roosevelt was once asked if she thought that her husband would have become President if he hadn't had poliomyelitis. She replied that, in her opinion, he would have become President but a different (lesser) President.

HELEN KELLER (1880-1968) Humanitarian and Author Who Overcame Handicaps

"My life has been happy because I have wonderful friends and plenty of interesting work to do. I seldom think about my limitations, and they never make me sad. Perhaps there is just a touch of yearning at times, but it is vague, like a breeze among flowers. The wind passes, and the flowers are content.... I slip back at times. I fall, I stand still. I run against the edge of hidden obstacles. I lose my temper and find it again, and keep it better. I trudge on. I gain a little. I feel encouraged. I get more eager and climb higher and begin to see widening horizons."[80]

Helen Keller

Helen Adams Keller was a model of what the human spirit can do when challenged. Helen Keller was above average in intelligence and in inquisitiveness. Her ability to overcome her triple handicaps of being blind, deaf, and mute is an inspiration to all of us. She could not have accomplished what she did without a very positive outlook and large measures of motivation and perseverance.

Helen was a normal infant until the age of nineteen months, when, due to an illness, she lost her sight, her hearing, and her ability to speak. Her resilience in overcoming her handicaps was exemplary. The accomplishments of her teacher, Anne Sullivan, were notable as well.

Helen led a life of achievement, writing articles and books and supporting causes for the handicapped, particularly the blind. She received considerable recognition for her accomplishments, including the St. Sava Order from King Alexander of Yugoslavia. Her academic honors included honorary degrees from Harvard University and the University of Berlin as well as a Doctor of Laws degree from the University of Glasgow and a Doctor of Humane Letters degree from Temple University. She was invited to the White House by every President from Grover Cleveland to John F. Kennedy, and, in 1964, she was awarded the Presidential Medal of Freedom by President Lyndon Johnson.

Helen Keller was born on June 27, 1880 in Tuscumbia, a town of 2,000 in northern Alabama near Muscle Shoals on the Tennessee River. Her father, Arthur H. Keller, who had been a captain in the Confederate Army, was the publisher of *The North Alabamian* and Marshal of North Alabama. Her paternal grandmother was a second cousin of Robert E. Lee. Helen's mother, Kate Adams Keller, was related to the Everett family of New England. Helen, the oldest of three children, had one sister, Mildred, and one brother, Philip. Arthur Keller was a prominent man in his community. He owned a large estate, but, like many of his neighbors, he was land poor.

The illness that deprived Helen of her sight, hearing, and ability to speak occurred in February 1882. It was described by doctors as "acute congestion of the stomach and brain" and "brain fever," but it was probably scarlet fever. Helen's doctor did not expect her to live.

Hope for Helen came when her mother read Charles Dickens's "American Notes," in which he described the progress made by Laura Bridgman. Laura, who was blind and deaf, had been educated by Dr. Samuel Gridley Howe at the Perkins Institution in Boston. Dr. Howe had been dead for a number of years when Kate Keller read this article in 1886.

At about the same time, Arthur Keller took Helen to Baltimore for a comprehensive eye examination by the highly regarded oculist, Dr. Chisholm. He gave no encouragement for improvement but suggested to Arthur Keller that he consult with Dr. Alexander Graham Bell in Washington. Dr. Bell, the Scottish-American inventor of the telephone, had a lifelong commitment to helping the deaf. He had been a teacher of speech for the deaf in Boston.

Dr. Bell suggested that the Kellers contact Michael Anagnos, Dr. Howe's son-in-law, who was his successor at the Perkins Institution. Anagnos recommended Anne

Sullivan, valedictorian of the Perkins Institution class of 1886, as a teacher for Helen. Anne had been nearly blind until she had two eye operations in her mid-teens that restored her sight.

Anne was apprehensive when she arrived in Tuscumbia to take up her new responsibilities. She was pleased to find a healthy young girl who indicated early that she was clever. However, Anne found that Helen was an unruly, undisciplined child whose behavior was out of control. Arthur and Kate Keller had tolerated it because they did not know how to deal with it.

Anne realized that she would have to establish her authority early if she hoped to succeed with Helen. Within several days, Helen demonstrated her unruliness by knocking out two of her teacher's front teeth. Helen would pinch Anne when she was disappointed and then lie on the floor and kick and scream. Helen threw her spoon on the floor, and Anne would make her pick it up. When Helen threw her napkin on the floor, Anne would make her pick it up and fold it.

Anne thought that faster progress could be made if she and Helen were off by themselves. The Kellers realized the importance of establishing discipline and suggested that Anne and Helen move to the garden house, which was a quarter mile from the homestead.

After two weeks in the garden house, Helen realized that Anne was trying to help her. The young student became not only obedient but loving. Anne was overjoyed. She wrote to Mrs. Hopkins, her old housemother at Perkins, that "the little savage has learned her first lesson in obedience." Helen began to show a definite interest in learning.

On April 5, 1887, just over a month after Anne arrived in Tuscumbia, a significant emotional event occurred for Helen. Anne described it in a letter to Mrs. Hopkins:

> I must write you a line this morning because something very important has happened.

Helen has taken the second great step in her education. She has learned that everything has a name, and that the manual alphabet is the key to everything she wants to know.... This morning, while she was washing, she wanted to know the word for "water" ... I spelled "w-a-t-e-r" and thought no more about it until after breakfast.... We went out to the pump house, and I made Helen hold her hand under the spout while I pumped. I spelled "w-a-t-e-r" in Helen's free hand.

The word coming so close upon the sensation of cold water rushing over her hand seemed to startle her. She dropped the mug and stood transfixed. A new light came into her face. She spelled "w-a-t-e-r" several times. Then she dropped on the ground and asked for its name and pointed to the pump.... Just then the nurse brought Helen's little sister into the pump house, and Helen spelled "baby" and pointed to the nurse.[81]

This was a major scene in *The Miracle Worker,* William Gibson's popular play based on *Anne Sullivan Macy: The Story Behind Helen Keller* by Nella Brady, Helen's friend. The play, starring Anne Bancroft as Anne Sullivan and Patty Duke as Helen, opened on Broadway in October 1959 and ran for 702 performances.

Helen was awakened to the possibilities now open to her; she learned at a frantic pace. During several hours in one day in April 1887, she added thirty words to her vocabulary. Obviously, the more abstract words, such as "love," were more difficult to learn. Her next goals were to learn to construct sentences and to learn how to read. In Helen's words:

> As soon as I could spell a few words, my teacher gave me slips of cardboard on which were printed words in raised letters. I quickly learned that each printed word stood for an object, an act, or a quality.... I found the slips of paper which represented, for example, "doll," "is," "on," "bed" and placed each name on its object; then I put my doll on the bed with the words "is," "on," "bed" arranged beside the doll, thus making a sentence of the words, and at the same time carrying out the idea of the sentence with the things themselves.[82]

In May 1887, Helen read her first story. Unfortunately, no standardized technique for printing books for the blind existed at this time. In 1829, Louis Braille had invented a system of printing books for the blind in which characters are represented by raised dots. Dr. Howe at the Perkins Institution did not like the Braille system so he invented "Boston Line Type" using embossed regular letters. Also, William Bell Wait, Superintendent of the New York School for the Blind, devised a system called "New York Point." In addition, a teacher at Perkins invented another system, "American Braille."

After instructing Helen for three months, Anne wrote to Michael Anagnos, telling him that "something tells me that I am going to succeed beyond all my dreams." Anagnos began to make Helen's accomplishments known to the public; however, since he was known as a flowery writer with a tendency toward overstatement, some were concerned that Helen's accomplishments were being exaggerated. Anagnos asked Anne to write about her progress to date. She was reluctant to do it, but Arthur Keller, with newspaperman's blood in his veins, prevailed upon her to provide the summary. Anne's account contributed significantly to Helen's name becoming known.

Anne suggested that Helen move to Boston to take advantage of all the materials available at the Perkins Institute to teach the blind. Also, Helen would have the opportunity to meet other children who shared her handicaps. In May 1888, Helen began to learn Braille at Perkins. Anne continued to work with Helen, teaching her during the day and into the evening. Helen was learning too fast to adhere to the usual classroom schedule.

Helen set a goal for herself to learn to speak. Anne did not think that this was a good way for Helen to spend her energy; however, Helen insisted. Her teachers gave in after hearing about a young blind and deaf girl in Norway who had been taught to speak.

In March 1890, Helen enrolled at the Horace Mann School for the Deaf in Boston. She described the method used by her teacher, Sarah Fuller, the principal: "She passed my hand lightly over her face, and let me feel the position of her tongue and lips when she made a sound. I was eager to initiate every motion and in an hour had learned six elements of speech: M, P, A, S, T, and I. I shall never forget the surprise and delight I felt when I uttered my first sentence: 'It is warm.'"[83]

One had to speak slowly for Helen to understand what a person was saying. Sarah Fuller also taught Helen how to lip read by placing her fingers not only on the lips of the person speaking but also on their throat.

In autumn 1894, Helen enrolled in the Wright-Humason School for the Deaf in New York, which had a strong reputation for teaching deaf people how to speak and how to read lips. Her expenses were paid by John Spaulding, who had made his fortune in the sugar business. Her two years of study there included courses in arithmetic, geography, French, and German. Helen was disappointed in her progress in being able to speak clearly; people had difficulty understanding her.

Helen made many friends in New York, including Mark Twain and William Dean Howells. She and Mark Twain became good friends; her close friendship with the author was second only to her friendship with Alexander Graham Bell.

Helen's sponsor from Boston, John Spaulding, passed away, and her father was struggling financially. Mr. and Mrs. Lawrence Hutton, who had introduced Helen and Anne to New York society, established a fund for Helen's education. In 1896, Helen enrolled at the Cambridge School for Young Ladies to prepare for the entrance examinations for Radcliffe College. She left after a year and moved to her friends, the Chamberlins', farm in Wrentham, twenty-six miles from Boston, where she was tutored by Merton S. Keith of Cambridge.

In June 1899, Helen took the entrance examinations for Radcliffe. Unfortunately, the mathematics portion of the exam was in American Braille, and she was familiar with only English signs and symbols. She overcame this obstacle and passed; however, she spent another year being tutored by Keith before she entered Radcliffe in the fall of 1890. Years later, President Woodrow Wilson asked her why she chose Radcliffe. She replied that she thought that they didn't want her at Radcliffe, and, because she was stubborn, she decided to go there.

Helen carried a full course load at Radcliffe. Anne went to all of her classes and spelled the contents of the lectures into Helen's hand. Helen was elected vice president of her freshman class. She completed seventeen and a half courses to fulfill the requirement for an BA degree without taking any courses in science or mathematics. In 1904, she graduated cum laude with "especial mention for her excellence in English literature." Her classmates, who gave her a standing ovation when she received her degree, wrote that "beside her task, our efforts pale." Helen and Anne did not stay and socialize after the degrees were conferred; they felt that Anne had not received the recognition that she deserved.

While at Radcliffe, Helen had enrolled in a composition course taught by a well-known Harvard professor, Charles

Copeland. Her writing attracted the attention of the editors of the *Ladies' Home Journal*, who asked her to write her autobiography. John Macy, a young English literature instructor at Harvard University, assisted her in writing the book, which was published in 1902. *The Story of My Life* was a success as it had been when published as a serial in the *Ladies' Home Journal*. Helen's second book, *Optimism,* based on a 7,000-word essay that she wrote on the goodness of life while an undergraduate at Radcliffe, was published in 1903.

While John Macy was helping Helen to write her autobiography, John and Anne fell in love. Although he was considerably younger than she, they were married in 1905. John had to agree with the stipulation that Helen would have first priority in the household.

Helen bought a farm on seven acres of land in Wrentham, Massachusetts with the proceeds from her books and by selling sugar stock that John Spaulding had given her. Helen and Anne moved there after Helen's graduation; they were joined by John after he and Anne were married.

In 1906, Helen was appointed to the Massachusetts Commission for the Blind. She pioneered in bringing the problems of blindness of the newborn to the attention of the public.

In 1909, Helen's third book, *The World I Live In,* was published, and the following year one of her poems, *A Song of the Stone Wall*, was published. Helen became interested in Socialism after reading H. G. Wells's *New Worlds for Old*. She was influenced by John Macy, who was an active Socialist. She was a member of the Socialist party in Massachusetts from 1909 until 1921, when she channeled her energies into causes for the blind. In 1913, her collection of essays on Socialism, *Out of the Dark,* was published.

In 1914, Helen and Anne went on the lecture circuit to supplement their income. They spoke in the Midwest and California as well as Canada. Also in 1914, John Macy left Anne. He found that when he had married Anne, because of her association with Helen, he had married an institution. He had never fully learned how to deal with that.

Helen and Anne were unable to support themselves with revenue from Helen's books and their lectures. Earlier, Andrew Carnegie had offered financial help to Helen, but she had refused it. In 1914, Helen accepted a $5,000 per year lifetime pension from the philanthropist.

Also that year, Mary Agnes (Polly) Thompson joined Helen and Anne as hairdresser, housekeeper, and secretary. They finally had someone to handle practical matters, such as making transportation arrangements and balancing the checkbook. In 1916, Anne became ill with what was incorrectly diagnosed as tuberculosis, and Helen had to rely more on Polly. Anne recovered in 1917, and they sold the farm in Wrentham and moved to Forest Hills, New York. They appeared in a film, *Deliverance,* based on an embellished story of Helen's life that, while critically acclaimed, was not a financial success.

In 1927, Helen's book, *My Religion*, was published and two years later, *Midstream: My Later Life* was published. Helen gave lectures sponsored by the American Foundation for the Blind and established the Helen Keller Endowment Fund. For those efforts, she was awarded the Achievement Prize by the *Pictorial Review*.

Helen, Anne, and Polly made several trips abroad. They were welcomed and entertained everywhere. In England, Helen met George Bernard Shaw. Lady Astor introduced Helen and explained that she was deaf and blind. Shaw replied, "Why, of course, all Americans are deaf and blind." Later, Shaw denied having made the comment, but he was heard by a roomful of people. Helen was surprised but not offended. She considered Shaw the "chief prosecutor of his time." While in Scotland, Anne heard that John Macy had died. Anne herself did not have long to live. She died on October 20, 1936.

Helen and Polly traveled to Japan, where they were greeted warmly. She had a special relationship with the Japanese people, and she aided their efforts to help the blind. When Helen and Polly returned to the United States, they moved to Westport, Connecticut, where the Pfeiffer family had built a house for them. They had many talented neighbors, including the sculptor, Jo Davidson, and the writer, Van Wyck Brooks.

In 1940, Helen wrote *Let Us Have Faith*, in which she discusses "the ultimate ability of man to conquer despair and tyranny." In 1955, her biography of Anne Sullivan Macy, *Teacher*, was published.

Helen underwent many medical tests during her lifetime. Surprisingly, an eminent neurologist found that her sense of smell, taste, and touch were average. He mentioned that, although those three senses were not elevated, Helen provided an example of what the human brain can do when pushed.

Helen died on June 1, 1968 of arteriosclerotic heart disease. Her ashes were placed in the National Cathedral in Washington, D.C., alongside those of Anne and Polly, not far from where the ashes of Woodrow Wilson were interred. Helen was an optimist over her entire lifetime. She said, "I believe that all through these dark and silent years, God has been using my life for a purpose I do not know. But one day I shall understand, and then I will be satisfied."[84]

GAIL BORDEN (1801-1874) Developer of Evaporated Milk

"If I miss it in one thing, I will hit it in another."[85]

Gail Borden

Gail Borden is an example of an individual who was not successful until late in life. He was almost fifty-six when he was granted a patent for his first successful product, evaporated milk—on his fourth attempt. He is a role model of a person who continues to strive and to persevere well into his later years.

An early Borden invention was an amphibious prairie schooner, called a "terraqueous machine," in which he almost drowned his friends and neighbors. His next invention was a meat biscuit that he tried to sell to the U.S. Army and to explorers for use on expeditions. The Army Review Board said that it was "not only unpalatable, but fails to appease the craving of hunger—producing headache, nausea, and great muscular depression."

After finally convincing the U.S. Patent Office that producing evaporated milk in a partial vacuum was indeed different from previous milk patents, Borden built a successful company that during the Civil War produced 14,000 quarts of evaporated milk daily from just one of his factories. In 1867, he retired as a successful businessman.

Gail Borden was born on November 9, 1801 in Norwich, New York, the oldest of four sons of Gail Borden and Philadelphia Borden. Gail Borden sold his farm and his half-interest in a sawmill in 1812 to participate in the westward movement. He transported his family to Pittsburgh and down the Ohio River to Cincinnati. The family lived across the Ohio River in Covington, Kentucky just long enough for their only daughter, Esther, to be born, and then they moved to New London, Indiana.

Young Gail completed his schooling in New London. At

the age of twenty-one, he had three options for earning a living: farming, surveying, and teaching. His first job was teaching school in Amite County, Mississippi on the Louisiana border. Borden supplemented his income by working as the county surveyor. He married Penelope Mercer of Amite County in February 1828.

Borden had heard about Texas from his brother, Tom, one of Stephen Austin's "Old Three Hundred," who had lived there since 1824. Tom convinced his parents to move to Texas in 1828, and Borden decided to join them. He and Penelope traveled to New Orleans on the schooner *Hope* and continued onward by boat to Texas. Borden was reunited with his father and brothers in Texas, but his mother and his sister, Esther, died during the journey.

Availability of land was a principal attraction of Texas. Mexico generously granted Borden a sitio (4,428 acres) of land in Fort Bend County. Initially, Borden farmed and raised cattle; he performed his brother's surveying duties for Stephen Austin when Tom went on extended trips.

In October 1835, Borden, Tom, and a partner began publishing a newspaper in San Felipe. *The Telegraph and Texas Register*, the first Texas newspaper to stay in business for more than two years, had a forty-year run. Eventually, publication was moved to Houston, where Borden sold his share before moving to Galveston.

In 1837, Borden was appointed collector for the port of Galveston by Sam Houston, President of independent Texas. Borden established the first customs office, and his attention to detail served him well in his new duties. According to the Texas Constitution, a President could serve only one term, and in 1838 Mirabeau Lamar succeeded Houston as President of Texas. Borden was a hard-working, conscientious collector, but the job was a political appointment; he was replaced by one of Lamar's men.

For twelve years, Borden served as the agent for the Galveston City Company, the organization that promoted and controlled Galveston's growth during its first seventy-five years. Galveston's population more than tripled during that time, and it became the largest city in Texas. In 1844, an epidemic of yellow fever struck Galveston; it took Penelope Borden's life and left Borden with five young children.

Borden had great quantities of nervous energy, and he didn't need as much sleep as most people. As he approached his fiftieth year, he was always in a hurry and frequently preoccupied. He was full of ideas; many considered him eccentric. While showing a friend around his home and yard, they walked by cast-iron kettles, empty barrels, and pieces of machinery. Borden explained:

> That was one of my ideas, just then I was full of hydraulic pressure. I would put in water, half a hogshead of sugar, and a cartload of fruit, figs say, into the kettle. Then, while hot, I would press the preserves into ten-pound canisters.... But I learned better. I never drop an idea except for a better one—never! You can do almost anything with everything. If you plan and think, and, as fast as you drop one thing, seize upon another.... The world is changing. In the direction of condensing.[86]

He used the word "condensing" in a general sense. To him, condensing meant giving short quotations to his son from the Bible instead of long lectures and eating a meal in fifteen minutes instead of an hour or more.

Borden invented an amphibious prairie-schooner that he called a "terraqueous machine" intended for use in crossing rivers. He invited his neighbors to a midnight meal and some unspecified "entertainment." Borden described the food:

> There are articles on this table from which, if you knew what they were in their original con-

dition, you would turn with loathing and hor-
ror. I have passed them, however, through certain processes by virtue of which they are deli-
cious. Out of the offal of the kitchens and the
streets, I have created ... a food for the poor
which will cost almost nothing. I have trans-
muted the dirt itself into delicacies.[87]

The feast included butter made by churning lard in milk,
bread made from ground bones, and jelly made from the
hoofs and horns of oxen.

The "entertainment" was a ride in his terraqueous
machine. As his neighbors boarded the floating wagon, the
owner of the livery stable where it was housed commented
that "we may all end up in eternity." Borden steered the vehicle toward the Gulf of Mexico, but the women on board began
to scream even before he was near the water. He turned the
wagon around and returned home.

Borden attempted a daylight run. He mounted a mast with
a square sail on the front of the wagon, assisted by wheels that
operated as propellers when the vehicle was in the water.
With a sail full of wind, he steered the wagon into the bay at
high speed. When the sail dropped, all of the passengers
moved to the landward side of the vehicle. The wagon cap-
sized, dumping its passengers into fifty feet of water. His
invention was a failure.

Next, Borden developed the "meat biscuit," similar to
Comanche food called pinole. It was compact, easy to transport, and travelers could subsist on it. The Indians prepared
pinole by grinding dried buffalo meat and mixing it with
crushed, dried hominy and mesquite beans. They ate pinole
dry or added water and baked it into a cake. On the trail, they
stuffed the mixture into a section of buffalo intestine and wore
it as a belt.

Borden began experimenting with meat biscuit in 1849.
He perceived that armies and navies would be ideal markets

for it. In early 1850, the U.S. Army expressed an interest in his meat biscuit. He packed the biscuit into canisters that Dr. Elisha Kane took on his Arctic expedition searching for the lost English explorer, Sir John Franklin. On February 5, 1850, Borden was granted a U.S. patent for his product.

Borden made meat biscuit by boiling eleven pounds of meat, usually beef, into one pound of extract and filtering the broth from the "solid nutritive portions." He boiled the broth until much of the water had evaporated; this formed a liquid of the consistency of "sugar-house syrup." He used a liquid gauge to ensure a consistent density and then added flour in the ratio of three pounds of flour to two pounds of extract. The five-pound mixture was kneaded, baked (resulting in a biscuit that weighed four pounds), and then prepared in a number of ways, including frying, further baking, or mixing into a pudding. Borden's main claim to originality was the addition of flour.

The meat biscuit was Borden's focus for two years. He wanted to stay close to the production site, so he asked Dr. Ashbel Smith, an old friend, to promote the biscuit to potential customers. The first test results of the meat biscuit by the U.S. Army were favorable. Brevet Colonel E. V. Sumner in Fort Leavenworth, Kansas wrote a glowing report to the War Department.

About $10,000 was required to buy production equipment, such as boilers, caldrons, pipe, and tubs. Borden raised most of the needed capital by mortgaging his property. He went another $5,000 into debt in 1851, the year of the Great Council Exhibition at the London World's Fair. To promote the product, Borden and Smith traveled to the fair, where they received a Gold Medal award for their entry. About this time, *Scientific American* reported the meat biscuit "one of the most valuable inventions that has ever been brought forward."

In June 1851, however, the results of the Army's extended trial were published. The board of six army officers was unanimous in rejecting the product in what was known as the

"Waco Report":

> The biscuit could not replace the ordinary
> army ration, it did not have the food value to
> sustain life and vigor, whilst on active duty ...
> even when increased to ... 12 ounces per ration
> (Borden recommended six ounces); the meat
> biscuit was "not only unpalatable, but fails to
> appease the craving of hunger—producing
> headache, nausea, and great muscular depres-
> sion"; furthermore, it "impairs the capacity of
> the healthy human-system to sustain much
> mental or bodily labor as it can be legitimate-
> ly called upon to perform; ... it diminishes the
> power of resisting the extremes of heat and
> cold."[88]

Borden's prospects of selling his meat biscuit to the U.S.
Army didn't recover from this critical report. By 1851,
Borden had spent $30,000, most of it from sales of his prop-
erty, on the business. Ultimately, he lost $60,000 on the meat
biscuit venture.

Borden contacted Dr. Elisha Kane upon his return from
the Arctic. Kane told Borden that his biscuit had too high a
gelatin content. Kane and the doctors that accompanied his
expedition decided to take pemmican on their next trip.
Borden tried to break into other markets, such as hospitals
and ships, without success. In 1853, Dr. Ashbel Smith backed
out of his agreement to market the biscuit in Europe. The last
order for meat biscuits was filled in 1855.

Borden's next project occupied him for the remainder of
his life. The development and sale of condensed milk began
when he gave up on the meat biscuit. He became aware of the
need for condensed milk on his return home from the Great
Council Exhibition in London. The voyage across the North
Atlantic was rough. The cows in the hold of the sailing vessel

were seasick and couldn't be milked to feed the large number of immigrant children on board. The crying of hungry babies disturbed Borden, and he was determined to do something about it. His goal was to treat milk so that it would keep for several weeks or longer, while retaining its nutritional value and purity.

The preservation of milk wasn't a problem; retaining its purity and palatability was. Previous attempts to preserve milk used brown sugar, which gave the resulting product an off color and an unappealing odor. Borden borrowed a vacuum pan from the Shaker Colony at New Lebanon, New York in an early experiment to retain the taste of the milk. When he had modest success with its use, he ordered his own vacuum pan.

The albumin in the milk that he was boiling stuck to the vacuum pan, causing foam and boiled-over milk. A local sugar-boiler told Borden that condensing milk using a vacuum pan wouldn't work. However, Borden discovered that the solution to the problem was easy; he just greased the pan like the housewife does when she bakes.

In May 1853, Borden applied for patents in the U.S. and England on his process for condensing milk. Two of the most important criteria for patent applications in the U.S. were that the inventions were "new" and "useful." In 1851, an inventor had been awarded a patent for condensing milk "in any known mode," including the use of a vacuum pan. Borden's London patent attorney, C. Barlow, told him that no previous inventor had actually used a vacuum pan to evaporate milk. Borden thought that this answered the complaint of the Patent Office that his process lacked novelty.

Patent Office authorities weren't convinced that condensing milk in a partial vacuum distinguished Borden's process from earlier patents. His patent application was denied. He immediately began collecting testimonials to support his next patent application. An early testimonial was from Robert McFarlane, editor of *Scientific American* and holder of a dye-process patent, who reported that he had stored Borden's condensed milk in a warm room for three months, and that it had stayed sweet.

Borden experimented with the condensation of other items, such as coffee, tea, and apple juice, but his principal studies were with milk. He wrote more letters to the Patent Office and visited Washington, D.C. again to plead his case. He persisted; he sought testimonials from additional scientists to support his claim. The acting Commissioner of the Patent Office failed to see the importance of the partial vacuum in the process and rejected Borden's second patent application.

Borden continued to lobby for his patent. In May 1856, his third application was rejected, but the Commissioner of the Patent Office, Charles Mason, left the door to approval open a crack. He wrote:

> Borden claims evaporation *in vacuo* to be a valuable feature of his discovery, and necessary. The Commissioner sees no reason to believe this. If it were really a discovery, Borden would be entitled to a patent. If Borden could prove that the removal of air in contact with the milk was important and that milk, taken fresh from the cow, and evaporated in the open air ... would not answer substantially the same purpose as when evaporated *in vacuo*, I would certainly grant to Mr. Borden the patent he is asking.[89]

Borden consulted again with scientists, including Dr. John Currie of New York. They studied all known methods of condensing milk and documented the results. Then they conducted more tests, prepared numerous charts, and wrote many affidavits. The results indicated that condensing milk *in vacuo* over low heat was superior to all other known methods; the exclusion of air was critical to its preservation.

The documentation was forwarded to London and Washington, D.C. Borden's U.S. patent application was granted on August 19, 1856, and his English patent application received final approval on August 26, 1856. It had taken three years and three months and four patent applications for Borden to receive U.S. patent no. 15,553. He was now almost fifty-six years old and was considered a failure by many of his acquaintances and friends.

Borden didn't have the financing to establish manufacturing facilities for the production of condensed milk. He recruited two partners, Thomas Green and James Bridge, to obtain financial backing; Borden retained three-eighths of the ownership for himself. His first factory was located in Wolcottville, Connecticut, west of Hartford. He sold his first output to stores in the region, but he realized that he needed a substantially larger market. A milk depot in New York provided the means of reaching that expanded market.

New Yorkers weren't yet interested in his product, however, and his partner, Bridge, refused to contribute more than $1,900 to the venture. Borden needed money to pay farmers for their milk; he couldn't convince these frugal New England farmers to wait for their money. If Borden couldn't pay them, other customers could. Borden was forced to close his factory at Wolcottville.

Borden signed over fifty percent of his milk patent and his further developments to reach an agreement with Green. Green convinced Bridge to reinvest in the venture with the three partners sharing expenses, profits (and losses), in the same proportion as their ownership of the patent. A second factory was established at Burrville, five miles north of Wolcottville. The country was in the middle of the Panic of 1857—not a good time to start a business or to expand one. Banks were failing and many companies were going out of business. Borden's partners were reluctant to advance any more money; the outlook for the enterprise was bleak.

Borden shut down operations at his factory and boarded a

train for New York to negotiate with his creditors. A serendip-itous event happened. Timing, being at the right place at the right time, can be a critical element of success. On the train to New York, Borden had the good fortune to sit next to Jeremiah Milbank, owner of a wholesale grocery business.

Thirty-nine-year-old Milbank would later become a suc-cessful banker, broker, and railroad director. According to *Harper's Weekly,* Milbank "was one of those merchants whose careers are the true glory of the metropolis ... farsee-ing, conservative, and enterprising, a conceiver of large schemes, a financier who did not fail, a friend to wise chari-ties."[90]

As they traveled to New York, Borden told Milbank of his development effort and of the importance of continuing with it. Borden spoke with conviction, sincerity, and with little break in his monologue. He was animated and enthusiastic; he impressed Milbank as being an honest man possessing considerable drive. Backing Borden was a substantial risk, however. The country was in the middle of a financial panic, and Borden's relationships with his partners were complicat-ed. Even so, Milbank's instincts told him to back "the old man with the stooped shoulders and the fire in his eyes."

In Milbank, Borden had a partner who knew that it took money to make money. Milbank realized that few economic shortcuts exist, and that you must be prepared to absorb short-term losses in order to be around for the long-term gains. Above all, you must be aggressive, persevering, and strong enough to overcome the inevitable setbacks. Venture capital-ists didn't exist in the mid-1800s, but Milbank came close to fitting the definition. In fact, he probably had a stronger inter-est and commitment to the enterprise than many of today's venture capitalists.

Milbank paid off Borden's $6,000 debt incurred at Burrville and negotiated with Green and Bridge to settle their patent claims. The company was renamed "The New York Condensed Milk Company" to reflect its largest market.

Borden imposed strict rules on the dairy farmers who sold milk to him, including:

- Barns must be kept clean; manure must be kept out of the milking stalls.
- Cow udders must be washed in warm water before milking.
- Milk strainers must be cleaned with boiling water and dried twice a day.
- No milk should be provided from cows who have calved within twelve days.
- No milk should be provided from cows that have been fed silage or turnips, which affect the taste of the milk.

In 1858, conditions in New York favored the sale of condensed milk. Thousands of babies and infants died each year due to unsanitary conditions in dairies and milk delivery wagons. Occasionally, manure and milk were hauled in the same wagon. New York's infant mortality rate was higher than Glasgow's and Liverpool's and was increasing.

By 1860, the business began to grow sufficiently for John Burr, owner of the Burrville factory site, to ask for additional remuneration for water use. Borden moved his factory across the New York-Connecticut state line to Wassaic, New York in dairy farm country on a branch of the New York Central Railroad.

Noah Gridley, one of Wassaic's town fathers, agreed to build the factory for Borden; then he pressed Borden for payment. Milbank reentered the scene, paid off Gridley, Green, and Bridge, and pushed for an aggressive sales campaign. When the business began to expand and Gridley realized the profitable opportunity he had lost, he shut off the supply of water to the factory. Borden built a reservoir with water lines to the plant.

With the outbreak of the Civil War, the New York Condensed Milk Company switched emphasis from expanding consumer demand to filling orders from its largest customer, the Union Army. The daily output of the Wassaic factory reached 5,000 quarts in 1860 and grew to 14,000 quarts a day by 1863. Capacity was 16,000 quarts daily.

Borden continued to improve his process and to apply for patents. He was granted additional patents in 1862, 1863, 1865, and 1866. Borden was personally involved in the details of running the factory, including routine maintenance and repair. Much of his redesign involved trial and error. He didn't have an engineering background, but he persisted in working on a design problem until he solved it.

Plants were established in other regions when orders for milk outstripped the plant's capacity. The company built a new plant in Elgin, Illinois, forty miles west of Chicago; the business expanded until, in 1866, the Elgin Milk Company processed over 300,000 gallons of milk per year. Brewster, New York, half way between Wassaic and New York City, was another important expansion site.

By 1867, Borden had overexpansion problems. Sales had tapered off dramatically in the years following the Civil War. The Elgin facility was closed in mid-1867. Overcapacity was addressed successfully, and Borden turned the business over to his sons.

When Borden retired from active management of the business in late 1867, he traveled to Texas to visit his many relatives there. In 1868, he returned to his home in White Plains, New York but spent the winters of 1871-73 in Texas. Borden died on January 11, 1874 in Texas. His funeral service was held in White Plains, where he was buried in Woodlawn Cemetery. Gail Borden's monument is a granite milk can inscribed with: "I tried and failed, I tried again and again, and succeeded."[91]

AL NEUHARTH (1924-   ) Creator of *USA Today*

"[Potential] headlines about the end of the world:
Wall Street Journal: STOCK EXCHANGE HALTS TRADING AS
 WORLD ENDS.
New York *Times*: END OF WORLD HITS THIRD WORLD
 HARDEST.
Washington *Post*: WORLD ENDS; MAY AFFECT ELECTIONS,
 SOURCES SAY.
USA Today: WE'RE GONE ... STATE-BY-STATE DEMISE ON 6A.
 FINAL SCORES ON 8C."[92]

John Quinn, in a speech to the National Press Foundation

While Chief Executive Officer of the Gannett Corporation, Al Neuharth was willing to innovate and to create new products. He paid great attention to detail and was a strong promoter of his visions. When *USA Today* losses continued at $10 million a month, he convinced employees to work harder, work leaner, and to provide a higher quality paper at a lower cost. Neuharth's strongest qualities in creating a new national newspaper were his drive, his determination, and his ability to implement a vision.

Al Neuharth, the younger of two sons of Daniel and Christina Neuharth, was born in Eureka, South Dakota in 1924. Daniel Neuharth farmed eighty acres until he injured his leg in a farm accident, developed tuberculosis, and died in 1926. Christina took in laundry and sewing and waited on tables to support the family. Her motto was "do a little bit more tomorrow than you did today, a little better next year than you did this year."[93]

At the age of eleven, Neuharth delivered the Minneapolis *Tribune,* and, at thirteen, he worked after school in the composing room of the Alpena *Journal.* In 1942, he graduated from high school and enrolled briefly at Northern State Teachers' College before enlisting in the U.S. Army as World

War II broke out. Serving as a combat infantryman, he won a Bronze Star and earned sergeant's stripes.

In 1946, Neuharth returned home and enrolled at the University of South Dakota on the G. I. Bill. He was a sports announcer for the college radio station before shifting his interest to the college newspaper, *The Volante*, and becoming its editor. In 1950, he graduated from the University of South Dakota and became a reporter for the Associated Press.

In 1952, with $50,000 from the sale of shares in the venture, Neuharth and a friend started *SoDak Sports*, a statewide sports weekly modeled on the national *Sporting News*. Within a year, circulation had increased to 18,000, but sales of advertising space were sluggish. Their few advertisers began to shift to television commercials.

In 1954, Neuharth and his partner tried unsuccessfully to sell their weekly; they declared bankruptcy, and their creditors received less than thirty-five cents on the dollar. Neuharth looked upon it as a learning experience. Their biggest error had been the lack of a business plan. They had not estimated projected sales revenue, advertising revenue, or profit and loss. It was a mistake that Neuharth would not make again.

Neuharth accepted a job as a reporter for the Miami *Herald*. He wrote a series of articles about mail order scams and was at the right place at the right time on some fast-breaking stories. His career took off, and he was given an assignment with the *Herald's* Washington bureau. In 1959, he was promoted to Assistant Managing Editor of the *Herald* and was chosen to open its Brevard County bureau to cover the news from the Cape Canaveral Space Center.

In the following year, Neuharth was appointed assistant to the Executive Editor of the Detroit *Free Press*. He worked in both the news and business operations. His performance was noticed both within Knight Newspapers and outside of the organization. In 1963, he accepted a position with the Gannett Corporation as General Manager of its Rochester, New York newspapers: the *Democrat and Chronicle* and the *Times-Union*. He was viewed as the heir apparent to Paul Miller, Chief Executive Officer of the Gannett Corporation.

Neuharth suggested to Miller that Gannett start a daily newspaper in Brevard County, Florida to serve the Cape Canaveral area. Miller had already tried unsuccessfully to buy a small Florida daily as a nucleus for expansion; he was receptive to Neuharth's suggestion even though it bucked the national trend of fewer daily newspapers. Neuharth bought the Cocoa *Tribune* for $1.9 million but, instead of revamping it, decided to start a new paper with a fresh format. He called it *Today: Florida's Space Age Newspaper* and supplemented the small staff with "loaners" from other Gannett newspapers.

He did not repeat the mistakes he had made in starting *SoDak Sports*. First, he authorized the preparation of a comprehensive business plan; second, he knew that he had sufficient funds to pay for the start-up. Neuharth was a hands-on manager. He was on-site in Cocoa functioning as the Managing Editor. He organized the new paper into three distinct sections: News, Business, and Sports. The comics section was printed in color, a *Today* innovation. *Today* was profitable in twenty-eight months, which was due mainly to the boldness, innovation, and determination of Neuharth.

In 1973, Neuharth became Chief Executive Officer of the Gannett Corporation and added the title of Chairman of the Board upon the retirement of Paul Miller in 1978. Neuharth had considered the idea of a national newspaper for ten years; finally, he decided to proceed with the idea, for professional and personal reasons. He thought that the newspaper journalism profession could do a better job than it was doing, and, personally, he needed new worlds to conquer.

Improvements in satellite communications helped to make the idea achievable. Neuharth's lack of humility was apparent in his goal: "We'll reinvent the newspaper." He wanted to create a newspaper so captivating that it would attract millions of readers, including many who currently read no newspaper. He also wanted to innovate the design and content of the new paper to "pull the rest of the industry into the twenty-first century, albeit kicking and screaming."

By late 1979, Gannett already had newspapers across the United States, including many in the major city markets. In areas where Gannett did not own a printing plant, it could make contract printing arrangements. Neuharth considered three start-up possibilities:

- a national sports daily, similar to the *Sporting News* and *Sports Illustrated*
- a daily and / or Sunday supplement for the Gannett community newspapers with national news and advertising
- a national general-interest daily newspaper

He sought the opinion of three key Gannett managers: John Quinn, the chief news executive; Jack Heselden, President of the newspaper division; and Douglas McCorkindale, the chief financial and legal officer. At the year-end Board of Directors' meeting, Neuharth announced that he was going to set aside $1 million in 1980 to "study what's new in newspapers and television and especially whether we can harness the satellite to deliver more news to more people in more ways."

The R & D effort was called Project NN, which denoted "National Newspaper." Outside of Gannett, Neuharth promoted the idea that it stood for "New Newspapers." Project NN soon became known outside of the company as "Neuharth's Nonsense." The five-person project team that assembled in Florida included:

- Tom Curley, a newsman with an excellent record in news research
- Paul Kessinger, a research and marketing guru
- Larry Sackett, an expert in satellite communications technology
- Frank Vega, a savvy circulation specialist

Neuharth chose Vince Spezzano, the veteran publisher of

Today in Florida, as coordinator of the team. The average age of the team's members, not including Spezzano, was thirty.

Neuharth courted the Board of Directors' support for his project and kept them informed. In October 1980, the Project NN report was presented to the Board and an additional $3.5 million was budgeted for planning and prototypes in 1981. In August 1981, research conducted by Lou Harris and Associates and Simmons Market Research Bureau was presented to the board, and the prototypes were reviewed. In December 1981, the Board of Directors voted to launch *USA Today* by a unanimous 12-0 vote, even though the finance organization of Gannett counseled against going ahead.

The next phase was called GANSAT, Gannett Satellite Information Network. The team members were:

- Moe Hickey, President and supervisor of business planning
- Ronald Martin, planning editor responsible for prototype development
- Chuck Schmitt, finance director
- Frank Vega, director of circulation

Neuharth personally worked on the news product and circulation planning; he continued to be a hands-on manager. John Quinn worked virtually full-time with Martin on prototype plans.

The team decided that *USA Today* must be different from existing papers, both in appearance and in content. The early goals were to include four highly organized sections, emphasis on color, easy-to-read stories, frequent use of charts and graphics, news from all fifty states, and a concentration on sports, TV, and weather. Neuharth used "intrapreneurship" on *USA Today* by obtaining "loaners" from the other Gannett papers. These loaners were gone from their parent newspapers for a average of four months. It provided a broadening experience for young newspaper journalists and introduced them to new techniques and technology.

On September 15, 1982, *USA Today* was launched at a

party in Washington, D.C. President and Mrs. Ronald Reagan, Speaker of the House "Tip" O'Neill, and Senate Majority Leader Howard Baker all attended. Red, white, and blue *USA Today* banners waved from the 60-foot-wide by 140-foot-long tent erected on the Mall. The 800 guests included Cabinet members, representatives, senators, publishers, and executives. The party on the Mall was followed by dinner at *USA Today* headquarters across the Potomac River in Rosslyn, where food from every state was served.

In 1983, circulation of *USA Today* passed 1,000,000. The only other newspapers with circulation over 1,000,000 were the *Wall Street Journal,* the New York *Daily News*, and the Los Angeles *Times*. Signing up advertisers was a problem, however, because the only official circulation numbers were those provided by the independent Audit Bureau of Circulations (ABC), which wouldn't look at circulation until after the first year of operation. Neuharth commissioned the public accounting firm of Price Waterhouse to conduct a circulation survey, which verified that circulation had surpassed 1,000,000. However, Madison Avenue didn't view the results as official. Finally, in late June 1984, ABC verified that annual sales were 1,280,000.

In August 1984, Neuharth estimated that *USA Today's* losses would be $124 million in 1984, $81 million in 1985, and $25 million in 1986, but that the business would break even in 1987. He also estimated that the cumulative losses since start-up would approach $400 million before taxes by the end of 1987. That evaluation of *USA Today's* finances was "as close as we ever came to folding the tent."[94] Advertising increased significantly after Cathleen Black was brought in from *New York* magazine as President of *USA Today* and placed in charge of advertising.

Losses continued at $10 million a month during 1984, which translated into $339,726 per day, $14,155 per hour, and $236 per minute. Neuharth decided that serious steps would have to be taken to save the paper. On Sunday, November 11,

1984, he held a meeting of *USA Today's* management committee at his Florida home. He told the committee that things could not continue in the current mode. He listed two alternatives: to quit or to make a concerted effort to make many changes.

He said that, to reduce their losses, they must substitute management for money by taking the following steps:

- "We must produce and present even more news, with fewer people, in less space, at lower cost.
- We must sell and present even more advertising, at higher rates, with fewer people, at lower cost.
- We must produce and print more newspapers, with even better quality, with fewer people, at lower cost.
- We must circulate and sell even more newspapers, at higher prices, with fewer people, at lower cost."[95]

He directed that payroll costs would be reduced by five percent by the end of 1985, and that all new hires would require either his or John Curley's approval signature. He also set a goal for 1985 losses of under $75 million.

USA Today was not considered a serious newspaper by many members of the journalism community; it was called "McPaper." *USA Today* staffers heard the name "McPaper" and commented that many papers were stealing their McNuggets. John Quinn admitted that if *USA Today* ever won a Pulitzer Prize, it would probably be for "the best investigative paragraph."

Gannett's other eighty-eight papers carried the financial load for *USA Today*. By mid-1985, however, the "Nation's Newspaper" began to turn the corner financially. Gannett reported a twenty percent earnings increase compared with the first half of 1984, an indication of the company's financial strength. Cathy Black increased the advertising revenue 106 percent compared with the previous year. The price was increased from thirty-five cents to fifty cents when the volume of the paper went to sixty pages. However, the losses were still staggering: $102 million in 1985 followed by $70 million in 1986.

In May 1986, Neuharth stepped down as the CEO of Gannett, but retained the title of Chairman. He recalled his difficult transition with Paul Miller and wanted to ensure that the transition with President John Curley was more orderly. He planned to stay on as Chairman until 1989, when he would be sixty-five.

In July 1986, Simmons Market Research conducted a survey noting that *USA Today* had 4,792,000 readers per day, the highest readership of any U.S. daily. The *Wall Street Journal's* paid circulation was still much higher, but each *USA Today* was read by three readers while the *Journal* was read by only two readers on the average. Increases in advertising followed the increases in readership.

On June 15, 1987, Curley sent a telegram to Neuharth, who was on a business trip: "McPaper has made it. *USA Today* broke into the black with a profit of $1,093,756 for the month of May, six months ahead of schedule."[96] "The Nation's Newspaper" became profitable faster than many other new media ventures: *Sports Illustrated* required ten years, *Newsweek* nine years, and *Money* magazine eight years to move into the black.

Neuharth's vision, motivation, and pure strength of will brought a daily national newspaper into existence when many said it couldn't be done. In his opinion:

> The most satisfying victories are those where the odds against your winning are the greatest. But long odds don't necessarily make the job more difficult. In fact, the more that people tell you that it can't be done, the more likely that you have a winner. That usually means that you know something that they don't know. Or that your idea is so different or so daring that they can't comprehend it. If your sights are clearly set on a goal, the fact that others say it

can't be done shouldn't slow you down. It should spur you on.[97]

CHAPTER 3

INEVITABLE WINNERS

"Discontent is the first step in progress. No one knows what is in him [or her] till he [or she] tries, and many would never try if they were not forced to."

Basil W. Maturin

This chapter provides the stories of five men and women whose success was predictable. Perhaps they should be called moral heroes instead of inevitable winners. The unfailing faith that fulfillment of their goals was inevitable motivated these heroes, but their own sacrifice made success possible.

Emmeline Pankhurst and her daughter, Christabel, were beaten, imprisoned, and scorned. Christabel became, in effect, the leader of the Women's Rights Movement in England. They spent significant portions of their adult lives striving to obtain rights for women that they should have had just by being citizens.

Carrie Chapman Catt was the executive-type manager that the Women's Rights Movement needed in the decade leading up to granting the vote to women in 1920. She was a highly organized individual who took charge of the state-by-state effort to pass the Amendment to the U.S. Constitution securing voting rights for women. She had a good working relationship with national leaders, including President Wilson, that helped to advance the women's cause.

Alice Paul was active in the trenches in the fight for women's rights. She organized and led the parades. She learned her trade working with the Pankhursts in England. She was imprisoned and force-fed when she wouldn't eat. Women like Alice Paul were willing to endure hardship and imprisonment to obtain fundamental rights for half of the population of the country.

Mother Teresa was happy teaching in her school at a convent walled off from the teeming masses of Calcutta. However, she knew the need that existed in the slums, and she was motivated to help. The case that she pleaded to her superiors was not received enthusiastically. She was asked to wait a year and a half before beginning to comfort the poor and destitute. Her effort began as a one-person support group and grew as other young sisters volunteered to help her. She devoted her life, unselfishly, to her cause and was successful beyond her dreams.

Nelson Mandela, the first Native-African President of the Union of South Africa, spent much of his life in prison. However, it was inevitable that when he was released from prison, he would have a responsible position in society. He had displayed leadership qualities as a young man and was widely respected. He retained his role as leader of the people throughout his long incarceration. When the vote was given to Native Africans, it was inevitable that Mandela would be elected President of the Union of South Africa. His personal strengths were vital in making the transition to a government of the majority.

The lives of these men and women show us the importance of driving toward a goal. They motivate us to strive toward our own goals.

EMMELINE and CHRISTABEL PANKHURST (1858-1928, 1880-1958) Women's Rights Leaders in England

"There was something quite ruthless about Mrs. Pankhurst and Christabel where human relationships were concerned.... Men and women of destiny are like that."[98]

Emmeline Pethick-Lawrence

Emmeline Pankhurst and her daughters played a major role in the Women's Suffrage Movement in England, which was much more militant than in the United States. Women realized that the only way to gain their rights, particularly the right to vote, was to organize protest marches and to destroy public property to get the attention of the government. Unlike women in the United States, when English women finally obtained the right to vote, it was granted in stages.

Emmeline, who was born in 1858, was the attractive, delicate eldest daughter of Robert Goulden, a wealthy cotton printer from Manchester. After returning from finishing school in Paris in 1878, Emmeline met Richard Pankhurst, a radical advocate who had been called to the Bar in 1867 after receiving the highest law degrees at London University.

In 1865, when Emmeline was only seven years old, Pankhurst had helped to found the Woman's Suffrage Society in Manchester. In 1870, he had drafted the Married Women's Property Bill that gave women the right to own property and to keep the wages they earned. Also that year, he drafted the first of many parliamentary bills to give women the right to vote.

Emmeline and Richard fell in love at first sight. She was captivated by his eloquence, his idealism, and his "beautiful white hands." They had a happy marriage, partly because they saw each other as kindred spirits ("Every struggling cause shall be ours").

Four children were born during the first six years of their

marriage: Christabel in 1880, Sylvia in 1882, Adela in 1885, and a son who died in childhood. Pankhurst thought of his four children as the four pillars of his home. He repeatedly told them that if they didn't grow up to help other people, they would not have been worth the upbringing. He continually counseled them that drudgery and drill are important elements of life, but that "life is nothing without enthusiasms."

The Pankhursts were politically active in Manchester. They were active Socialists as well as feminists. Women's rights was Pankhurst's highest priority, and he was a strong influence on his wife and daughters. As one who opposed exploitation of all kinds, he couldn't tolerate half of the population being held back economically and politically.

In 1890, the usually calm Pankhurst erupted after a meeting of the Women's Franchise League in their home. He burst out, "Why don't you force us to give you the vote? Why don't you scratch our eyes out?"[99] Christabel and Sylvia were startled by his outburst; Emmeline was astonished at the vehemence of his feelings. Financial problems plagued the family. Years of overwork caught up with Pankhurst; he developed gastric ulcers.

In 1895, Emmeline was elected to the Chorlton Board of Guardians. When she was told that the Guardians couldn't provide relief to the "able bodied poor," she organized food kitchens. She was horrified by conditions in the workhouses and incensed by the treatment of young women with illegitimate babies. Years later, she wrote that although she had been a suffragist before, she began to view the women's vote not only as a right, but as a vital necessity.

In 1898, Richard Pankhurst died suddenly of a perforated ulcer, leaving no money to the family. Pankhurst had frequently asked his children what they wanted to be when they grew up. He had always advised them to work at something that they liked to do and could do well. However, at the time of his death, none of the children was educated or trained to help their mother support the family. Eighteen-year-old

Christabel had considered both ballet dancing and dressmaking, but she wasn't encouraged to do either.

Emmeline accepted a position as Registrar of Births and Deaths with the Chorlton Board of Guardians. Christabel enrolled in courses at the University of Manchester, where she actively participated in discussions. Her perceptive responses brought her to the attention of Eva Gore-Booth and Esther Roper of the Suffrage Movement.

After the death of Lydia Decker, their dynamic leader, the suffragists in England were divided about the amount of political involvement that they should have. Lydia's successor was Millicent Fawcett, a capable leader but one without Lydia's drive. Eva and Esther, who were looking for dynamic women to work in the Movement, asked Christabel to join their cause. Emmeline's interest in the Suffrage Movement was elevated by her daughter's participation; she worked actively for the Women's Rights Movement, thereby establishing an extraordinary mother-daughter partnership.

Christabel discovered that she was a natural leader and speaker. Her intelligence, pleasant appearance, and forceful personality impressed her audiences. Christabel had an internal need to dominate her environment. The Suffrage Movement provided her with a forum to display her strengths.

In 1903, Emmeline invited Labour Party women to a meeting at her home and founded the Women's Social and Political Union (WSPU). Their motto was: "Deeds, not Words"; their slogan was: "Votes for Women." For the next eleven years, the WSPU disseminated the views of this remarkable mother-daughter partnership.

Many English women were upset with the government. They realized that relying on private Members' bills wasn't the path to success; the government must legislate. An attempt was made to pass a bill to help the unemployed in an economy with increasing unemployment. Prime Minister Balfour's government attempted to postpone the bill. Several thousand destitute workers marched from the East End to

Westminster in protest. In Manchester, mobs of enraged unemployed men marched in the streets, and four men were arrested. Ten days later, Arthur Balfour backed down, and the bill became law.

This success was not lost on the women of the WSPU. They realized that the threat of violence had caused the government to act. If a threat of violence was required to get bills passed into law, then they would become increasingly militant. The Pankhursts were thrust into a nationwide militant movement operating out of Manchester and led by Christabel.

Esther Roper, who was impressed with Christabel's skill in arguing issues, suggested to Emmeline that her oldest daughter should study law. Christabel enrolled at Manchester University's law school, while continuing to participate in suffrage work.

Christabel's coworker, Annie Kenny, wondered where and how she studied because she worked for the Movement every day and almost every night. However, as her final examination approached, Christabel withdrew from all other activities to concentrate on preparing for it. In June 1906, she graduated with honors and used her new skills to support the women's cause. Christabel focused on one overriding issue—obtaining the vote for women. All other causes, including social reform issues, would have to wait.

Christabel's first unladylike step occurred in 1904 at a Liberal Party meeting at the Free Trade Hall in Manchester at which Winston Churchill launched the campaign for the general election. When a resolution supporting free trade was agreed upon and the speeches were over, Christabel rose from her chair on the platform and asked the chairman if she could propose an amendment on women's suffrage. The chairman denied her request amid cries from the audience, and Christabel backed down.

Later, she recalled, "This was the first militant step—the hardest for me because it was the first. To move from my place on the platform to the speaker's table in the teeth of the astonishment and opposition of the will of that immense throng, those civic and county leaders and those Members of Parliament, was the most difficult thing I have ever done." Nevertheless, it was "a protest of which little was heard and nothing remembered—because it did not result in imprisonment!"[100] She formed the opinion that she must go to prison to arouse public opinion; she must become a martyr.

In 1905, Christabel and Annie Kenney attended a Liberal Party rally in Manchester. Christabel had told her mother, "We shall sleep in prison tonight." They carried a banner that asked "Will you give votes for women?" Both Annie and Christabel asked the question on their banner. The Chief Constable of Manchester told them that their question would be answered later. It was ignored, so they asked it again. The crowd responded, "Throw them out!" Stewards bruised and scratched them while attempting to remove them from the hall.

Christabel realized that they hadn't done enough to be taken to prison. She knew that she was going to have to do more to be arrested; however, she wasn't sure how to do that with her arms being held behind her back. Finally, she was arrested and charged with "spitting at a policeman."

Her account of the incident was, "It was not a real spit, but only, shall we call it, a 'pout,' a perfectly dry purse of the mouth. I could not really have done it, even to get the vote, I think."[101] Christabel was kept in jail for seven days; Annie was jailed for three days. Christabel received the publicity that she sought.

Sylvia and Annie interrupted a speech in Sheffield by Henry Asquith, Chancellor of the Exchequer, and were jostled by the stewards. Men in the crowd hit them with fists and umbrellas as the women were roughly forced from the hall. The Pankhursts decided to spread their activities to London. Unfortunately, they didn't have the finances to do it. They sent Annie Kenney to London with £2 in her pocketbook to spread their version of militant suffrage activity. Emmeline

Pankhurst instructed her to "go and rouse London."

The necessary financing did come to them. Frederick and Emmeline ("the other Emmeline") Pethick-Lawrence were visiting South Africa when they heard of the suffragist activities in England. They hurried home to see what they could do to help. The Pethick-Lawrences were philanthropists who had contributed to university settlements and women's hospitals and had founded boys' clubs. They expanded the scope of their monthly newspaper, the *Labour Record*, from supporting the Labour Party cause to supporting the Suffrage Movement.

Initially, Emmeline Pethick-Lawrence hesitated before backing the Pankhursts. In her autobiography, she observed, "I had no fancy to be drawn into a small group of brave and reckless and quite helpless people who were prepared to dash themselves against the oldest tradition of human civilization as well as one of the strongest governments of modern times." She was moved by Annie Kenney's willingness to "rouse London" with £2 in her pocketbook. "I was amused by Annie's ignorance of what the talk of rousing London would involve and yet thrilled by her courage."[102]

The "other Emmeline" attended a suffrage meeting at Sylvia Pankhurst's lodgings and was impressed with the audacity of the six women who were there. Pethick-Lawrence said, "I found there was no office, no organization, no money—no postage stamps even.... It was not without dismay that it was borne on me that somebody had to come to the help of this brave little group, and that the finger of fate pointed to me."[103] Emmeline Pethick-Lawrence helped to establish the Central Committee of the WSPU and became its honorary treasurer.

Not only was Emmeline Pethick-Lawrence an effective treasurer, she was also a source of many good ideas. Money began to flow into the Movement, including generous contributions from Frederick Pethick-Lawrence. The Pethick-Lawrences allowed the Pankhursts to use their house at

Clements Inn as their base of operations, retaining only the upstairs apartment for their own use in addition to one room as an office for the *Labour Record*. They treated Christabel as a favored daughter.

The *Daily Mail* called the militant suffragists "suffragettes," a name that Christabel liked. In her opinion, the suffragists merely desired the vote, but, if you pronounce the hard "g," the suffragettes "mean to get it." Membership in the WSPU grew rapidly. Middle class women joined because they were looking for "wider and more important activities and interests."

Women of the upper class were drawn to the WSPU for other reasons: "Daughters of rich families were often without personal means, or permitted a meager dress allowance, and when their parents died, they were often reduced to genteel penury, or unwelcome dependence on relatives.... It offered an outlet from an empty, purposeless existence to an active, exciting part in ... the most important work in the world."[104]

The command of the Movement became a triumvirate: Christabel and the two Emmelines. There was no question as to who was in charge; it was Christabel. Some women were surprised how willingly Emmeline Pankhurst followed the direction of her oldest daughter.

In early 1906, thirty women carrying banners marched in front of the residence of the Chancellor of the Exchequer, Henry Asquith. The marchers were punched and kicked by police, who attempted to break up the march. Annie Kenney and two other suffragettes were sent to jail for six weeks, and Emmeline Pankhurst was handled roughly for asking a question at one of Asquith's meetings. In October 1906, ten women were arrested for making speeches in the lobby of Parliament.

Prisons had three divisions or levels of treatment. In the Third Division, the lowest division, the women were considered common criminals. They ate prison food, were subjected to coarse treatment, and wore prison clothing. Treatment in the Second Division was marginally better. Prisoners in the First Division enjoyed many privileges, including the right to have friends visit, to wear their own clothing, and to have food, writing materials, and other amenities from the outside world.

In 1907, the triumvirate called a Women's Parliament near Westminster to coincide with the opening of Parliament. When they heard that there had been no mention of women's suffrage in the King's Speech, 400 women stormed Parliament. Sylvia described the activities of the constables:

> Mounted men scattered the marchers; foot police seized them by the back of the neck and rushed them along at arm's length, thumping them in the back, and bumping them with their knees in approved police fashion. Women, by the hundred, returned again and again with painful persistence, enduring this treatment by the hour. Those who took refuge in doorways were dragged down by the steps and hurled in front of the horses, then pounced on by the constables and beaten again.[105]

Fifty women were arrested, including Christabel. Sentences ranged from one to three weeks. This time, the women were placed in the First Division.

In 1908 at the by-election in mid-Devon, Emmeline Pankhurst and a fellow suffragist were attacked by a gang of young Liberal toughs, who were unhappy that their candidate had lost to the Tory candidate. Mrs. Pankhurst was knocked unconscious into the mud and injured her ankle. The young toughs were about to stuff her into a barrel and roll her down main street, when she was rescued by mounted police. The effects of the ankle injury persisted for months and motivated her to work harder to obtain the vote.

Christabel decided that the next step was for her mother to

go to jail. From a small cart, the injured Emmeline led a delegation of thirteen women who marched on Parliament. The thirteen women were sent to prison for six months in the Second Division. In her first visit to prison, Emmeline tolerated the stripping, the body search, the bath in filthy water, and the patched and stained prison clothing made of coarse material.

She knew that the cold cells and the plank bed would be uncomfortable, but she was unprepared for the sobbing and foul language of the other prisoners. In particular, she was affected by the claustrophobic living conditions of many women in a small cell. Within two days, dyspepsia, migraine headaches, and neuralgia caused her to be moved to the prison hospital.

Another march on Parliament was planned. They weren't sure which verb to use. They considered "besiege," "invade," "raid," and "storm," and finally settled on "rush," which was enough of an action word to provoke the government. They circulated a leaflet with the message, "Men and Women— Help the Suffragettes to Rush the House of Commons," and Christabel and Emmeline spoke in Trafalgar Square. Their call to action was heard by Lloyd George, Chancellor of the Exchequer, and they were charged with "inciting the public to a certain wrongful and illegal act—to rush the House of Commons."

Christabel conducted her own defense at her trial at Bow Street. The magistrate rejected her request for a trial by jury; nevertheless, she called Lloyd George and Herbert Gladstone, the Home Secretary, as witnesses. The public was captivated by a young woman lawyer cross-examining Cabinet Ministers. The Suffrage Movement received much publicity, but, after two days, Emmeline was sentenced to three months in the Second Division and Christabel to ten weeks.

During the trial, writer Max Beerbohm was impressed with Christabel. He wrote in the *Saturday Review*: "She has all the qualities which an actress needs and of which so few actresses have any.... Her whole being is alive with her every meaning, and if you can imagine a very graceful rhythmic dance done by a dancer who uses not her feet, you will have some idea of Miss Pankhurst's method." Furthermore, he noted "the contrast between the buoyancy of the girl and the depression of the statesman [Lloyd George]."[106]

During a rally at Albert Hall where Lloyd George spoke, the suffragettes were abused again. They were bruised, and their clothing was disarranged. Some had their corsets ripped off and their false teeth knocked out. One woman had been whipped with a dog whip, and another had a wrist burned by a man using it to put out his cigar while other men struck her in the chest. The Manchester *Guardian* reported that the women had been treated "with a brutality that was almost nauseating."

The more activist members of the Movement began to become impatient with the government's delays. They threw stones wrapped in WSPU literature through the windows of government buildings. When they were arrested, they went on hunger strikes. Women who were prevented from attending public meetings climbed onto the roof of the hall and used axes to chop off slates. One woman was imprisoned for throwing an iron bar through the window of an empty railroad car on the train carrying the Prime Minister to London.

Women were given sentences ranging from two weeks to four months. Many of them went on hunger strikes. The Home Secretary ordered that they be forcibly fed using rubber tubes through their mouth or nose. In one case, the feeding tube was accidentally passed into the trachea instead of the esophagus, and the woman developed pneumonia from broth forced into her lung.

Sylvia Pankhurst described being forcibly fed in graphic terms. She experienced shivering and heart palpitations when told that she was going to be forcibly fed. Six big, strong wardresses pushed her down on her back in bed and held her by her ankles, knees, hips, elbows, and shoulders.

A doctor entered her room and attempted unsuccessfully to open her mouth. He then tried to push a steel gag through a gap between her teeth, making her gums bleed. Next two doctors thrust a pointed steel instrument between her jaws, which were forced open by the turn of a screw, and pushed a tube down her throat. While Sylvia panted and heaved, she tried to move her head away. She was almost unconscious when they poured the broth into her throat. As soon as the tube was withdrawn, she vomited. She said, "They left me on the bed exhausted, gasping for breath, and sobbing convulsively." The women were subjected to this treatment twice a day.

Some women died for their beliefs in the women's cause. In December 1910, Celia Haig, a sturdy, healthy woman, died of a painful illness from injuries incurred when she was assaulted at a public gathering. Mary Clarke, Emmeline Pankhurst's sister, died of a stroke after being released from prison "too frail to weather this rude tide of militant struggle." Henria Williams, who had a weak heart, died in January 1911 from injuries suffered during a rally.

Early in 1912, Emmeline Pankhurst broke several windows at the Prime Minister's residence at 10 Downing Street. She went to jail for two months with 218 other women. In March 1912, the police raided WSPU headquarters and arrested Emmeline and Frederick Pethick-Lawrence. Christabel had recently moved into an apartment and wasn't at Clements Inn when the police arrived. It was obvious to Christabel that the "ringleaders" were being rounded up. She fled to France to ensure that the Movement's leaders weren't all in jail. Annie Kenney became her link with Clements Inn.

Frederick and the two Emmelines were sent to prison for seven months in the Second Division. Emmeline Pankhurst refused to be treated as she had been on her first trip to prison. Sylvia described the scene: "Mrs. Pankhurst, ill from fasting and suspense, grasped the earthen toilet ewer and threatened to fling it at the doctors and wardresses, who appeared with the feeding tube. They withdrew and the order for her release was issued the next day."[107] Emmeline Pethick-Lawrence was forcibly fed once, and her husband for five days; they, too, were released early.

The militant wing of the Movement set fire to buildings, including churches, historic places, and empty buildings. They tried to set fire to Nuneham House, the home of Lewis Harcourt, an anti-suffragist Minister. Mary Leigh and Gladys Evans attempted to burn down the Royal Theatre in Dublin, where Herbert Asquith was scheduled to speak.

Christabel's mother convinced her that increased militancy was the direction in which they should move. This caused a rift with the Pethick-Lawrences, who preferred a more moderate approach. When they returned from a trip to Canada, the couple who had contributed so much to the campaign found that they had been forced out of the leadership.

Frederick commented on their falling out in unselfish terms: "Thus ended our personal association with two of the most remarkable women I have ever known.... They cannot be judged by ordinary standards of conduct; and those who run up against them must not complain of the treatment they receive."[108] Emmeline Pethick-Lawrence did not accept the split with the Pankhursts as easily as her husband did. She was offended by being dumped by them after contributing so much time and money to their mutual cause.

However, Frederick and Emmeline Pethick-Lawrence recognized Christabel's intelligence and political acumen as well as her appeal to young men and women. They also appreciated Mrs. Pankhurst's ability to move an audience with her appeals to their emotions by modulating her voice.

The level of destruction caused by the suffragettes stepped up as they became increasingly frustrated with the delay in obtaining the vote. Their acts included:
- widespread burning with acid of the message "votes for women" on golf greens
- cutting telephone wires

- burning boathouses and sports pavilions, including the grandstand at Ayr racecourse
- slashing thirteen paintings at the Manchester Art Gallery and the Rokeby *Venus* at the National Gallery
- destroying with a bomb a home being built for Lloyd George
- smashing the glass orchid house at Kew Gardens
- breaking a jewel case in the Tower of London
- burning three Scottish castles and the Carnegie Library in Birmingham
- flooding the organ in Albert Hall
- exploding a bomb in Westminster Abbey

Emmeline Pankhurst was charged with "counseling and procuring" the bombing of the house being constructed for Lloyd George at Walton-on-the-Hill. That bombing was done by Emily Wilding Davison, one of the most impulsive suffragettes. To protest not being granted the vote, Emily waited at the turn at Tattenham Corner and committed suicide by throwing herself under the King's horse at the Derby.

The militancy of the Movement in England ceased with the outbreak of World War I. Christabel moved back to England, confident that the government would have more on its mind than pursuing her. She announced, "This was national militancy. As suffragettes we could not be pacifists at any price. We offered our service to the country and called upon all our members to do likewise."[109] Christabel supported Prime Minister Asquith in the war effort as fervently as she had opposed him prior to the war.

In August 1916, Asquith surprised the House of Commons by declaring that if the voting franchise were expanded, women had an "unanswerable" case for obtaining the vote. He said that "during this war, the women of this country have rendered as effective a service in the prosecution of the war as any other class of the community."[110]

In February 1917, a committee recommended that the vote be granted to all men over twenty-one and women over thirty who were university graduates or local government electors (owners or tenant householders), or the wives of both. The bill was extended to the wives of all voters and became law in January 1918. Eight and a half million women were enfranchised. Ten years later, the remaining political limitations on women were removed.

Emmeline Pankhurst died in June 1928, a month before her seventieth birthday. Christabel wrote, "The House of Lords passed the final measure of Votes for Women in the hour her body, which had suffered so much for that cause, was laid in the grave. She, who had come to them in their need, had stayed with the women as long as they might still need her, and then she went away."[111]

Christabel became a Second Adventist and in 1936 was made a Dame Commander of the British Empire for "public and social services." She moved to the United States and died in Santa Monica, California in 1958.

The Pankhursts were a family of achievers. Perhaps the single characteristic that most led to their many accomplishments was best summarized by Frederick and Emmeline Pethick-Lawrence: "Their absolute refusal to be deflected by criticism or appeal one hair's breadth from the course they had determined to pursue."[112]

CARRIE CHAPMAN CATT (1859-1947) U.S. Women's Rights Leader

"This world taught women nothing skillful and then said her work was valueless. It permitted her no opinions and and said she did not know how to think. It forbade her to speak in public, and said the sex had no orators. It denied her the schools, and said the sex had no genius. It robbed her of every vestige of responsibility, and then called her weak. It taught her that every pleasure must come as a favor from men, and when to gain it she decked herself in paint and fine feathers, as she had been taught to do, it called her vain."

Carrie Chapman Catt, 1902

Carrie Chapman Catt was the executive and visionary of the latter phase of the Women's Rights Movement in the United States, which led to women winning the right to vote in 1920. She succeeded Susan B. Anthony as President of the National American Woman Suffrage Association in 1900 and led the Association in the critical years 1915-20. Chapman Catt also founded the organization that became the League of Women Voters.

Carrie Clinton Lane, the second of three children and only daughter of Lucius and Maria Clinton Lane, was born on January 9, 1859 in Ripon, Wisconsin. In 1866, the Lane family, attracted by the availability of prairie land, moved to a farm near Charles City, Iowa. Carrie was strongly influenced by growing up on the frontier. She was an active child who did many household chores, including cooking, and she learned to ride. She was self-reliant and did not consider females weak or inferior.

Carrie was a serious reader who graduated from Charles City High School in three years. Her father did not support her ambition to go to college, so she obtained a teacher's certificate and taught school for a year to earn money for college.

In the spring of 1877, she entered Iowa State College as a sophomore and supported herself by washing dishes and working in the library. In November 1880, she graduated with a BS degree and worked in a law office for a year in preparation for attending law school.

In 1881, Carrie gave up her plans for law school and accepted the position of Principal in the Mason City High School. Two years later she became Superintendent of Schools, a position rare for a young woman at the time. On February 12, 1885, Carrie married Leo Chapman, owner and publisher of the Mason City *Republican*. She left her job with the school district to become Assistant Editor of the newspaper. She met women's rights leader Lucy Stone while attending a convention of the American Woman Suffrage Association that year.

In 1886, Leo Chapman sold the Mason City *Republican* and traveled to San Francisco to buy another newspaper. He contracted typhoid fever, and Carrie started for the West Coast to be with him; however, he died before she reached California. Carrie worked a year for a newspaper in San Francisco before returning to Charles City, Iowa, where she earned a living on the lecture circuit. In 1887, she joined the Iowa Woman Suffrage Association. She became its unsalaried state organizer, with only her expenses paid.

In 1890, Carrie, as a member of the Iowa Woman Suffrage Association, attended the first convention of the combined National and American Woman Suffrage Associations. She heard Elizabeth Cady Stanton speak as the President of the new combined organization, the National American Woman Suffrage Association (NAWSA). Carrie addressed the convention and began to acquire a reputation as a gifted speaker.

In the summer of 1890, Carrie participated in a women's suffrage campaign in South Dakota, where she was appalled by the campaign's lack of organization. She wrote to South Dakota's campaign headquarters:

> With the exception of the work of a few
> women, nothing is being done. We have
> opposed to us the most powerful political ele-
> ments in the state. Continuing as we are, we
> cannot poll 20,000 votes. We are converting
> women who "want to vote" by the hundreds,
> but we are having no appreciable effect on the
> men.[113]

Of course, only men could vote. The results of the South
Dakota referendum were 22,000 votes for women's suffrage
and 45,000 votes against. Carrie defined the requirements for
winning a referendum:
- endorsement by the large citizens' organizations
- endorsement by the two major political parties
- possession of a sufficiently large campaign fund

She vowed that she would never again participate in an effort
doomed to failure because of lack of planning and adequate
preparation.

On June 10, 1890 in Seattle, Carrie married George W.
Catt, a structural engineer who became President of his own
construction company. Catt was a college acquaintance with
whom she had become reacquainted in San Francisco. He was
an advocate of women's rights, and, before they were married, he signed a legal agreement that Carrie would have two
months in the spring and two months in the fall each year to
devote to suffrage work. He encouraged her to do the reform-
ing for both of them while he earned a living to support them.
They had no children.

In 1892, they moved to New York City. That summer,
Chapman Catt returned to Iowa to organize a Missouri Valley
women's suffrage conference in Des Moines. Susan B.
Anthony was impressed with the results of her efforts, and
Chapman Catt was appointed finance chair of the NAWSA.

In 1895, Chapman Catt suggested that the NAWSA establish an organization committee to direct its work in the field. As chair of the committee, she operated as the Executive Secretary, forming new branches, raising money, and dispatching organizers to the field organizations. She became known for careful planning, for attention to detail, for constantly searching for better ways of doing things, and, generally, for her organizational efficiency.

Chapman Catt was an attractive woman with a magnetic personality, a commanding stage presence, and an element of brashness that served her well. She delivered her well-conceived and logical speeches with a pleasant voice and clear enunciation. Because of her strong personal characteristics, she advanced to increasingly responsible positions within the Women's Rights Movement.

In February 1900, when Susan B. Anthony retired as President of the NAWSA, Carrie Chapman Catt was elected to take her place. In her first speech as President, she said:

> The papers have spoken of the new President as Miss Anthony's successor. Miss Anthony will never have a successor. A President chosen from the younger workers is on a level with the association....

> The cause has gotten beyond where one woman can do the whole. I shall not be its leader as Miss Anthony has been; I can only be an officer of this association. I will do all I can, but I cannot do it without the cooperation of all of you.[114]

Chapman Catt built up the national organization, expanded the treasury, and provided a foundation of sorely needed administrative procedures. However, in 1904, due to her husband's poor health, she announced that she would not stand for reelection.

In 1905, Chapman Catt was asked to direct a campaign in Oregon, but she declined: "All I have done for the suffrage cause during the last fifteen years, I have been able to do by my husband's generosity.... I would dearly love to undertake the work in Oregon, but my husband needs me now, and is going to need me more and more, and I will not leave him."[115] George Catt died soon afterward at the age of forty-five, leaving her financially independent and able to focus her life on reform causes.

After her husband's death, Chapman Catt restricted her suffrage activities to New York City and New York State as well as the international movement. In 1909, she consolidated the splintered New York City groups into an Interurban Suffrage Council, which evolved the following year into the Woman Suffrage Party. Also, she built up the International Woman Suffrage Alliance's membership from eight branches to twenty-five branches. In 1910-11, she traveled across Europe on behalf of the international Women's Suffrage Movement and met many notables.

In 1913-14, Chapman Catt was chair of the Empire State Campaign Committee leading the effort to pass a state suffrage referendum. She resigned from the presidency of the International Woman Suffrage Alliance in 1915 to lead the New York State campaign. The campaign failed but won forty-two percent of the vote. The New York *World* observed that this was "a revelation of the astonishing growth of the movement." The results of this campaign effort drew attention to her political skills.

In 1915, Chapman Catt was reelected President of the NAWSA, replacing Anna Shaw, who had led the Association for eleven years. Chapman Catt inherited a divided organization that was not clearly focused. One division had begun in 1912, when Alice Paul had formed within the NAWSA a Congressional Committee that two years later became an independent organization, the Congressional Union. In 1916, the Congressional Union became the National Woman's

Party. The new organization emphasized a federal suffrage amendment, an effort that had been neglected by the NAWSA for years. Alice Paul and her organization blamed the incumbent Democratic party for the failure to pass an amendment granting the vote to women.

Chapman Catt's efforts as the newly elected President of the NAWSA were aided by a legacy of almost a million dollars from the estate of Mrs. Frank Leslie, widow of the publisher of *Leslie's Weekly*. Chapman Catt was directed to use the money as she saw fit to further the cause of woman suffrage, to which she had devoted much of her life.

Chapman Catt placed the NAWSA on a path that supported the passage of a federal amendment and simultaneously continued to push for obtaining the right to elective franchise for women in the states. The NAWSA's efforts in the states took three different paths: by the amendment of State constitutions by referenda, by the vote of State Legislatures in conferring presidential suffrage, and by obtaining the right to vote in primaries.

With the United States entry into World War I, Chapman Catt directed the Association to push both the war effort and the women's suffrage cause. In Great Britain, the Women's Rights Movement had been set aside until the end of the war. She did not want to see that happen in the United States, since it would merely delay women's victory. Although some questioned her patriotism, she stayed with a decision that she believed was right. She served on the Women's Committee of the Defense Council while continuing to be active in striving to achieve the NAWSA's goals.

In January 1918, President Wilson made a commitment to the passage of a women's suffrage amendment. The evolution of his stance on this issue was based on his respect for the good judgment, stewardship, and tact of Carrie Chapman Catt and his appreciation of the series of state suffrage victories through 1917. The bill for the Amendment to the U.S. Constitution granting women the right to vote passed the

House of Representatives on January 10, 1918 and the Senate on June 4, 1919.

The Nineteenth Amendment, the "Susan B. Anthony Amendment," was ratified on August 26, 1920, over seventy-two years after the first Women's Rights Convention in Seneca Falls. Its passage was the capstone to the life's work of Carrie Chapman Catt and many other capable women.

Chapman Catt placed great demands on others, but she placed the greatest demands on herself. She was known for her leadership qualities, and she was widely loved despite her aloof personality. American women owe their right to vote to Carrie Chapman Catt more than to any individual except Susan B. Anthony, who devoted over fifty-five years of her life to the cause.

In 1920, Chapman Catt presented to the NAWSA the idea for an organization that would become the League of Woman Voters. She proposed a nonpartisan political organization to educate women on how to use their newly gained rights. She envisioned a league that worked for child labor reform, for protective legislation for working women, and for the reduction and elimination of political corruption. The first President of the League of Woman Voters was Maud Wood Peck.

After the passage of the Nineteenth Amendment, Chapman Catt continued with her international suffrage work, particularly with the International Woman Suffrage Alliance, which became the International Alliance of Women. She was also a strong supporter of the peace movement, including the effort to establish a League of Nations and later to found the United Nations.

Chapman Catt and Nettie R. Shuler wrote *Woman Suffrage and Politics: The Inner Story of the Suffrage Movement*. Chapman Catt received honorary degrees from the University of Wyoming, Iowa State University, Smith College, and the Moravian College for Women. She received a citation of honor from President Roosevelt in 1936 and the gold medal of the National Institute of Social Sciences in 1940.

On March 9, 1947, Carrie Chapman Catt died of a heart attack at the age of eighty-eight in New Rochelle, New York. She placed winning the right to vote for women in perspective. She said, "Winning the vote is only an opening wedge. To learn how to use it is a bigger task."[116]

ALICE PAUL (1885-1977) American Social Reformer

"She [Alice Paul] has in the first place a devotion to the cause which is absolutely self-sacrificing. She has an indomitable will. She recognizes no obstacles. She has a clear, penetrating, analytic mind which cleaves straight to the heart of things. In examining a situation, she always bares the main fact; she sees all the forces which make for change in that situation. She is a genius for organization, both in the mass and in the detail. She understands perfectly, in achieving the big object, the cumulative effect of multitudes of small actions and small services. She makes use of all material, whether human or otherwise, that comes along.... Her inventiveness and resourcefulness are endless."[117]

Maud Younger, suffragist

Alice Paul organized the picketing and the suffrage parades in Washington, D.C. She didn't mind getting her hands dirty and being thrown in jail to aid the cause of obtaining the right to vote for women. In her later years, she was an active sponsor of the Equal Rights Amendment.

Alice Paul was born in Moorestown, New Jersey in 1885 to upper-middle-class Quaker parents. Her father was a successful farmer and banker. She attended the Friends' elementary and high school in Moorestown and then enrolled in Swarthmore College, which her grandparents had helped to found. She had read English literature and history widely, so she majored in biology, a subject about which she knew little.

In her senior year at Swarthmore, Paul's interest shifted to economics and political science. After graduating, she was awarded a one-year graduate scholarship at the School of Philanthropy in New York, which later became part of Columbia University. Her fellowship involved work in the College Settlement, which was her first exposure to a heterogeneous group of people. In fact, 1905-06 was a peak of immigration to the United States, and the lower East Side of

Manhattan was truly a melting pot.

Paul received a degree in social work and completed a number of assignments in the field, which was one of the few majors other than nursing and teaching open to women at the time. The following year, she received a Master's degree at the University of Pennsylvania with a major in sociology and a double minor in economics and political science.

In 1907, Paul went to England to study on a fellowship at the Quakers' Woodbrooke Institute. She enrolled in Woodbrooke's combined program at the University of Birmingham, which consisted of courses in economics and training in social work. Her fellowship included work at the Summer Lane Settlement. Her lifelong career decision was made, or was thrust upon her, while she was a student at the University of Birmingham.

Paul attended a public meeting sponsored by the University. She described the experience:

> So I went to this public meeting—after school hours, you see. It was Christabel Pankhurst. I don't know that I had ever heard her name before.... She was [suffrage leader] Mrs. Pankhurst's daughter.... She was a very young girl and a young lawyer.... Quite an entrancing and delightful person, really very beautiful I thought. So she started to speak. And the students started to yell and shout, and I don't believe anybody heard one single word that Christabel said. So she kept on anyway for her whole speech. She was completely shouted down.
>
> So I just became from that moment very anxious to help in this movement.... I thought, "That's one group now that I want to throw in all the strength I can give to help."[118]

When Paul finished the program at the Woodbrooke Institute, she enrolled at the London School of Economics. She joined the Women's Social and Political Union, did some administrative work for the Pankhursts, and marched in a large suffrage parade through London.

Paul learned how to speak in public, usually on street corners, and how to sell the idea of "votes for women." She also learned how to use the cry "votes for women" to disrupt the speeches of the British political leaders. She was sent to prison three times, where she engaged in a hunger strike and was forcibly fed. She soon became an assistant to Mrs. Pankhurst.

At the London School of Economics, Paul's own social thinking was evolving. She was influenced by Professor Westermark, a Dutch anthropologist, who wrote the classic book, *The History of Human Marriage*. Paul concluded that there were certain female traits that were evident in all cultures that distinguished women's personality characteristics and motivations from those of men.

In 1910, Paul declined a paid position with Mrs. Pankhurst and returned to the United States, where she worked with the Philadelphia suffrage organization. She enrolled in graduate school at the University of Pennsylvania and received a PhD degree in June 1912. Her interests were widening into the field of law, and her doctoral dissertation was "The Legal Position of Women in Pennsylvania."

Later that year, Paul worked with Jane Addams and became chair of the Congressional Committee of the National American Woman Suffrage Association (NAWSA). The NAWSA's emphasis had been to get suffrage referenda passed in all forty-eight states. Her role was to push for a women's suffrage amendment to the Constitution. These were difficult times for the Suffrage Movement; referenda had failed to pass in several states, which wasn't surprising since only men could vote.

Paul organized a large suffrage parade in the nation's capital; boisterous crowds caused considerable disorder along the parade route. The cavalry was called out to control the rowdy counter-demonstrators. Paul then mobilized women voters in the western states, who had already been granted the right to vote, to hold Woodrow Wilson and the Democrats—the party in power—responsible for their failure to obtain the elective franchise for women.

Paul established a new organization, the Congressional Union, to push for a women's suffrage amendment. The NAWSA would not allow it to be an auxiliary of their organization; so she split her organization off from the NAWSA. The Congressional Union evolved into the National Woman's Party. In 1917, she organized women picketers who carried bright purple, white, and gold anti-Wilson banners outside the grounds of the White House. When mobs attacked the suffragists, police arrested the women. In prison, she and the other suffragists went on hunger strikes and were forcibly fed.

Paul was allowed no visitors in prison, not even her lawyer. Also, she was not permitted to receive mail. Prison psychiatrists interviewed her several times. They asked her questions about her feelings toward President Wilson, and, in particular, if she considered him her enemy. They told her that one signature on an admission form was all that was required to commit her to an insane asylum.

Visits from the head physician of the District of Columbia jail were particularly threatening to Paul. She admitted that "I believe I have never in my life before feared anything or any human being. But I confess I was afraid of Dr. Gannon, the jail physician. I dreaded the hour of his visit. He said, 'I will show you who rules this place. You think you do. But I will show you that you are wrong'"[119]

After her release from jail, Paul, with the help of a capable staff, directed the fund-raising, lobbying, and publicity efforts of her growing organization. She was good at fund-raising; Mrs. Alva Vanderbilt Belmont was a major contributor. President Wilson's government felt the increasing pressure of their activity. The work of the National Woman's Party was called "militant," but Paul considered it "nonviolent." She counseled her picketers to dress well and not to indulge in conduct unbecoming a lady, such as screaming. Their efforts were viewed by the courts as civil disobedience because their picketing was considered "obstructing traffic."

Paul focused her organization on women's right to vote. She believed in wider social reform, but, in order to concentrate her effort on obtaining the elective franchise for women, she did not work toward other reform objectives, such as child labor laws, equal pay for equal work for women, or welfare. Although she looked forward to the end of World War I, she was not distracted by the peace movement. From 1916 to 1920, the NAWSA, the organization from which Alice had broken off, also pushed forcefully for a women's suffrage amendment.

In August 1920, American women were granted the right to vote. Paul and her staff were exhausted. However, she continued to work to pay off the debts of the National Woman's Party. She also worked to get discriminating laws replaced in several states. She earned three degrees in jurisprudence by attending classes early in the morning and in the evening.

Paul began to work toward an Equal Rights Amendment, which was submitted to Congress for the first time in 1923. She worked with women attorneys to document the laws affecting the family and women in all states to show the need for a federal Equal Rights Amendment. Not all reformers were in favor of an amendment, partly because of its potential impact on protective labor legislation. Some feared that hard-fought legislation for women such as maximum hours, minimum wage, restrictions on hours of work at night, and limitations on the weight workers could be required to lift might be lost or watered down.

In the 1920s, Paul and the National Woman's Party pushed to expand the concept of equal rights beyond the United States. In Paris, Mrs. Alva Vanderbilt Belmont corresponded with forty-five feminists in twenty-six countries to form an International Advisory Council of the National Woman's Party.

In 1926, the National Woman's Party joined the Open Door Council, an equal rights group based in England. Two years later the Party attended the Sixth Pan-American Conference in Havana, at which the Inter-American Commission of Women was established. Paul was appointed to head a committee to prepare a survey of all member nations' laws for nationality requirements. The comprehensive document was called "Alice Paul's Golden Book" by James Brown Scott, an authority on international law.

In 1928, the National Woman's Party participated in a meeting of the Open Door Council in Berlin at which a Charter of Economic Rights for Working Women was prepared. The Open Door Council opened an international office in Geneva to track the activities of the League of Nations and the International Labor Office. During the 1930s, the International Advisory Committee of the National Woman's Party worked for equal rights.

In 1938, Paul was a driving force in establishing the World Woman's Party, which was modeled on the National Woman's Party, to concentrate on equal rights for women in international rights and treaties. The headquarters, near the League of Nations and the International Red Cross in Geneva, became a refuge for women and their families fleeing the battlefields after World War II began in Europe in 1939. She shifted her efforts to the resettling of refugees.

After World War II, Paul continued to push for the passage of the Equal Rights Amendment in the U.S. She ensured that it was introduced in each session of Congress until 1972, when it passed from Congress to the states for ratification. Alice Paul died in 1977. That year ratification was three states short of passage.

Alice Paul's contributions to the Women's Rights Movement will always be remembered, particularly her work to keep the pressure on President Wilson and his administration to support women's suffrage. Like Susan B. Anthony, Alice Paul never married but devoted her entire career to the Women's Rights Movement and social reform.

MOTHER TERESA (1910-1997) Comforter of the Destitute

"Someone will ask, 'What can I do to help?' Her response is always the same, a response that reveals the clarity of her vision.... 'Just begin, one, one, one,' she urges. 'Begin at home by saying something good to your child, to your husband or your wife. Begin by helping someone in need in your community, at work, or at school. Begin by making whatever you do something for God.'"[120]

Mother Teresa, from an interview in "Words to Love By"

Sister Teresa was happy as a teacher with the Sisters of Loreto in Calcutta. However, she felt challenged to do more to help the people of the slums. She knew that to reach the poor she would have to work outside of the convent. Earlier, she had received a call to be a nun; on September 10, 1946, while traveling on a train to Darjeeling, she received "the call within a call":

> And when that happens the only thing to do is to say "Yes." The message was quite clear—I was to give up all and follow Jesus into the slums—to serve Him in the poorest of the poor. I knew it was His will that I had to follow Him. There was no doubt that it was to be His work. I was to leave the convent and work with the poor, living among them. It was an order. I knew where I belonged, but I did not know how to get there.[121]

In 1950, Mother Teresa formed the Missionaries of Charity with the Pope's blessing. By the late twentieth century, 300 houses of the Missionaries of Charity were located in over seventy countries. During a time when vocations dwindled in the Catholic Church, the Missionaries of Charity expanded to over 4,000 sisters and brothers.

On August 27, 1910, Agnes Gonxha, the third and last child of Drana and Nikola Bojaxhiu, was born in Skopje, Macedonia. Nicola Bojaxhiu was a successful merchant who had moved with his wife from Albania to Macedonia, which was part of the Ottoman Empire at the time. Drana and Nicola were deeply religious Catholics who ensured that their children had a strict Catholic upbringing.

Nicola became ill at a meeting of Albanian Nationalists in Belgrade and died the following day. Political opponents were suspected of poisoning him. Drana, an accomplished seamstress, became a dressmaker to support the family. She was very active in church activities.

Young Agnes enjoyed reading and was a good student. When she was twelve, she realized that the religious life was to be her vocation. As a member of the Sodality of the Blessed Virgin Mary, a church society for young girls, she heard about the Church's missionary work around the world. The idea to become a missionary occurred to her when she was fourteen. At the age of eighteen, she joined the Loreto Order of nuns who worked in India.

In September 1928, Agnes boarded a train to begin her trip to the Loreto Abbey in Dublin, Ireland, where she would learn English to enable her to teach in India. She traveled to Ireland by way of Paris, where she met the Mother Superior of the Loreto Order. In November, Agnes began a seven-week sea voyage to India via the Suez Canal, the Red Sea, and the Indian Ocean. She arrived in Calcutta in January 1929.

On May 24, 1931, Agnes took her first vows of poverty, chastity, and obedience as a nun. She chose the name Teresa after Saint Thèrése of Lisieux, the little flower of Jesus, a Carmelite nun who believed that the most menial tasks were forms of worship if they were done to help others or to serve God. Saint Thérèse expressed her faith by going "the way of trust and absolute self-surrender" to God; she called it her "Little Way."

Sister Teresa's first assignment was at the Loreto convent school in Darjeeling, where she also helped at the hospital. She was introduced to poverty and suffering; conditions were worse than she had expected. Later she wrote: "Many have come from a distance, walking for as much as three hours. What a state they are in! Their ears and feet are covered in sores. On their backs are lumps and lesions, among the numerous ulcers. Many remain home because they are too debilitated by tropical fever to come."[122]

After her assignment in Darjeeling, Sister Teresa taught geography, history, and catechism to Indian and Anglo-Indian girls from wealthy families at St. Mary's, the Loreto convent school in the Entally district of Calcutta. She studied the Bengali and Hindu languages. On May 14, 1937, she took her final vows as a Sister of Loreto. She became Principal of St. Mary's School.

From her bedroom window, Sister Teresa could see the slums of Motijhil. She wanted to go there to help the needy, but the nuns were only allowed out of the convent for emergencies, such as going to the hospital. Sister Teresa also saw the poverty first-hand when going back and forth through the bustee, or slum, to teach at St. Teresa's School, another Loreto convent school. She enjoyed her work at the convent schools for almost twenty years as a novice and as a nun, but she wanted to do something to help the poor and those dying from starvation and disease.

On September 10, 1946, when Sister Teresa received "the call within a call," she knew that she had to go into the slums to help the poorest of the poor. She discussed her call with her spiritual director, Father Celeste Van Exem, a Belgian Jesuit priest. He said that he would discuss it with Archbishop Ferdinand Perier of Calcutta at an opportune time. The Archbishop was reluctant to allow Sister Teresa to go out into the slums to establish a new congregation, so he postponed making the decision for a year.

Sister Teresa sent a letter to the Mother General of the

Loreto Order describing her request. In February 1947, Archbishop Perier sent the Mother General's reply along with a copy of his letter to the Pope. Permission was granted by the Vatican six months later.

On August 16, 1948, Sister Teresa took off the cumbersome Loreto habit that she had worn for seventeen years and put on a white cotton sari with a coif around the head with one wide and two narrow blue stripes. It was more practical and cooler than the heavy habit for her work in the slums. She spent several months with the medical mission sisters in Patna to add to her knowledge of nursing. She learned how to give injections, to set broken bones, and to assist in delivering babies.

Initially, Sister Teresa planned to live on a meager diet of rice and salt. Mother Anna Dengel of the medical mission advised against it. In working with disease, Mother Dengel pointed out that Sister Teresa would have to maintain her own health. Sister Teresa ensured that she and the young sisters who volunteered ate a well-balanced diet and never went into the slums in the morning without a breakfast of chapattis, Indian unleavened bread. Also, they washed thoroughly after a day's work and wore a clean sari every day.

Sister Teresa was thirty-eight years old when she began her work in the slums. She had no detailed plan; in her opinion, leaving the Loreto convent was a great sacrifice, probably the most difficult thing that she ever did. Initially, she lived with the Little Sisters of the Poor, whose mission was to help destitute elderly people.

Sister Teresa started a school in Motijhil, the slum adjacent to the Loreto convent. She had no money for school equipment and supplies, so she began by scratching letters in the dirt with a stick. Her five students the first day grew to forty very quickly. Someone donated a table, another person brought a chair, and a third gave her a chest. It was lonely work, however, and her problems seemed insurmountable. She entered her thoughts into her diary:

God wants me to be a lonely nun, laden with
the poverty of the cross. Today I learned a
good lesson. The poverty of the poor is so
hard. When I was going and going until my
legs and arms were paining, I was thinking
how they have to suffer to get food and shelter.
Then the comfort of Loreto came to tempt me.
But God, out of love for you, and by my own
free choice, I desire to do whatever be your
holy will. Give me courage now, this
moment.[123]

She realized that to understand the poor, she had to live
among them.

Father Van Exem helped Sister Teresa find a place to live.
Michael Gomes, an Indian-Catholic teacher let her have a
small room on the second floor of his home. She used a pack-
ing crate for a desk and wooden cartons for chairs. In March
1949, one of her students at Loreto, Subhasini Das, joined her
in her mission. Within a year, ten young sisters had volunteered to help her in her work. In 1949, Sister Teresa became
an Indian citizen. She wrote, "I feel Indian to the most profound depths of my soul."[124]

Archbishop Perier of Calcutta applied to the Office of the
Propagation of the Faith in Rome for independent status for
Sister Teresa's organization. She prepared a constitution that
added a fourth vow of "wholehearted free service to the poorest of the poor" to the vows of poverty, chastity, and obedience. On October 7, 1950, she became Mother Superior of the
Missionaries of Charity.

Mother Teresa drafted a decree for the new order:

"To fulfill our mission of compassion and love to the poorest
of the poor we go:
  —seeking out in towns and villages all over the

world even amid squalid surroundings the
poorest, the abandoned, the sick, the infirm,
the leprosy patients, the dying, the desperate,
the lost, the outcasts;
—taking care of them,
—rendering help to them,
—visiting them assiduously,
—living Christ's love for them, and
—awakening their response to His great love."[125]

In *A Gift for God*, Mother Teresa offers advice to novices in caring for the poor and the sick: "Speak tenderly to them. Let there be kindness in your face, in your eyes, in your smile, in the warmth of your greeting. Always have a cheerful smile. Don't only give your care, but give your heart as well."[126] In her opinion, "The poor deserve not only service and dedication but also the joy that belongs to human love." In each of the "poorest of the poor" to whom she ministered, she "saw her God himself, in distressing disguise." She said, "It is Christ you tend in the poor. It is his wounds you bathe, his sores you clean, his limbs you bandage."

Mother Teresa and her young helpers expanded into all of the rooms on the second floor of her friend Michael Gomes's home and then outgrew those rooms. Father Julien Henry helped the nuns look for larger quarters. He mentioned the need to a Muslim friend who was moving to Pakistan. His friend went into the Mosque and prayed. When he came out, he told Father Henry that the Missionaries of Charity could have his house in Calcutta for a mother house because "I got the house from God; I give it back to Him."

Mother Teresa calmly confronted those in authority on behalf of the poor. In 1954, for example, she found a woman dying in the gutter. When she tried to get the woman admitted to a hospital, the medical community at the hospital was reluctant to admit her. Mother Teresa told them that she would stay on their doorstep until they admitted the woman. Mother

Teresa asked Calcutta's public health organization for their support in caring for terminally ill patients. It found an abandoned building that she could use adjacent to a Hindu shrine to the goddess Kali. The Missionaries of Charity established Nirmal Hriday, Place of the Immaculate Heart, in the building.

Nirmal Hriday accepted the destitute and dying of all faiths, including Christians, Hindus, and Muslims. All were provided the opportunity to die with dignity; no attempt was made to convert members of other faiths to Catholicism. Initially, Hindu leaders opposed the idea of Catholic nuns establishing a home for the dying on the site of a Hindu shrine. After visiting the home in operation, however, a senior Hindu leader observed: "In the temple we have a goddess in stone; [in Mother Teresa] you have a living goddess."[127]

Mother Teresa's objective in establishing the home, or Kalighat—the Home for the Dying, was to provide "beautiful deaths." She said, "A beautiful death is for people who lived like animals, to die like angels—loved and wanted." Kalighat housed men and women with many diseases, including cancer, dysentery, malaria, malnutrition, leprosy, and tuberculosis.

Mother Teresa paid particular attention to sufferers of Hansen's disease, or leprosy. She knew that administering sulfone drugs and providing a balanced diet brought improvement in virtually all cases of leprosy. In fact, the disease was curable if caught early enough. Mother Teresa opened rehabilitation centers for lepers. She was also instrumental in founding Shanti Nagar, the Town of Peace, 200 miles from Calcutta.

When a poor woman with children died at Kalighat, the Missionaries of Charity cared for the orphans. By 1955, so many children needed housing and food that Mother Teresa rented a building near the Order's headquarters and founded Nirmala Shishu Bhavan, the Children's Home of the Immaculate Heart. Young teenage girls were brought in off the street to help take care of the young children. Mother Teresa provided a small dowry for these girls when they were of marriageable age. Without a dowry, a young girl would never find a husband and have the security of marriage.

In 1960, Mother Teresa made one of her first trips outside of India. She was invited by the National Council of Catholic Women to speak at its convention in Las Vegas, Nevada. She made a tour of the United States, and donations began to flow in to support her many projects. She also spoke with a representative of the World Health Organization at the United Nations about conditions facing lepers in India. In New York, she met Bishop Fulton J. Sheen and Dorothy Day, co-founder of the Catholic Workers Movement, which published the *Catholic Worker.* Mother Teresa and Day remained friends until Day's death in 1980.

Mother Teresa expanded the Missionaries of Charity outside of Calcutta in the early 1960s. Contributions from supporters in Germany financed the building of a home for the dying in Delhi. Houses to aid the poor and the dying were established in Agra and Jhansi, and a leprosy clinic was established in the Asansol district of Bengal. By 1962, nuns had been sent to thirty centers outside of Calcutta in the states of Bihar, Kerala, Maharashtra, and Punjab.

In March 1963, Mother Teresa added a group of young men to perform charitable services similar to those provided by the nuns. Twelve young men and a priest went to Shisu Bhaven as the first members of the Missionary Brothers of Charity. Mother Teresa could not be the head of a male congregation, so her friend, Father Julien Henry, directed the brothers' spiritual education until Father Ian Travers-Ball, an Australian Jesuit priest, left the Society of Jesus and became the director.

Brothers could work in areas that were difficult for nuns, such as Phnom Penh, Cambodia and Saigon, Viet Nam. They fed and sheltered boys from the streets and were responsible for the men's ward at the Home for the Dying. They worked with the sick and the terminally ill, drug addicts, juvenile delinquents, lepers, and mental patients. Within a short time, they had hundreds of volunteers and had established forty-four houses around the world.

In 1965, Mother Teresa opened her first mission outside of India, in Venezuela. Two years later, a mission was established in Ceylon. In the middle of her career, Mother Teresa summarized her outlook on her calling:

> In these twenty years of work amongst the people, I have come more and more to realize that it is being unwanted that is the worst disease that any human being can ever experience. Nowadays we have found medicine for leprosy and lepers can be cured.... For all kinds of diseases there are medicines and cures. But for being unwanted, except there are willing hands to serve and there's a loving heart to love, I don't think this terrible disease can ever be cured.[128]

Mother Teresa's work was recognized and appreciated. She collected many awards, including:
- Pope John XXIII Peace Award, 1971
- John F. Kennedy International Award, 1971
- Jawaharlal Nehru Award for International Understanding, 1972
- Templeton Prize for Progress in Religion, 1973
- Albert Schweitzer International Prize, 1975
- Honorary Doctor of Divinity degree from Cambridge University, England, 1977
- Balzam International Prize from President Pertini of Italy, 1979
- Nobel Peace Prize, 1979
- Bharat Ratna (Jewel of India), India's highest civilian award, 1982

- Honorary Doctor of Law degree from Harvard University, 1983
- England's Order of Merit, 1983
- U.S. Presidential Medal of Honor from President Ronald Reagan, 1985

If we were to look for an example of a person motivated to serve God by helping others, we would need to look no further than Mother Teresa. What can one person do to address the world's ills? Mother Teresa showed us.

NELSON MANDELA (1918-   ) First Native-African President of the Union of South Africa

"During my lifetime, I have dedicated myself to this struggle of the African people. I have fought against white domination, and I have fought against black domination. I have cherished the ideal of a democratic and free society in which all persons live together in harmony and with equal opportunities. It is an ideal which I hope to live for and to achieve. But if needs be, it is an ideal for which I am prepared to die."[129]

Nelson Mandela, 1963

Nelson Mandela spent over twenty-seven years in the Union of South Africa's prisons for political activism in the cause of eliminating racial segregation and improving the economic conditions of South African blacks. In February 1990, he was released from prison and was overwhelmed by the enthusiasm with which he was greeted.

In April 1994, for the first time in the history of South Africa, black people voted to elect leaders of their choice. On May 19, 1994, Nelson Mandela was inaugurated as the first black President of the Union of South Africa.

Nelson Rolihlahla Mandela was born on July 18, 1918 at Qunu in the Transkei reserve on the east coast of South Africa. He was the eldest son of Henry and Nonqaphi Mandela, members of the royal family of the Thembu, a Xhosa-speaking people. His Xhosa name, Rolihlahla, means "stirring up trouble." Henry Mandela was the chief councilor to the leader of the Thembu people and served on the Transkeian Territories General Council.

Young Nelson worked on the family farm plowing the fields and tending the cattle and sheep. He attended the local school run by white missionaries. When Nelson was twelve, Henry Mandela became ill and sent his son to live with the Chief of the Thembu. Nelson was raised with the Chief's son and attended the Methodist High School.

In 1936, Mandela enrolled in Fort Hare College, a Methodist college in eastern Cape Province. At Fort Hare, he met many future activist leaders, including Oliver Tambo, who later became the leader of the African National Congress. Mandela's political activism began in college. After three years of college, he was suspended for boycotting the Students' Representative Council, of which he was a member, because the college administration had reduced the powers of the council.

Mandela returned to the Transkei. The Chief was disappointed in Nelson and encouraged him to cooperate with the college administration. Mandela moved to Johannesburg, the center of the gold-mining region in the Transvaal, to avoid the arranged marriage that the Chief had planned for him.

Cosmopolitan Johannesburg, the "city of gold," was a shock to Mandela, who was used to rural and small-town life. Like all "Bantus," the whites' name for black Africans, he lived in a township on the outskirts of the city with no electricity or sewers. Initially, he worked as a guard at a mining compound. He had to carry a government-issued pass at all times. In the township of Alexandra, he met Walter Sisulu, owner of a real estate agency, who lent him money to complete his college degree through correspondence courses.

Sisulu also helped Mandela find a job with a Johannesburg law firm to finance his part-time law studies at the University of Witwatersrand. While studying for a law degree, he met a young nurse, Evelyn Mase, whom he married. They lived in Soweto (Southwest Townships) in Orlando Township, where their son, Thembi, was born.

Sisulu, a member of the African National Congress (ANC), suggested to Mandela that he join their organization, which had been formed by journalists, lawyers, teachers, and tribal chiefs to work to end segregation. They were convinced that they had to become more militant and use mass action to fight apartheid, the government's program of racial separation and white supremacy. Black South Africans wanted to be able to buy property and to be elected to Parliament.

In 1943, Mandela helped revive the moribund Youth League of the ANC. The Youth League planned to push the ANC to fight white domination by participating in protests of the white government and by spurring blacks into militant action. In September 1944, Anton Lembede was elected President of the ANC, and Mandela, Sisulu, and Tambo (Mandela's friend from college), were appointed to the executive committee.

The ANC stated its philosophy: "The Congress must be the brains-trust and power-station of the spirit of African nationalism; the spirit of African self-determination; the spirit that is so discernible in the thinking of our youth. It must be an organization where young African men and women will meet and exchange ideas in an atmosphere pervaded by a common hatred of oppression."[130]

In 1946, 70,000 black African mine workers participated in a strike for better wages. Seven mines were shut down; the country's booming economy was slowed. The government reacted violently. Police, aided by army units, cut off all food and water to workers' living quarters, arrested the leaders of the strike, and used batons to beat protesters who would not return to work.

Workers were killed; the strike was broken within a week. The ANC learned lessons from the strike. It realized that in numbers alone black South Africans had the power to make social change happen. Mandela noted that they had a strong ideology; they had to find a way of carrying that ideology to the people.

In 1949 at the ANC annual conference, the Youth League implemented a new policy of action employing strikes, civil disobedience, and noncooperation. In 1950, the ANC allied with the Indian National Congress, which was better-financed than the ANC.

Mandela learned about the passive resistance campaigns

waged by Mohandas Gandhi in Africa earlier in the twentieth century. He respected the Indians' hard work and dedication to their cause, but he felt that the African movement should be separate. The Indian National Congress worked closely with the South African Communist Party. Mandela did not believe that Communism could flourish in Africa.

Mandela completed his law studies in 1950 and established a law practice in Johannesburg with Oliver Tambo. Most of their cases involved victims of apartheid laws. Tambo observed, "South African apartheid laws turn innumerable innocent people into 'criminals.' ... Every case in court, every visit to the prison to interview clients, reminded us of the humiliation and suffering burning into our people."[131]

On May 1, 1950, the ANC scheduled a one-day national work stoppage. Over half of African workers stayed home. The strike was successful; however, nineteen Africans were killed in Johannesburg when police attacked demonstrators. Mandela observed: "That day was a turning point in my life, both in understanding through firsthand experience the ruthlessness of the police, and in being deeply impressed by the support African workers had given to the May Day call."[132]

In 1951, as newly elected national President of the Youth League, Mandela was asked to lead a Defiance Campaign. He toured the country to sign up volunteers. In June 1952 in Port Elizabeth, the Defiance Campaign began their "defiance" by singing African freedom songs, calling out freedom slogans, and using the "Europeans only" entrances to post offices and railroad stations.

In Johannesburg, Sisulu, Mandela, and fifty Defiance Campaign volunteers were arrested for violating the 11:00 p.m. curfew. A volunteer broke his ankle when a guard pushed him down a flight of stairs; he was refused medical attention. When Mandela protested to the policeman, he was beaten with a nightstick. By the end of December 1952, over 8,000 Defiance Campaign volunteers had been arrested.

Mandela and other ANC leaders were tried in December

1952. Over fifty of the ANC's most capable leaders were prohibited from participating further in the organization. Mandela was forbidden to travel outside of Johannesburg for two years, and he was not permitted to attend political meetings. By the end of 1952, ANC membership had grown to 100,000, however.

Mandela was away from home most of the time, which put considerable strain on his marriage. Evelyn was raising their children by herself, and, with his commitment to the ANC, she could foresee no improvement in their relationship. He was never out of the view of undercover police. She moved with the children to Natal, where she studied to become a midwife. She decided not to return to Johannesburg, and finally Mandela and Evelyn were divorced.

On December 5, 1956, 156 people, including Mandela, Sisulu, and Tambo, were arrested and charged with treason as members of "a countrywide conspiracy, inspired by communism, to overthrow the state by violence." The "Treason Trial" lasted for six years, during which time Mandela, who helped to prepare the defense, was alternately in jail and out on bail. During one of the times that he was out of jail, Mandela was introduced to Winnie Nomzamo Madikizela by Oliver Tambo and his fiancée, Adelaide Tsukudu.

Winnie's Xhosa name, Nomzamo, means "she who strives." Winnie, whose parents were both teachers, graduated from Shawbury High School and enrolled in the Jan Hofmeyr School of Social Work in Johannesburg. Upon graduating with honors from the Hofmeyr School, Winnie won a scholarship to study for an advanced degree in sociology in the United States. Instead, she accepted a position at the Baragwanath Hospital in Soweto and became the first black medical social worker in South Africa.

Mandela was thirty-eight years old when he met Winnie. She was nervous because he was a national figure sixteen years older than she. A white resident of Cape Town at the time observed, "I noticed people were turning and staring at the opposite pavement and I saw this magnificent figure of a man, immaculately dressed. Not just blacks, but whites ... were turning to admire him." While they were dating, Winnie commented, "Life with him was a life without him. He did not even pretend that I would have a special claim on his time."[133]

In June 1958, Nelson and Winnie were married in the Methodist church in Bizana, Pondoland. They moved into a home in the Orlando West township of Soweto. Winnie joined the ANC and enrolled in a course in public speaking. Soon after their marriage, they were awakened in the middle of the night by security police who searched their home but found nothing incriminating.

At a mass demonstration organized by the Women's League of the ANC, Winnie and 1,200 other female protesters were arrested and imprisoned. Winnie, who was pregnant, was struck several times and almost lost her baby. After her release from prison, Winnie was told that she had been fired from her position at the hospital. She found a job with the Child Welfare Society.

In 1959, a militant group split off from the ANC because they did not want to cooperate with other racial groups; they advocated "Africa for Africans" and called themselves the Pan Africanist Congress (PAC). In the following year, the PAC planned a campaign against the requirement for all blacks to carry a pass.

On March 21, 1960 in Sharpeville, 10,000 protesters gathered in peaceful support of the ban on passes. The police panicked and fired into the unarmed crowd killing sixty-seven Africans, including eight women and ten small children. Most were shot in the back while running away.

Later, the police fired into a peaceful crowd in the township of Langa, outside of Cape Town, killing fourteen and wounding many others. The government of the Union of South Africa was universally condemned by world opinion.

The United Nations Security Council spoke out against the government of the Union of South Africa for the first time. The ANC decided to send one of their leaders outside of the country, beyond the jurisdiction of the police of South Africa. Oliver Tambo was chosen to go.

In March 1961, the chief judge announced a verdict of not guilty in the "Treason Trial." The spectators cheered and shouted "Nkosi Sikelel iAfrika" (God Bless Africa). Mandela had conducted the defense, cross-examined witnesses, and given testimony himself. He emphasized that the ANC through their Defiance Campaign had conducted nonviolent activities and maintained that, in the long run, civil disobedience would free all Africans. His defense brought him an international reputation and increased his standing within the ANC; he was now considered its strongest leader.

Mandela had responded to the accusation that the freedom of the ANC was a threat to Europeans (whites): "No, it is not a direct threat to the Europeans. We are not anti-white; we are against white supremacy and in struggling against white supremacy we have the support of some sections of the European population.... We said that the campaign we were about to launch was not directed at any racial group. It was ... directed against laws which we considered unjust."[134]

After spending a brief time with his family, Mandela went on the road. His first stop was the All-in-Africa Conference in Pietermaritzburg, where he was the keynote speaker. He was elected head of the National Action Council. He decided to go underground to plan further protests.

Mandela became known as the "black pimpernel," after the fictional English character who always eluded his enemies during the French Revolution. He stayed underground for a year and a half, surfacing only for meetings. On one occasion, he had to climb down a rope from an upstairs window in the back of a house while police entered the front.

Winnie would be given a message to meet someone in a car at a certain location. She would change cars frequently:

"By the time I reached him I had gone through something like ten cars.... The people who arranged this were ... mostly whites. I don't know to this day who they were. I would just find myself at the end of the journey in some white house; in most cases when we got there they were deserted."[135]

One day at work, Winnie was told to drive to a particular part of the city. She described the incident: "When I got there, a tall man in blue overalls and a chauffeur's white coat and peaked hat opened the door, ordered me to shift from the driver's seat and took over and drove. That was him. He had a lot of disguises and he looked so different that for a moment, when he walked toward the car, I didn't recognize him myself."[136]

By June 1961, the ANC realized that the tactic of nonviolence had failed. They were going to have to "answer violence with violence." A new organization was formed, the Umkhonto we Sizwe (Spear of the Nation, or MK), to conduct violent attacks against the government. The MK was not a terrorist organization; it limited its attacks to sabotage, mainly of power plants, railroad freight cars, and transmission lines where innocent bystanders wouldn't be injured. If caught, MK saboteurs faced the death penalty. The police stepped up their search for Mandela.

In January 1962, Mandela traveled out of South Africa for the first time. Oliver Tambo asked him to speak at the Pan African Freedom Conference in Addis Ababa, Ethiopia. For leaving the country without a passport, Mandela was charged with an additional "crime." He was moved by the open environment outside of South Africa: "Free from white oppression, from the idiocy of apartheid and racial arrogance, from police molestation, from humiliation and indignity. Wherever I went, I was treated like a human being."[137]

Mandela returned to South Africa. On August 5, 1962, he was captured returning to Johannesburg from a meeting in Natal as the result of a tip by an informer. He was accused of inciting a strike in 1961 and of leaving the country illegally.

At the beginning of his trial in Pretoria, Mandela shouted to the gallery, "Amandla!" (power), and the crowd in the gallery answered "Ngawethu!" (to the people).

Mandela told the court, "I consider myself neither legally nor morally bound to obey laws made by a Parliament in which I have no representation. In a political trial such as this one, which involves a clash of the aspirations of the African people and those of whites, the country's courts, as presently constituted, cannot be impartial and fair."[138] He was found guilty on both charges and sentenced to ten years of hard labor. He was imprisoned in Pretoria, where he sewed mailbags, and then was transferred to the maximum-security prison on Robben Island in the Atlantic Ocean seven miles off Cape Town.

On July 12, 1963, the police raided the ANC's Rivonia farm and captured Walter Sisulu. They found many ANC documents, including Mandela's diary of his tour of Africa and incriminating evidence that documented his role in the MK violence. In court, he stated: "I do not ... deny that I planned sabotage. I did not plan it in a spirit of recklessness, nor because I have any love of violence. I planned it as a result of a calm and sober assessment of the political situation that had arisen after many years of tyranny, exploitation, and oppression of my people by the whites."[139]

On June 11, 1964, Mandela was sentenced to life imprisonment. A staff writer for the New York *Times* observed, "To most of the world, the Rivonia defendants are heroes and freedom fighters, the George Washingtons and Ben Franklins of South Africa." The London *Times* added: "The verdict of history will be that the ultimate guilty party is the government in power."[140]

On Robben Island, Mandela had a seven-feet-square cell without electricity or sanitary facilities. It was furnished with a mat, a bedroll, two light blankets, and a bucket. He was issued cotton shorts, a khaki shirt, and a light jacket. The guards told him that he was going to die there. He rejected the offer of a special diet and did not use his international reputation to obtain special privileges. All prisoners at Robben Island considered him their leader and spokesperson. He worked in a limestone quarry chained to another prisoner.

Every six months, prisoners were permitted one half-hour visit and were allowed to mail one letter of 500 words and to receive one letter. On Winnie's first visit, she was instructed that they could not speak in the Xhosa language, and that political subjects could not be discussed. She could not bring any presents, and their daughters could not visit their father until they were fourteen. They communicated with microphones and headsets through a glass partition that gave a distorted view of the other party.

Winnie was forced to leave her job at the Child Welfare Society. To support her family, she worked at menial jobs— in a dry cleaners, a furniture store, and a laundry—but lost even those jobs when the security police threatened the owners with reprisals. Spies and informers were everywhere, and the police maintained an ongoing program of harassment.

The children suffered. Winnie was frequently in jail, and friends and neighbors had to care for the young girls. On one occasion, she spent seventeen months in jail; the first five in solitary confinement in filthy living conditions. This hardship made her a stronger person, however. Finally, she sent their daughters to Swaziland to attend school. She lived on the charity of her friends and her supporters.

On June 16, 1976, during a mass protest in Soweto, the brutality of the government was again displayed. A Soweto leader observed,

> I saw a stream of schoolchildren marching
> past my house.... They had just reached the
> Orlando West school when the police tried to
> stop them marching any further. The children
> kept on walking so the police released dogs....
> Then the police panicked and fired into the

mass of children.... I will never forget the bravery of those children. They were carrying [trash can] lids to protect themselves and deflect the bullets.... The police had dogs and tear gas and batons, but they chose instead to use bullets against those unarmed kids. The saddest sight anyone can see is a dying child crippled by bullets.[141]

The people of Soweto responded with an uprising. Over 1,000 protesters died, and over 4,000 were injured. Across South Africa, over 13,000 were arrested, 5,000 of whom were under eighteen. Again, the government of the Union of South Africa was condemned in world news. The government was not influenced by international opinion, however.

Later, in September 1977, Steve Biko, the student leader of the Black Consciousness Movement died in jail from beatings and torture. This incident also received attention in the international press.

In an attempt to minimize her role as a leader, the South African government banished Winnie to Brandfort in the Orange Free State in May 1977. For ten years, she lived in a three-room concrete-block house without running water, electricity, or plumbing. It had a dirt floor; access was through openings in the front and side walls that could not be closed. Communication was difficult. Local people spoke only the African languages, Sotho and Tswana; Winnie spoke English and Xhosa. To communicate with the outside world, Winnie used the international press.

Winnie received an honorary Doctor of Laws degree from Haverford College, and two Scandinavian newspapers awarded her the Freedom Prize. In January 1985, U.S. Senator Edward Kennedy visited Winnie at Brandfort while on a trip to South Africa.

While Winnie was receiving international attention, Mandela continued to lead the movement, even while in prison. The United Democratic Front stated, "You [Nelson Mandela] are a true leader of the people. We will not rest until you are free. Your release and the release of all political prisoners is imperative. Your sacrifice for your people is affirmed. We commit ourselves anew to a free South Africa in which the people shall govern." Bishop Desmond Tutu said, "The government has to come to terms with the fact that the black community now says, 'Our leader is Nelson Mandela and any other persons are just filling in.'"[143]

The government offered to release Mandela if he would reject violence unconditionally. He responded, "Only free men can negotiate. Prisoners cannot enter into contracts.... I cannot and will not give any undertaking at a time when I and you, the people, are not free. Your freedom and mine cannot be separated. I will return."[144]

In 1985, British Conservative Lord Bethell described Mandela after visiting him in prison:

> A tall lean figure with silvering hair, an impeccable olive-green shirt and well-creased navy blue trousers. He could almost have seemed like another general in the South African prison service. Indeed his manner was the most self-assured of them all, and he stood out as obviously the senior man in the room.
>
> He was, however, black. And he was a prisoner, perhaps the most famous in the world, the man they write songs about in Europe and name streets after in London, the leader of the African National Congress, a body dedicated to the destruction of the apartheid system, if necessary by force.[145]

Samuel Dash, who had been chief counsel for the U.S. Senate Watergate Committee, observed on a visit that the guards treated Mandela "as though he were their superior, unlocking gates and opening doors on his command as he led me on a tour of his building." When Dash commented on the whites' fear of the black majority, Mandela pointed out that "unlike white people anywhere else in Africa, whites in South Africa belong here—this is their home. We want them to live here with us and to share power with us."

Dash noted, "I felt that I was in the presence not of a guerrilla fighter or radical ideologue, but of a head of state." Mandela reiterated the principles of the ANC to Dash:

- "A unified South Africa without artificial 'homelands'
- Black representation in the central Parliament
- One man, one vote"[146]

On February 11, 1990, Nelson Mandela was released from prison after twenty-seven years of incarceration. His first speech was in Cape Town at the Grand Parade, a large square in front of the old City Hall. As Mandela, Winnie, and ANC leaders were driven to the Grand Parade, they could see that a huge crowd had gathered. Their driver became nervous as the crowd enthusiastically charged the car.

After some delay, the reception committee got Mandela to the balcony of the old City Hall where he spoke:

> Friends, comrades, and fellow South Africans.
> I greet you all in the name of peace, democracy, and freedom for all! I stand here before you not as a prophet but as a humble servant of you, the people. Your tireless and heroic sacrifices have have made it possible for me to be here today. I therefore place the remaining years of my life in your hands.[147]

In late February, Mandela traveled to Lusaka to attend a meeting of the National Executive Committee of the ANC. He enjoyed being reunited with comrades that he hadn't seen in many years. He also spoke with heads of state of other

African countries, including Angola, Botswana, Mozambique, Uganda, Zambia, and Zimbabwe.

After the conference, Mandela traveled around Africa and visited the Egyptian president, Hosni Mubarak, in Cairo. While in Egypt, Mandela stated at a press conference that the ANC was "prepared to consider a cessation of hostilities." This was a message for the government of South Africa.

After Mandela returned to South Africa, the ANC leadership, including Mandela and Walter Sisulu, met with government officials in a first round of talks to discuss their differences. In early June, Mandela went on a six-week trip to Europe and North America. He met with world leaders in France, Switzerland, Italy, Ireland, and England as well as the United States and Canada. After visiting Memphis and Boston, he traveled to Washington and addressed a joint session of Congress.

When he returned to South Africa, Mandela realized that violence was continuing to obstruct the peace process. He traveled around the country in an attempt to soothe some of the ill feelings. On December 20, 1991, the first serious negotiations, called the Convention for a Democratic South Africa (CODESA), started between the ANC, other South African parties, and the government.

On June 3, 1993, negotiations resulted in setting a date for the first non-racial, one-person-one-vote national election in South Africa: April 27, 1994. For the first time in the history of South Africa, black voters could elect the leaders of their choice. In 1993, Mandela and President F. W. de Klerk shared the Nobel Peace Prize. Mandela accepted the prize on behalf of the people of South Africa. He acknowledged that Mr. de Klerk had made a vital contribution to the peace process.

Mandela and de Klerk had one television debate before the election. In concluding his remarks, Mandela looked at de Klerk and said, "Sir, you are one of those I rely upon. We are going to face the problems of this country together." Mandela extended his hand to de Klerk and added, "I am proud to hold your hand for us to go forward."[148] The gesture surprised de Klerk, but he took Mandela's hand and agreed to work together.

Mandela won the election with 62.6 percent of the vote. He realized that now he would have to heal the country's wounds, to promote reconciliation, and to instill confidence in the leadership of the government. At his inauguration ceremony in Pretoria, Mandela declared:

> We have, at last, achieved our political emancipation. We pledge ourselves to liberate all our people from the continuing bondage of poverty, deprivation, suffering, gender, and other discrimination. Never, never, and never again shall it be that this beautiful land will again experience the oppression of one by another.... The sun shall never set on so glorious an achievement. Let freedom reign. God bless Africa.[149]

After his swearing-in ceremony, the ranking generals of the South African Defense Force and the security police saluted the new President and affirmed their loyalty as jet fighters, multi-engine aircraft, and helicopters of the South African Air Force flew overhead. Ceremonies were concluded with blacks singing "Die Stem," the anthem of the republic, and whites singing "Nkosi Sikelel iAfrika."

In *Long Walk to Freedom*, Nelson Mandela comments:

> I have walked that long road to Freedom. I have tried not to falter; I have made missteps along the way. But I have discovered the secret that after climbing a great hill, one only finds that there are many more hills to climb.

> I have taken a moment to rest, to steal a view

of the glorious vista that surrounds me, to look back on the distance I have come. But I can rest only for a moment, for with freedom comes responsibilities, and I dare not linger, for my long walk is not yet ended.[150]

CHAPTER 4

VALUE UNAPPRECIATED

"To be what we are, and to become what we are capable of becoming, is the only end of life."

Baruch Spinoza

This chapter provides profiles of men and women who labored without receiving the recognition that they deserved. With one exception, they were sufficiently self-motivated to persevere with their talent. Herman Melville's most productive time as a novelist was in his late twenties and early thirties. He did little writing after 1860, although he lived for another thirty years. He is the exception in this group of five individuals; the others persevered even though their talent was unappreciated. What might Melville have created had he continued to write?

Emily Dickinson was a recluse who didn't want her poems published during her lifetime. The few that were published while she was alive were published anonymously. She was a perceptive writer who ranged from the whimsical to the serious and the revealing; her work displayed her wisdom and her depth. She was one of the founders of modern American poetry.

Vincent Van Gogh had to paint; he had no other interest in life. Some of his personal characteristics were not those of a role model; nevertheless, he is an example of a highly motivated individual. After the age of twenty-seven, he did nothing but paint. His brother, Theo, supported him financially and gave him moral support. Vincent Van Gogh died relatively young, leaving much of his work undone.

Amedeo Modigliani also had to paint. Many of his artist friends worked to support themselves when their art didn't sell; Modigliani didn't. He was fortunate to receive an allowance from his family in Italy. Like Van Gogh, Modigliani's personal characteristics were not all those of a role model; however, he is another example of a talented person who was driven.

Robert Goddard was the "father of rocketry." Much of his rocket design was done in the first half of the twentieth century, but its importance was not appreciated. Only after Germany developed V-1 and V-2 rockets during World War II and the space race began after the war was his work recognized.

Most of us need feedback on how we are doing; otherwise, we don't know whether to continue on the path that we're on, or to modify our approach. None of these individuals received positive feedback on their work; nevertheless, with the exception of Melville, they persisted in their efforts and continued to be productive. How much more might they have written, painted, or developed if their efforts had been encouraged?

HERMAN MELVILLE (1819-1891) Author Who Was Unappreciated in His Lifetime

"Melville's values were not the values of his generation. He never strove for fame, 'the triumph of insincere mediocrity.' He was not sure of anything, including mankind, never unreservedly affirmative. Unable to accept the the sweeping optimism of Longfellow, Emerson, and Whitman, he adds his skepticism to that of Hawthorne and Poe. Against the happy yea-sayers he pits his tragic and challenging "no." Instead of Emerson's peaceful rainbow, he presents thunderheads; instead of Whitman's splendid sun, he calls up heroic blackness. His stature constantly increasing, Melville not only measures up to the American giants but towers darkly above them."[151]

Louis Untermeyer, *Makers of the Modern World*

During his lifetime, Herman Melville was considered only a moderately successful author. He did most of the writing for which he is known from 1846 until 1852, between the ages of twenty-seven and thirty-two. During that span of time, his work was considered obscure; a later generation interpreted his work more fully and established his reputation as a leading author of romantic fiction. Rarely has an author faded from popularity and experienced an almost total obliteration of his reputation as Melville did. From 1860 until 1921, Melville was an almost totally forgotten author.

Melville's renaissance began in 1921 when Raymond M. Weaver published *Herman Melville: Mariner and Mystic*. In 1922, a comprehensive edition of Melville's work was compiled in London and published as a sixteen-volume set in 1924. Many biographies and essays were written about Melville and his work from the 1920s through the 1950s. He became one of America's most widely read and analyzed and highly regarded authors.

Herman Melville was born on August 1, 1819 in New

York City. His paternal grandfather was Major Thomas Melville, a participant in the Boston Tea Party; his maternal grandfather was General Peter Gansevoort, who had successfully defended Ft. Stanwix against General Burgoyne and his Indian allies.

Melville's father, Allen Melville, was a successful importer and commission merchant until 1830, when he was forced into bankruptcy during a general business depression. He moved his family to Albany to be near his wife's relatives. Weighed down by his financial failure, he was a defeated man. He became physically ill and died of a stroke in his forties.

Herman Melville's oldest brother, Gansevoort, undertook the responsibility of supporting the family by attempting to maintain what was left of their father's business. Herman attended the Albany Academy and the Albany Classical School; however, Gansevoort's business did not prosper, and Herman had to drop out of school. He worked in a bank for a while, and then taught school in Pittsfield, Massachusetts.

Melville's introduction to the sea, which is the principal subject of his books, was in 1829 at age twenty when he signed on as cabin boy on the *St. Lawrence* bound for Liverpool. He made an entry in his diary:

> I was conscious of a wonderful thing in me, that responded to all the wild commotion of the outer world and went reeling on and on with the planets in their orbits and was lost in one delirious throb at the center of the All. A wild bubbling and bursting at my heart, as if a hidden spring gushed out there.... But how soon these raptures abated, when after a brief interval, we were again set to work, and I had a vile commission to clean out the chicken coops and make up the beds of the pigs in the long boats. Miserable dog's life is this of the

sea: commanded like a slave and set to work like an ass; vulgar and brutal men lording it over me, as if were an African in Alabama.[152]

However, his reservations about life at sea during his first voyage were not enough to prevent him from signing on for another voyage of three years' duration. He sailed on the whaler *Acushnet* from New Bedford on January 3, 1841 with a tyrannical captain and a near-mutinous crew. They sailed around Cape Horn and up the west coast of South America to the Galapagos Islands and continued westward. Conditions eventually became unbearable, and he and a friend, Richard Tobias Greene, jumped ship when they reached the Marquesas.

Nevertheless, Melville was aware of the wealth of knowledge and experience he had accumulated on the whaler. He made the following diary entry:

> If I ever deserve any real repute in that small but high-bushed world which I might not unreasonably be ambitious of; if hereafter I shall do anything that, upon the whole, a man might rather have done than left undone; if at my death, my executors or more properly my creditors find any precious manuscripts in my desk, then I prospectively ascribe all the honor and glory to whaling; for a whaleship was my Yale College and my Harvard.[153]

The island of Nuku Hiva in the Marquesas, where Melville and Toby Greene escaped from the *Acushnet*, was inhabited by a tribe of cannibals called Typees (Taipis). He and his friend were treated simultaneously as prisoners and honored guests. However, despite the peaceful life and the attention of the native girls, Melville and Greene were not ready to turn their back on civilization forever.

Greene returned to Anna Maria Bay to look over a French warship and did not return. Melville escaped later and made his way out to an anchored Australian whaler, the bark *Lucy Ann*. The combination of a captain who was ill and a drunken first mate made conditions on the *Lucy Ann* no more tolerable than the *Acushnet*. When the *Lucy Ann* put into Papeete, Melville refused to go any further with the ship and was put into prison on shore. The natives allowed him to escape.

Melville signed up as harpooner on the *Charles and Henry* out of Nantucket for the voyage to the next port. In May 1843, he was discharged from the *Charles and Henry* in Lahaina, Hawaiian Islands. He went to Honolulu, where he worked as a storekeeper and a pinsetter in a bowling alley while awaiting passage home. In August, he signed on the frigate *USS United States;* he was discharged when the ship reached Boston in October 1844.

Melville joined his family at Lansingburgh, near Albany. At the age of twenty-five, he was glad to be home; he was welcomed by a family who were spellbound by his story-telling of his adventures at sea. He began to write shortly after his return home. The narrative of his adventures on Nuku Hiva became *Typee*. His storytelling is so elevated that it is difficult for the reader to determine where fact leaves off and imagination begins.

Melville's older brother was appointed to a diplomatic post in London and took the *Typee* manuscript with him to submit to John Murray, the English publisher, who accepted it for his Home and Colonial Library. Since Murray claimed in his advertising that his books were true but were as exciting as fiction, he asked for proof of the story's authenticity. Toby Greene came forward and verified Melville's story. He told Melville that he had been pressed aboard the French warship at Nuku Hiva and had left against his will. Greene became a journalist and editor and served at the headquarters of General Grant during the Civil War.

Typee was a moderate success, and, although some critics

objected to Melville's description of native customs, this success encouraged him to continue to write. Next, he wrote *Omoo* (beachcomber), a narrative of the events after he escaped from the Typees and made his way to Tahiti. He learned from his experiences with publishers on *Typee; Omoo* was essentially a sequel to *Typee* but Melville wrote it in a more straightforward and believable style. As with *Typee*, *Omoo* was a blending of Melville's actual experiences and his imagination, in which he built upon his memory and extrapolated what might have happened to enhance his story. *Omoo* was also a minor success; Melville was optimistic about his future prospects.

Melville courted Elizabeth Shaw, daughter of Lemuel Shaw, Chief Justice of Massachusetts, who had been a friend of Melville's father. Melville had known Elizabeth since childhood; she was one of his sister's friends. They were married on August 4, 1847 and bought a house in New York, where his editor, Evert Duychinch, was located. Melville considered himself a professional writer, and, in addition to beginning a third novel, he wrote reviews for *Literary World*.

After settling in New York, Melville read more widely, including the works of Dante, Rabelais, Spenser, Robert Burton, Coleridge, and Sir Thomas Browne. In particular, he was moved by Shakespeare; he found it hard to believe that he had not encountered Shakespeare previously in his twenty-nine years.

Melville's third book, *Mardi*, was a departure from his earlier works. He attempted a different style of writing in which he was influenced by his recent reading. *Mardi* confused critics as well as readers; it did not sell. It was his first unsuccessful book, and it caused him to return to telling stories about the sea.

Melville's next book was *Redburn*, the story of his first voyage as a cabin boy aboard the *St. Lawrence*. He relates his experiences aboard ship and in Liverpool. In this book, he became more of a novelist. The plot is fiction; nevertheless, some of the characters are the actual people who sailed with him. It was not one of his better books; however, he was now writing for income.

After *Redburn*, Melville wrote *White Jacket*, based on his experiences aboard the frigate *USS United States*. *White Jacket* was an indication that he was maturing as an author, and it was a book with a purpose. In it, Melville documented a cruel shipboard practice, flogging. As a result of his description and the public outcry at the time, flogging was abolished by the U.S. Navy.

By this time, Melville had written five books in five years and was in need of a change of pace. He borrowed money from his father-in-law to buy Arrowhead, the Melville farm in western Massachusetts, where he had worked as a boy to help his uncle. If he were looking for a change to inspire him, he was successful. At Arrowhead, he planned and wrote *Moby Dick*, his greatest achievement.

In August 1850, while writing *Moby Dick*, Melville invited some of his New York friends to Arrowhead, including Evert Duychinch, his editor; Cornelius Mathews, the critic; and James Fields, the publisher. While they were there, he invited Nathaniel Hawthorne and Dr. Oliver Wendell Holmes, who had summer homes in the Berkshires, to Arrowhead for a house party.

They picnicked at Monument Mountain near Stockbridge, where they read a poem by William Cullen Bryant and speculated on the influence of geography on creativity and intelligence. Melville, who was thirty-one at the time, was impressed by being in company with authors of the caliber of Hawthorne and Holmes. Hawthorne had just published *The Scarlet Letter* and was working on *The House of Seven Gables*. Melville sought the counsel and companionship of Hawthorne, whose summer home was only six miles away. For a time, Nathaniel and Sophia Hawthorne socialized with the Melvilles.

Sophia Hawthorne had formed a comprehensive impression of Melville:

> I am not quite sure that I do not think him a
> very great man.... A man with a true, warm
> heart, and a soul and an intellect—with life at
> his finger tips; earnest, sincere, and reverent;
> very tender and modest. He has a very keen
> perceptive power; but what astonishes me is
> that his eyes are not large and deep. He seems
> to me to see everything accurately; and how
> can he do so with his small eyes, I cannot tell.
> His nose is straight and handsome, his mouth
> expressive of sensibility and emotion. He is
> tall and erect, with an air free, brave and
> manly.
>
> When conversing, he is full of gesture and
> force, and loses himself in his subject.... Once
> in a while, his animation gives place to a sin-
> gularly quiet expression out of those eyes to
> which I have objected: an indrawn, dim look,
> but what at the same time makes you feel that
> he is at that moment taking deepest note of
> what is before him. It is a strange, lazy glance,
> but with a power in it quite unique. It does not
> seem to penetrate through, but to take you into
> itself.[154]

Moby Dick begins as a story about whale fisheries and
becomes a complex narrative that can be interpreted in many
ways. Melville's story of Captain Ahab of the whaling ship
Pequod pursuing the malicious great white whale that had
taken off his leg in a previous encounter draws upon whaling
lore. It includes folklore, descriptions of shipwrecks, legends,
and as many details of the whaling trade that Melville could
incorporate. It combines the strengths of all of his earlier

books and adds something uniquely its own.

Included in *Moby Dick* are the descriptions of the tropics in *Typee* and *Omoo*, the allegory and satire of *Mardi*, the narrative quality of *Redburn*, and the well-drawn characters of *White Jacket*. Melville stated that he did not consciously write *Moby Dick* with the idea of an allegory in mind. However, over time, the complexity of the book and its different meaning to different people are factors that promoted its later popularity.

In explaining his contention that he did not intend *Moby Dick* to be an allegorical work, Melville said, "I had some vague idea while writing it, that the whole book was susceptible to an allegorical construction, and that parts of it were—but the speciality of many of the particular subordinate allegories were first revealed to me after reading Mr. Hawthorne's letter."[155] Hawthorne had exclaimed, "What a book!" when he wrote Melville that he understood the book and the allegorical references made by Melville.

The view of *Moby Dick* as an allegory has persisted with a wide range of meanings generated from the story. A French critic noted that Captain Ahab wanted to harpoon Moby Dick because he could not harpoon God. Richard Chase viewed it similarly, "Ahab is the American cultural image: the captain of industry and his soul.... Moby Dick is God incarnate in the whale."[156] In *Great Novelists and Their Novels*, W. Somerset Maugham observes that:

> According to Ellery Sedgwick, Ahab is Man—man sentient, speculative, religious, standing his full stature against the immense mystery of creation. I find this hard to believe. A more plausible interpretation is Mumford's. He takes Moby Dick as a symbol of Evil, and Ahab's conflict with him as the conflict of Good and Evil in which Good is finally vanquished.... Why have all the commentators

assumed that Moby Dick is a symbol of evil?

Why should the White Whale not represent goodness rather than evil? Splendid in beauty, vast in size, greater in strength! Captain Ahab with his insane pride is pitiless, harsh, cruel and revengeful; he is evil.... Or, if you want another interpretation, you might take Ahab with his dark wickedness for Satan and the White Whale for his Creator.... Fortunately, *Moby Dick* may be read, and read with passionate interest, without a thought of what allegorical significance it may or may not have.[157]

Unfortunately, when *Moby Dick* was published, it was not a success. It failed to impress either the critics or the reading public. A critic wrote in *The New Monthly Magazine* that the book was "mad as a March hare; gibbering, screaming, like an incurable Bedlamite, reckless of keeper or straitjacket."[158] Writing *Moby Dick* seemed to have sapped Melville's energy, and yet the economics of raising a family—his second son had just been born—and of running a farm motivated him to write. The poor response to *Moby Dick* seemed to have taken the spirit out of him.

Melville wrote Hawthorne, to whom he had dedicated *Moby Dick*, in 1851:

I am so pulled hither and thither by circumstances. The calm, the coolness, the silent grass-growing mood in which a man ought always to compose—that I fear can seldom be mine. Dollars damn me; and the malicious Devil is forever grinning in upon me, holding the door ajar.... What I feel most moved to write, that is banned—it will not pay. Yet write

another way, I cannot. So the product is a final
hash, and all my books are botches.... What's
the use of elaborating! Though I write the
Gospels in this century, I should die in the gutter. What reputation H. M. has is horrible.
Think of it! To go down in history as the man
who lived among the cannibals![159]

Melville continued to write but his remaining years were
not happy ones, at least not in terms of literary success. In a
sense, he had peaked before he was thirty-two. He attempted
a novel without any reference to the sea, *Pierre*, and it did not
sell. In 1853, Melville became a contributor to *Putnam's
Monthly Magazine*. In December of that year, one of his first
short stories was published, *Bartleby the Scrivener: A Story of
Wall Street*. In this story, Melville describes a passive hero
who is defiant and refuses to crawl in the dirt and to conform
to all of his environment's expectations of him.

In his late thirties, Melville published a long short story,
Benito Cereno; a novel, *The Confidence Man*; and a collection of short fiction pieces, *The Piazza Tales*. He began to lose
the motivation to write. Also, he suffered from neurasthenia,
rheumatism, and sciatica; he had the appearance of a much
older man. His health deteriorated to the point that his family
was concerned that he would have a breakdown. His father-
in-law advised him to give up his writing and paid for a trip
abroad for him. He visited Greece, Turkey, and Egypt as well
as Italy and England. Upon his return, he went on the lecture
circuit, but he found that it was neither financially rewarding
nor to his liking.

Over the years that his books were not selling, Melville
had on several occasions attempted to obtain a government
appointment, including applying to Hawthorne's friend,
Franklin Pierce, for a diplomatic post abroad. He did not
obtain one, but he persisted in pursuing a job that would give
him financial security.

At age forty-seven, Melville was appointed Inspector of Customs for the Port of New York, requiring that he move his family from Pittsfield to New York. His post was in the Surveyor's Department, and, although it was not challenging, it provided him with the security that he had been seeking. He worked in this post for almost twenty years, until a legacy from Mrs. Ellen Marett Gifford allowed him to retire on December 3, 1885. Mrs. Gifford was the daughter of an associate of Melville's father who had been at least partly responsible for his bankruptcy. This action had been on her father's conscience, so she did what she could to compensate the Melville family.

At age fifty, Melville turned from writing novels to writing poetry. Two of his most notable efforts were a book of short poems about the Civil War, *Battle Pieces*, and a narrative poem about the Holy Land, *Clarel*. His story of a young man's search for religious faith was not a popular work; the cost of its publication was paid by his uncle, Peter Gansevoort.

Melville's last work was *Billy Budd, Foretopman*, the story of a young sailor who was falsely accused of treason by the Master-at-Arms. Since Billy stammered when he was excited, he was unable to respond to the accusation. Instead, he struck his libeler on the temple, killing him. Since this happened in front of the Captain, Budd was sentenced to death by hanging.

In 1842, a similar incident had occurred on the frigate *USS Somers* involving Philip Spencer, the son of the Secretary of War. Melville's cousin, Guert Gansevoort, the first lieutenant on the *Somers*, presided over the court martial that handed down the sentence. Lieutenant Gansevoort became a target of congressional investigations and was threatened with arrest. This incident formed the plot for Melville's last book.

Herman Melville died on September 28, 1891 of "cardiac dilation." Attacks of erysipelas had enlarged his heart. Most

New York newspapers carried no notice of his death; the New York *Press* was an exception: "There died yesterday at his quiet home in this city a man who although he had done almost no literary work during the past sixteen years, was once one of the most popular authors in the United States. Herman Melville probably reached the height of his fame about 1852, his first novel having been printed about 1847 [1846]."[160] The New York *Daily Tribune* printed a brief paragraph in which the observation was made that *Typee* was Melville's best work.

Melville's principal achievements during his lifetime were his successful early efforts: *Typee, Omoo*, and *Redburn*. His master work, *Moby Dick*, was considered too difficult to understand. A narrative that concluded with the destruction of the captain, crew, and ship, with the narrator the only one left to tell the story, was not to the public's liking. Melville was a twentieth-century author writing in the nineteenth century. His masterpiece and some of his other works were not appreciated until twenty-one years into the twentieth century, thirty years after his death.

EMILY DICKINSON (1830-1886) Poet and Recluse

> "I'm nobody! Who are you?
> Are you nobody, too?
> Then there's a pair of us—don't tell!
> They'd banish us, you know!
>
> How dreary to be somebody!
> How public, like a frog,
> To tell your name the livelong day
> To an admiring bog!"[161]
>
> Emily Dickinson

Emily Dickinson spent her days as a recluse in her parents' home writing poetry. By the late 1860s, she had discontinued virtually all contact with the outside world, except for a small group of relatives and friends. Her mentor, Thomas Wentworth Higginson, observed upon meeting her, "She was much too enigmatical a being for me to solve in an hour's interview, and an instinct told me that the slightest attempt at cross-examination would make her withdraw into her shell; I could only sit still and watch, as one does in the woods."[162]

During her lifetime, Dickinson published only seven poems, all anonymously. After her death in 1886, Lavinia Dickinson found 900 of her sister's poems in a locked trunk in her bedroom. Later, 875 additional poems were discovered. Dickinson's highly crafted and usually short poems were written in a conversational idiom about a wide variety of topics. She was a pioneer in the use of rhyme and measured poetic patterns; she was an original and is considered a founder of modern American poetry.

Louis Untermeyer summarized Dickinson's poetry in *Makers of the Modern World:*

> She wrote both as a bereaved woman and a happy, irresponsible child. Often, indeed, her

writing is almost too coy for comfort. There is, at times, an embarrassing affectation, a willing naiveté, as though she were determined to be not only a child but a spoiled child—a child who patronizes the universe and is arch with its Creator. But the pertness suddenly turns to pure perception, and the teasing is forgotten in revelation.

There is no way of analyzing her unique blend of whimsicality and wisdom, of solving her trick of turning what seems to be cryptic *non sequiturs* into crystal epigrams, no way of measuring her deceptive simplicity and her startling depths. The mystery of Emily Dickinson is not the way she lived but the way she wrote, a mystery which enabled a New England recluse to charge the literature of her country with poems she never cared to publish.[163]

Emily Dickinson was born to Edward and Emily Norcross Dickinson on December 10, 1830 in Amherst, Massachusetts. She was a middle child; her brother Austin was two years older, and her sister Lavinia was two years younger. Emily was born in a large, brick house called the Homestead, built by her grandfather, Samuel Dickinson, a founder of Amherst College. Samuel, a successful lawyer, was such a strong supporter of the College that he spent his savings on the struggling school in its early days. After finishing college and entering law practice, Emily's father supported his parents and his siblings.

Edward was a strict disciplinarian with his children. Emily's view of him was that his "heart was pure and terrible, and I think no other like it exists." Nevertheless, he believed in education and ensured that his daughters were well educated. Emily's mother was a literate woman; however, Emily once said of her: "Mother does not care for thought." Later in life, Emily told her mentor that she "never had a mother." Like his father, Edward was the treasurer of Amherst College. He also served as a member of the Massachusetts General Court and as U.S. Congressman for two terms.

As a member of a religious Congregationalist family, Emily was discouraged from reading fiction in her adolescent years; nevertheless, she was allowed to read the novels of Nathaniel Hawthorne, Charles Dickens, and Sir Walter Scott. She also read the works of Ralph Waldo Emerson, Henry Wadsworth Longfellow, Henry David Thoreau, and British writers, including the Brontë sisters, Elizabeth Barrett Browning, and George Eliot.

After attending Amherst Academy, Emily enrolled at the Mt. Holyoke Female Seminary established by Mary Lyon, who had been a student of Edward Hitchcock, the President of Amherst College. The program at Mt. Holyoke was a combination of academic courses and religious services. Students were encouraged to "convert" into becoming committed Christians. Emily's religious beliefs were continually questioned, and she was admonished daily to save her soul. She hesitated to convert because "it is hard for me to give up the world." She left Mt. Holyoke after one year because of the religious pressures and homesickness.

When she returned home, Dickinson found that many of her friends had left Amherst. She became a good friend of Susan Gilbert, who later became her sister-in-law. Dickinson was close with her sister, Lavinia, throughout their lifetimes. In 1850, following a religious revival near Amherst, Susan Gilbert as well as Dickinson's brother, Austin, and sister, Lavinia, converted. Dickinson's hesitancy about religion remained; she did not convert. She expressed her feeling in verse:

> I shall know why—when Time is over—
> And I have ceased to wonder why—

Christ will explain each separate anguish
In the fair schoolroom in the sky—
He will tell me what "Peter" promised—
And I—for wonder at his woe—
I shall forget the drop of anguish
That scalds me now—that scalds me now.[164]

In 1850, Austin went to Cambridge for four years to attend Harvard Law School. Dickinson wrote to him almost every day. She wrote poetry throughout the decade of the 1850s. Her first two published poems were valentines, printed in the *Amherst College Indicator* and the Springfield *Republican*. Both poems were published anonymously.

Dickinson was encouraged in her writing by Benjamin Newton, a clerk in her father's law office from 1847 to 1849. He was a prolific reader nine years her senior, who helped her with her evolving style. She wrote to Susan, "I have found a beautiful new friend." It is probable that they were just friends; however, some biographers consider Newton Dickinson's first love interest. Three years after meeting Dickinson, Newton married a woman twelve years older than he. He died of tuberculosis in 1853.

Dickinson's friendship with Susan Gilbert was enhanced by their mutual interest in literature. Susan was also well educated. She and Dickinson were a good intellectual match; however, their relationship was sometimes strained. In 1856, Susan and Austin Dickinson were married and moved into their home, Evergreen, next door to the Homestead. Susan was loved by the Dickinson family; nevertheless, the relationship between Susan and Lavinia was occasionally tense.

Emily Dickinson rarely left Amherst, but in 1855 she visited Philadelphia and Washington, D.C. with her father. In Philadelphia, she met Charles Wadsworth, a young minister with personal magnetism. Many of Dickinson's biographers think that she had a romantic relationship with Wadsworth, a married man. In 1862, Wadsworth received a call from

Calvary Church in San Francisco and moved there. Dickinson expressed her feelings in a sad poem:

> I cannot live with You—
> It would be Life—
> And Life is over there—
> Behind the Shelf
>
> ....
> So we must keep apart—
> You there—I—here—
> With just the Door ajar
> That Oceans are—and Prayer—
> And that White Sustenance—
> Despair—[165]

Wadsworth visited Amherst twice, in 1860 and 1880; he and Dickinson corresponded regularly.

In 1860-61, Dickinson wrote moving letters to her "Master":

> I am older—tonight, Master—but the love is
> the same—so are the moon and the crescent. If
> it had been God's will that I might breathe
> where you breathed—and find the place—
> myself—at night—if I [can] never forget that I
> am not with you—and that sorrow and frost
> are nearer than I.... I want to see you more—
> Sir—than all I wish in this world—and the
> wish—altered a little—will be my only one—
> for the skies.[166]

Dickinson wrote one of her more passionate love poems in 1861:

> Wild Nights—Wild Nights!
> Were I with thee
> Wild Nights should be
> Our luxury!

Futile—the Winds—
To a Heart in port
Done with the Compass—
Done with the Chart!
Rowing in Eden—
Ah, the Sea!
Might I but moor—Tonight
In Thee![167]

She did not date her poems. Thankfully, her handwriting changed over the years; handwriting analysis was helpful in assigning an approximate date to her work.

Martha Dickinson Bianchi, Dickinson's niece, thought that Wadsworth was her aunt's "fate," and that they had fallen in love at first sight. Dickinson destroyed most of her correspondence before she died; however, three letters addressed to her "Master" were found among her papers, which caused much speculation. Wadsworth died in 1882. Dickinson wrote a poem that biographers speculate refers to the deaths of Newton and Wadsworth:

My life closed twice before its close;
    It yet remains to see
If immortality unveil
    A third event to me,
So huge, so hopeless to conceive,
    As these that twice befell.
Parting is all we know of heaven,
    And all we need of hell.[168]

Late in the decade of the 1850s, Dickinson began to withdraw increasingly from society. As she retreated from society, her output of poetry increased significantly. However, her brother and sister-in-law were very active socially, and Dickinson met many famous people at Evergreen, the house next door. In 1857, Ralph Waldo Emerson stayed at

Evergreen during a series of lectures at Amherst College, and Austin and Susan also hosted Harriet Beecher Stowe, author of *Uncle Tom's Cabin*, and Samuel Bowles, editor of the Springfield *Republican*. Bowles, an ambitious, charismatic man, published several of Dickinson's poems in the 1850s.

In 1860, Dickinson stopped attending church. She commented that some people kept the Sabbath by going to church, but that she kept it by staying at home.

In the early 1860s, Dickinson's eyesight began to fail. Her vision was blurred, and her eyes were extremely sensitive to light. She visited ophthalmologists in Boston and was advised to use her eyes less, a heart-rending prescription for a person like her. Worried that her ailment might be progressive, she stepped up her production of poems. Fortunately, her eyesight improved during the late 1860s.

Dickinson had a high regard for the literary opinions of her sister-in-law, Susan. She sent 267 poems over the years to her, soliciting suggestions for improvement. Susan did not always respond, causing some friction between the two women. In 1861, Susan had her first child, Edward; raising a family put increased demands on her time.

Dickinson responded to an essay in the newspaper, "Letter to a Young Contributor," by Thomas Wentworth Higginson, who became her mentor. She sent four poems to him and asked for his advice, and then didn't take it. He asked her to visit him in Boston so that he could introduce her to his literary friends. She didn't make the trip to Boston, but she invited him to Amherst. After corresponding for eight years, he finally visited her at her home.

When Higginson entered the house, Dickinson presented him with two lilies and said, "These are my introduction. Forgive me if I am frightened; I never see strangers and hardly know what to say." He remembered that, "She talked soon and henceforward continuously for her own relief, and wholly without watching its effect on her hearer." She told Higginson, "If I read a book [and] it makes my whole body so cold no fire can ever warm me, I know that is poetry. If I feel physically as if the top of my head were taken off, I know that is poetry. These are the only ways I know it." Higginson admitted, "I never was with anyone who drained my nerve power so much. Without touching her, she drew from me.... I am glad not to live near her."[169]

Initially, Dickinson was too obscure for him to understand her well. She experimented with meter and rhyme, including eye rhymes: words that are spelled similarly but do not rhyme, such as sword and word. However, she was meticulous in her choice of words. Although Higginson encouraged her, she never sought publication of her poems.

As Dickinson's poetry became more profound, she socialized less and less. During the 1860s, she was a prolific writer of poetry. She wrote her poems on large sheets of paper and organized them into small bundles by folding the sheets and sewing the pages together. Thirty-nine of these packets, containing a total of 811 poems, were found after her death.

By 1869, Dickinson rarely ventured out of the house. She said, "I do not cross my father's ground to any house or town." Lavinia commented on the family's spheres of activity: "Emily had to think—she was the only one of us who had that to do.... Father believed; and mother loved; and Austin had Amherst: and I had the family to keep track of."[170]

Friends admired Dickinson's work and suggested that she publish her poems; she resisted. One was her childhood friend, Helen Fiske, who married E. B. Hunt and was widowed during the Civil War. She then married W. S. Jackson, and as Helen Hunt Jackson became the best-known woman poet in America at the time. In particular, she wanted Dickinson to publish the following poem:

> Success is counted sweetest
> By those who ne'er succeed.
> To comprehend a nectar
> Requires sorest need.

Not one of all the purple Host
Who took the Flag today
Can tell the definition
So plain of Victory

As he defeated—dying
On whose forbidden ear
The distant strains of triumph
Break, agonizing clear![171]

The poem was published with the title "Success" in *A Masque of Poets* anthology in 1878.

Dickinson's third romance was with Judge Otis Phillips Lord, a friend of her father nineteen years her senior. Lord was an Amherst alumnus who returned regularly for reunions and visited the Homestead, even after Edward's death. Friendship evolved into romance. One year after the death of Lord's wife, Dickinson wrote in one surviving letter, "I confess that I love him—I rejoice that I love him—I thank the Maker of Heaven and Earth—that gave him me to love."[172] It is not known whether he ever proposed to her. He passed away in 1884.

Dickinson's reputation as an eccentric grew. Mabel Loomis Todd, who was married to an Amherst professor, moved to town in the fall of 1881 and wrote to her parents about the "nun of Amherst": "I must tell you about the character of Amherst; it is a lady whom the people call the 'Myth.' She is a sister of Mr. Dickinson and seems to be the climax of all the family oddity. She has not been out of her own house in fifteen years, except once to see a new church, when she crept out at night and viewed it by moonlight."[173] Mabel Loomis Todd first listened to Dickinson's poems at Evergreen and thought that they were "full of power."

Dickinson had a reputation for remaining behind half-closed doors instead of mixing with visitors to the

Homestead. In her later years, she always wore white. She liked children, but would not go outside to talk with them. She lowered candy and cookies to them in a basket from her bedroom window.

Mabel Loomis Todd and her husband, David Peck Todd, socialized with Austin and Susan Dickinson as well as with Lavinia Dickinson. Shortly after her first visit to Evergreen, Loomis Todd and Austin Dickinson began a love affair that continued until he died in 1895. They made no attempt to hide their emotions.

In the spring of 1884, Dickinson became ill with the kidney disease that ultimately caused her death. On May 13, 1886, she went into a coma; she died two days later. Her obituary appeared in the Springfield *Republican*: "Very few in the village, except among the older inhabitants, knew Miss Emily personally, although the facts of her seclusion and her intellectual brilliancy were familiar Amherst traditions.... As she passed on in life, her sensitive nature shrank from much personal contact with the world, and more and more turned to her own large wealth of individual resources for companionship."[174]

Shortly after Dickinson's death, Lavinia Dickinson discovered her sister's poems. In 1890, the first edition of *Emily Dickinson's Poems* was published. William Dean Howells, America's dean of letters at the time, praised the volume as a "distinctive addition" to the country's literature. During her later years, Dickinson wrote her poems on scraps of paper and the flaps of envelopes as thoughts occurred to her. This made editing her work extremely difficult. In 1891, Loomis Todd and Higginson edited a second volume of Dickinson's poetry, and, in 1893, Loomis Todd published another volume of Dickinson's poetry.

After Austin Dickinson died in 1895, Lavinia Dickinson, who had been working with Loomis Todd editing her sister's poems, decided that she no longer wanted Loomis Todd to edit the remaining poems. Tension had built up over the more than ten-year duration of Loomis Todd's affair with Austin Dickinson. Loomis Todd put the poems that she had been editing in the attic of her house, where they stayed for thirty years.

In 1914, Martha Dickinson Bianchi, Dickinson's niece, published 143 of her aunt's unpublished poems. In 1930, Millicent Todd Bingham, Loomis Todd's daughter, and Alfred Leete Hampson edited and published *Further Poems of Emily Dickinson*. Subsequent collections were published in 1935 and 1945. In 1955, *The Poems of Emily Dickinson*, all 1,775 original poems in three volumes, was published.

The principal insight into Dickinson's inner life is in her poetry, not her biographies. She provided at least a limited view of her thoughts about her verse:

> This is my letter to the World
> That never wrote to Me—
> The simple News that Nature told—
> With tender Majesty
> Her Message is committed
> To Hands I cannot see—
> For love of Her—Sweet countrymen—
> Judge tenderly—of Me.[175]

VINCENT VAN GOGH (1853-1890) Artist Who Sold Only One Painting in His Lifetime

"I should like to paint which would appear after a century to the people living then as apparitions. So I do not endeavor to achieve this by a photographic resemblance, but by means of our impassioned expressions, using our knowledge of and our modern taste for color as a means of arriving at the expression and the intensification of the character."[176]

Vincent Van Gogh, in a letter to his sister, Wil Van Gogh

Van Gogh sold only one painting in his lifetime. In 1890, the year of his death, *The Red Vineyard* sold for 400 francs (approximately eighty dollars) at the Brussels exhibition of Les Vingt, an organization of artists and authors. Another member of Les Vingt, painter Henry de Groux, would not permit his paintings to be displayed in the same exhibition as "the abominable pots of sunflowers." In 1987, one of Van Gogh's seven paintings of sunflowers was sold at an auction at Christie's in London for $39.9 million.

In *Makers of the Modern World*, Louis Untermeyer summarized Van Gogh's approach to painting:

> Vincent Van Gogh was only thirty-seven when he killed himself, and he had been a painter less than ten years. Yet in that decade he had crowded the time with some of the most passionate and personal canvasses ever conceived. His spirit struggling with agonized love and fear of life is shown as explicitly in those canvasses as in his revealing correspondence. Painting with him was a vehement confession, a tortured sacrament rather than a source of pleasure. He combined beauty and squalor, exultation and misery, to turn despair

into affirmative creation. "I want," he cried "to paint humanity, humanity, humanity." ...

There is drama in Van Gogh's very touch, the packed lines and turbulent colors mounting to a blaze of rapture. Frenzied and tormented, Van Gogh never ceased to be concerned with the troubled human comedy; even in his paroxysms he responded to its moral force. Everything he did was another attempt to add mortal passion and pity to the immortal humanity of art.[177]

At the age of twenty-seven, after unsuccessful careers as an art gallery manager and as a lay preacher, Van Gogh moved to the Hague to study with artist Anton Mauve, who was married to Van Gogh's cousin. Mauve was very helpful, particularly in assisting Van Gogh to get established in a studio and in teaching him oil techniques. Mauve gave Van Gogh an appreciation for color. However, Van Gogh did not accept critical advice well and when Mauve suggested that he practice sketching with plaster statues, Van Gogh smashed the plaster casts; he said he wanted to draw life.

In the spring of 1882, Van Gogh completed his first large painting, *The Potato Eaters,* which is considered the precursor of Expressionism. Along with Paul Cézanne and Paul Gauguin, Van Gogh is revered as one of the founders of modern art.

In February 1886, Van Gogh moved to Paris, where his brother, Theo, was manager of an art gallery. Vincent enrolled at Cormon's studio where he met Toulouse-Lautrec, who became his friend and a defender of his art. Through Theo, Vincent became familiar with the works of the Impressionists, such as Renoir and Manet. Pissaro had a definite influence on Van Gogh, particularly in the treatment of bright colors.

Van Gogh did not try to replicate on canvas the exact

images that his eyes perceived. In his words: "Instead of trying to produce exactly what I have before my eyes, I use color more arbitrarily so as to express myself more forcibly. I should be in despair if my figures were 'correct.' My great longing is to learn to make those very corrections, those deviations, remodelings, changes of reality, that may become, yes, untruth—but more truth than the literal truth."[178]

In Paris, Van Gogh awakened to the world of art. He visited the Louvre to see the old masters Rembrandt and Delacroix, and the art galleries to view the work of the Impressionists. He discovered the composition and color of Japanese prints, and he painted steadily; unfortunately, his work did not sell. He met many of the artists active in Paris, including Degas, Pissarro, and Gauguin, who was the one artist whom Van Gogh admired and respected; they became friends. Van Gogh frequented Père Tanguy's art supply shop as well as the Café Tambourin, a small restaurant where he hung his art on the walls and hoped that it would sell. He was finally in an environment in which he could mingle with other artists.

While living with his brother in Paris, Theo wrote to his mother, "There are two human beings in Vincent, the one extraordinarily gifted, sensitive, and gentle, the other selfish and insensitive. I am sure he is his own enemy, for he poisons not only the lives of others, but his own life, yet the seeds of greatness are in him too."[179]

After two years Van Gogh tired of the Paris scene. Many of the artists did not get along with one another. For example, Monet would not let his paintings hang in a gallery that included the works of Gauguin. Also, Van Gogh felt that he would experience brighter colors if he moved south; Toulouse-Lautrec encouraged him in this.

In February 1888, Van Gogh moved to Arles, an old Roman town in Provence. He made few friends and was lonely. He subsisted on a small allowance from Theo and was considered an oddity by the townspeople. He hoped that Gauguin would join him in Arles; he wanted to start a small artists' colony in southern France with himself and Gauguin as the nucleus.

Van Gogh was discouraged, but he persevered with his painting. Finally, in October 1888, Gauguin arrived in Arles and moved into a house with Van Gogh. Van Gogh was pleased to see him to relieve his loneliness. At this time, he viewed himself as a pupil of Gauguin; he was not aware that Gauguin was his inferior. Gauguin was impressed with the progress that Van Gogh had made in his art. They were different individuals. Gauguin was assertive, confident, and outgoing and had unusual tastes. His looks were striking, and he appealed to women.

Van Gogh, who was accustomed to living in poverty, did not possess much self-confidence; he was aware that his appearance tended to set him apart. Both Gauguin and Van Gogh viewed color as extremely important in their work, but they took different approaches to it. Van Gogh stressed primary colors and juxtaposed complementary ones, whereas Gauguin usually painted with the nonprimary colors and used related colors side by side, such as pink and orange, violet and purple.

Inevitably, differences of opinion arose between the two artists; Van Gogh described their arguments as "electric." Gauguin was critical of Van Gogh's work, and Van Gogh did not like to be criticized. They disagreed on who the great artists were. Van Gogh admired Daumier and Rousseau but did not care for the work of Ingres or Degas, whom Gauguin liked. One evening while they were drinking in a cafe, Van Gogh threw his drink at Gauguin. Gauguin took Van Gogh by the arm and led him home.

Van Gogh began to break down. Shortly after the scene in the cafe, Gauguin was walking near their yellow house on the Rue Lamartine when he heard someone behind him. He turned and saw Van Gogh with a open razor in his hand. When he asked Van Gogh what he was doing, Van Gogh turned and ran into the house without speaking. In his over-wrought state, Van Gogh cut off the lower part of his right ear with the razor. He wrapped a towel around his ear to stop the bleeding, placed the severed portion of the ear in an envelope, and sent it to a young woman in return for teasing him about his big ears.

Gauguin had written earlier to Theo, who as a dealer was selling his art, that he and Van Gogh were incompatible and too different in temperament to live peacefully in Arles. Gauguin returned immediately to Paris after these incidents. Before he left, he sent a telegram to Theo suggesting that he come to Arles. Theo came and took his brother back to Paris. Van Gogh was treated at St. Paul's Hospital. His condition improved, and he returned home after a stay of two weeks. He started to paint again. His first painting was *Self-Portrait with Cut Ear.*

However, the increased activity caused further attacks that were viewed more as a form of epilepsy than schizophrenia. After an especially bad attack, the townspeople asked him to leave Arles. His doctor recommended that he enter the asylum at Saint-Remy. He continued to paint after he moved there in May 1889.

Van Gogh accomplished some of his most notable work at Saint-Remy. Paintings of this period reflect his overexcited emotions, and he painted as though he were in a supercharged atmosphere. He increased his use of natural colors and captured the actual tones of the surrounding countryside. Although Van Gogh was technically under the care of a doctor, the treatment provided to patients at the asylum was minimal. Some of his paintings done at Saint-Remy were *Yellow Wheat, Starry Night,* and a series of country scenes that he called "Impressions of Provence," which included works such as *Quarry Near Saint-Remy.*

The duration of Van Gogh's attacks lengthened. After a year at Saint-Remy, Theo placed his brother under the care of Dr. Gachet at Auvers on the Oise River near Paris, where he and his wife, Joanna, could visit him. Dr. Gachet was a talented etcher as well as a connoisseur of art and a friend of Pissarro and Cézanne. Dr. Gachet realized that the best treatment for Van Gogh was his work. He encouraged Van Gogh to paint.

During the evening of July 27, Van Gogh wrote a letter to Theo:

> I shall always consider you to be something else than a simple dealer in Corots, that through my mediation you have your part in the actual production of certain canvasses, which will retain their calm even in catastrophe....[180]

He did not finish the letter. He went for a walk in the fields, taking a revolver with him. After shooting himself, he stumbled back to the inn where he had a room. Theo was called immediately and came to Auvers to be with his brother. At age thirty-seven, Vincent Van Gogh passed away with his brother and lifelong friend, Theo, at his side.

Van Gogh did not begin his art career until he was twenty-seven years old. He was a productive artist for only ten years. However, he was a prolific painter and over 1,700 of his works have survived him. He painted in spurts of creativity in which he averaged a painting a day over a period of several weeks. He created over forty self-portraits, more than any of the masters except Rembrandt.

Van Gogh was right in thinking that: "I cannot help it if my pictures do not sell. The time will come when people will see that they are worth more than the price of the paint and my own living—very meager, after all—that are put into them."[181] In 1988, a picture of irises painted while he was in the insane asylum at Saint-Remy was sold for $53.3 million. In May 1990, his *Portrait of Dr. Gachet* was sold for $82.5 million.

AMEDEO MODIGLIANI (1884-1920) Artist Who Refused to Do Anything but Paint

"For the distillation of Modigliani's quality as a man, when all is said, is found in the masterpieces he left behind him. They are more really himself than anything that has been recorded about the personality that produced them. Perhaps I have now got to the root of the matter. An artist should be judged not by his extravagances, intoxications, quarrels, vehement and silly letters, inability to be a bourgeois husband, lapses from being a "perfect gentlemen," and so forth, but solely by the extent of his achievement. By these standards, Modigliani is among the immortals and requires no justification."[182]

Douglas Goldring, *Artist Quarter*

The subjects of most of Modigliani's art were the human figure and face. He rarely painted landscapes or still lifes, and yet he was influenced by Cézanne. His work usually involved the single human form, in contrast with Cézanne's later paintings of multiple figures. The public was slow to gain an appreciation for Modigliani's distorted, elongated figures with tilted oval heads and long, pendulous noses. He varied his painting of eyes, from wide-open green eyes to lidded eyes that avoided eye contact.

Some of Modigliani's most notable works are his paintings of nude women. They are adult, erotic nudes in which physical realism is stressed, which was something that earlier artists either concealed or modified. The public in Paris during Modigliani's time was not ready for such openness in their art. That did not prevent Modigliani from providing it.

One catalog of Modigliani's works contains a list of 309 paintings dated from 1914 to 1920. It does not include the works destroyed by the artist. In his early years, he moved frequently. He was evicted for nonpayment of rent many times. On many of these occasions, he left hurriedly to escape arrest; many of his sketches and paintings were left behind and were destroyed by the enraged landlord. Estimates of his production during the years 1914-20 are as high as 450 paintings.

Amedeo Modigliani began to paint at age fourteen in his hometown of Leghorn, Italy with the local painter, Guglielmo Micheli. He left high school in 1899 to study painting full-time and enrolled in the Scuoli Di Nudo in Florence in May 1902. A year later, he moved to Venice, where he attended the Institute of Fine Arts for three years. In late 1905, Modigliani's mother visited him in Venice to give him money to travel to Paris.

In January 1906, Modigliani arrived in Paris to attend the Academie Colorossi. His "studio" in the *maquis* area of Paris was a rickety, run-down hut made of wood and corrugated steel. Louis Latourettes, a fellow artist, visited Modigliani in the *maquis* and said that he "had lots of promise but felt that, in general, the artist was rather uncertain of himself and fumbling for a road he had not found."

Modigliani agreed with him. He told Latourettes, "My damned Italian eyes are to blame. Somehow they can't get used to this Paris light.... None of this stuff is any good. All junk."[183] He told Latourettes that the only painters he admired were Pablo Picasso and Henri Rousseau. Since he wasn't able to approach their standards, he destroyed all of his paintings; he saved only a few drawings.

Modigliani received a small allowance from home, spent it as soon as he received it, and lived in poverty. He tried to sell his drawings in Montmartre and was continually looking for portrait customers. He found few customers, and, when he did, they paid him a nominal fee. It never occurred to him to do another type of work. His friend, Max Jacob, worked as an art critic and took part-time jobs to earn an income. Vlaminck worked nights in the market at Les Halles.

Picasso lived with an art colony in the Bateau-Lavoir, a large, dilapidated building at 13 Place Ravigon, where most of the artists did some type of odd jobs for spending money. Picasso did not need outside work; his art had been selling since his discovery by Gertrude Stein and her brother, Leo.

Modigliani frequently visited the Bateau-Lavoir, which came to be known as the birthplace of Cubism. The Bateau-Lavoir had been a habitat for artists and authors since the days of Gauguin. It was a ramshackle structure located on top of the Butte area of Montmartre, consisting of a rabbit warren of rooms.

Max Jacob gave the old factory its name because it reminded him of the washing boats or laundry barges that were tied up in the Seine River. Both the Bateau-Lavoir and the laundry barges creaked in the wind, and both were entered from the top. The Bateau-Lavoir was entered from the third floor. Visitors had to walk down rickety stairs to a maze of hallways, which led to individual studios. Many artists, in addition to Picasso, lived and worked there.

The Bateau-Lavoir also contained small workshops for tailors and seamstresses. Modigliani was not a member of the inner group of artists at the Bateau-Lavoir because he was not a member of any school of artists; he did not join in the fashionable activity of rejecting the work of earlier painters.

The Lapin Agile (Agile Rabbit) was one of Modigliani's hangouts in the Montmartre area. It was a noisy, smoky place and the site of uninterrupted conversation, drinking, and entertainment. Some of the entertainment was provided by the owner, Frédéric Gérard (Frédé), who played the guitar and sang bawdy songs.

In addition to being an artists' haunt, the Lapin Agile was frequented by *apaches*, members of the Parisian underworld. They added to the atmosphere of the place; however, Frédé had to keep an old pistol handy to break up riots. Picasso and his fellow artists from the Bateau-Lavoir were regulars at the Lapin Agile.

Modigliani met Maurice Utrillo there. Utrillo was the son of Suzanne Valadon, who was once Renoir's model and was a talented artist herself. Utrillo, like Modigliani, had a drinking problem. He began drinking at an early age and would sell one of his drawings for a drink. Modigliani and Utrillo admired each other's work; when they met, they paid each other compliments. Each called the other the world's greatest painter. When the other disagreed, they argued at length before settling down and going to a bistro for several bottles of wine.

Modigliani considered Suzanne Valadon his "elected mother." He confided his sufferings to her. Occasionally, when he had too much to drink, he would run up the stairs to the apartment Suzanne shared with Monsieur Utter, tear off his clothes and enter the apartment stark naked, dancing in a wild manner. Suzanne and Utter would give him a bath and put him to bed. She did not think of Modigliani as a rowdy alcoholic, but as a gifted artist tormented by a touch of madness.

One morning Modigliani woke up in the bright sunlight and was alarmed because he couldn't move. Two street cleaners were laughing at him. They helped him out of his predicament. Apparently he had passed out in a bar the previous evening and had been carried out and jammed into a trash can while bent double. He could not stand when helped out of the trash bin because his circulation had been cut off, and his muscles ached. He laughed at his situation and took it as a joke. His only observation was, "A god in a dust bin!"[184]

Dr. Alexandre, Modigliani's earliest patron in Paris, established a colony for artists where Modigliani worked briefly. In 1908, Dr. Alexandre convinced him to join the Société des Artistes Independents and to show his work at their salon that year.

Many of Modigliani's contemporaries had moderate success selling their art in the pre-World War I era. However, his work did not sell. In 1913, Modigliani became associated with Monsieur Cheron, an art dealer who was the son-in-law of one of the best-known art dealers in Paris. Cheron had been a bookmaker and wine merchant; he had no deep-seated love for art. In his opinion, an art dealer was a businessman. Cheron provided Modigliani with canvasses, paints, brushes, and a place to work in the basement of his shop on the Rue de la Boétie.

Modigliani produced one or two paintings a day for a louis, a gold coin worth twenty francs. Cheron also provided his young maid as a model and a bottle of cognac for Modigliani. Modigliani was locked in the basement as though he were a prisoner, and when he was done with his work he had to kick the door to be let out. The arrangement didn't last long.

Paul Guillaume, an intellectual who appreciated art, became interested in Modigliani when he left Cheron. Guillaume was a collector of African art who was interested in modern artists. Max Jacob introduced Modigliani to Guillaume. Jacob tried to arrange a sponsor for his friend similar to Gertrude Stein's sponsorship of Picasso. However, Guillaume was a very cautious, conservative individual who did not take substantial risks in advancing large amounts of money to unknown painters.

In 1916, Modigliani became associated with Leopold Zborowski, who was more a poor but determined art peddler than a professional dealer. Although he was considered an amateur in art circles, he worked hard for the artists he represented. He did more than anyone to make Modigliani's reputation as one of the modern masters.

Zborowski really cared for his artists as individuals. Frequently, he provided money to artists whose work he was trying to sell by skimping on living expenses for his family. Although Guillaume was probably the first serious dealer to represent Modigliani, he remained aloof and did not push hard to sell Modigliani's work. Zborowski pushed Modigliani's art relentlessly and became a friend, confidant, and advisor.

Zborowski convinced a gallery owner, Berthe Weill, to

have a Modigliani show. The paintings were hung in her gallery on a Sunday, and a private showing was held the next day. A Modigliani nude, a painting of a long-haired woman with her head tilted, was displayed in the window and attracted a crowd immediately.

The office of the Division Police Commissioner was located across the street from Berthe's gallery. The Commissioner sent a policeman over with orders to remove the painting from the window. Berthe complied with the request, although the patrons at the private showing snickered because there were many more paintings of nudes inside the gallery.

The crowd outside became larger, and finally the same policeman returned and summoned Berthe to the Commissioner's office. The Commissioner, who had been told by the policeman that the paintings inside the gallery were as "bad" as the nude in the window, ordered Berthe to remove the nudes from her gallery. If she didn't, he would send policemen over to confiscate all of the paintings. The show, which had not yet officially opened to the public, was over. To compensate Zborowski for the disaster, Berthe bought two of the paintings. Also, two were sold at the truncated private showing. The incident brought Modigliani's name before the public.

World War I depressed the Paris art market, which delayed interest in Modigliani's art. Paris endured air raids. The Germans lobbed heavy shells into the city from three large railway cannons (big Berthas) 100 kilometers away. Panic spread through the city, and everyone who could afford to or who had relatives in the provinces left the city. Zborowski planned a trip to Nice, which he hoped was a better art market than the depressed Paris market. It wasn't, and the visit to Nice was not productive. Zborowski was unsuccessful in finding art buyers in the Nice-Cannes area. He also made a selling trip to Marseille without success.

Modigliani returned to Paris in May 1919. He continued

to paint, but late in 1919 he began to cough and spit blood. He became weaker. On January 22, 1920, he lost consciousness and was taken to Charity Hospital in an ambulance. He never regained consciousness and died two days later of tuberculosis. On January 27, a cortege bore his body through the streets of Paris, and he was buried in Père-Lachaise Cemetery. An estimated 1,000 people attended his funeral, including most of his artist friends.

Recognition of Modigliani began after his death when his work as an artist replaced the legend of Modigliani, the bohemian. He was always an individualist in his painting. The slow acceptance his work is partially explained by his differences from other artists active in Paris at the time. He had considerable strengths as a draftsman when the Fauves school of artists gave color a dominant role in art. For example, Cézanne's goal was to attempt to present perspective by using color. After being influenced in his early work by the style of the 1890s, such as that of Toulouse-Lautrec, Modigliani matured as a painter at about the time the Cubists were emerging to the forefront of art in Paris. He was influenced by the distortions of Cézanne, the economy of Cubism, and the triangular shapes of African sculpture.

The market for Modigliani's work at the time of his death was a classic case of speculation in art. Interest in Modigliani's art increased significantly when he became seriously ill. Art speculators knew that the value of an artist's work increased sharply after his death. Leopold Zborowski, Modigliani's agent, was pressed to sell Modigliani's works within days of his death, but he held off. Before his death, Modigliani's paintings sold for 100-150 francs. Zborowski received an offer during his client's funeral procession of 40,000 francs for fifty paintings, or 800 francs each.

One dealer heard two days before Modigliani's death that he probably wouldn't recover. He hurried around Paris buying all of Modigliani's work that he could find. The dealer ran around saying, "Have I luck! Right up to his death watch, I still picked up some Modiglianis for nothing. It was about time."[185]

The day after Modigliani's death, a customer in an art gallery in Paris asked for a Modigliani. The Swiss painter Fornerod said that the dealer went into his back room for a Modigliani marked 300 francs, added a zero, and sold the painting for 3,000 francs.

The paintings that Modigliani left at the Cité Falguiere studio were used by the landlord to reupholster his furniture. After Modigliani's death, when his paintings increased in value, the landlord disassembled the couch and chairs to sell Modigliani's works to a dealer for 10,000 francs. However, his wife had removed as much of the "dirty paint" as she could. The landlord became so furious about his lost windfall that he died of apoplexy.

In *Modigliani*, Pierre Sichel comments on Modigliani's life:

> Modi's art is the vindication of his life. He believed in himself and his art, and, truly, nothing else mattered. If he managed triumph only after his death, because he was his own worst enemy, it does not matter. How he lived his life does not matter; he did triumph—and so very few of us do.

> And in the tragic and peculiar fashion in which he achieved his posthumous triumph, Claude Roy compares him "with one of those exiled princes disguised as beggars whom we read of in fairy tales, and who at the story's end, casting off their rags, triumphantly ascend the throne." Perhaps that very throne Modi wrote of in his poem: up atop the black mountain on which sits the king, "the chosen-to-rule, to command," who "weeps the tears of a man who could not reach the stars."[186]

Modigliani was motivated to create his style of art without public recognition or appreciation for his work in his lifetime. An example of the increase in value of Modigliani's paintings is *The Pretty Shopkeeper*, which was sold for $12 million in November 1990 at an auction in Paris.

ROBERT GODDARD (1882-1945) Rocketry Pioneer

"The secret of discipline is motivation. When a man [or a woman] is sufficiently motivated, discipline will take care of itself."

Sir Alexander Paterson

On October 19, 1899 at age seventeen, Robert Goddard climbed a large cherry tree in the backyard of his home to prune dead branches. He had recently read H. G. Well's *War of the Worlds*, which at least partially explains the significant emotional event that occurred.

He climbed down from the tree and made the following entry in his diary: "As I looked toward the fields at the east, I imagined how wonderful it would be to make some device which has even the possibility of ascending to Mars, and how it would look on a small scale, if sent up from the meadow at my feet.... I was a different boy when I descended the tree from when I ascended, for existence at last seemed very purposive."[187]

That phrase, "for existence at last seemed very purposive," was a great motivator for Goddard's subsequent endeavors. He felt that he now had a purpose in life and a goal to develop something that would go higher than anything had gone previously. Every year for the remainder of his life, he viewed October 19 as his "Anniversary Day."

Goddard began his research with rockets as an undergraduate at Worcester Polytechnic Institute and as a graduate student at Clark University. While recovering from an illness in 1913, he developed rocket designs. During this time, he applied to the U.S. Patent Office for the first two of approximately 200 patents he was granted in his lifetime. His first patent described the characteristics required by all modern rockets: a combustion chamber with a nozzle, a pump to force fuel into the combustion chamber, and the propellant, either solid or liquid, which burns in the combustion chamber.

Goddard's second patent outlined the concept of the multi-stage rocket that is the forerunner of all high-altitude rockets in use today. Earlier, Goddard investigated the efficiency of rocket fuel. A simple rocket using gunpowder placed in a cylinder closed at one end and ignited uses only about two or three percent of the energy of the fuel. Goddard's two principal goals were to improve the basic design of the rocket and to develop an improved propellant.

By the fall of 1914, he was well enough to resume work on a part-time basis on the faculty of Clark University. Within a year, he had built some of the rockets that he had designed. He developed a nozzle design to improve propellant efficiency and to generate more thrust. By the summer of 1915, working with solid-fuel rockets, he had achieved a fuel efficiency of forty percent and was recording ejection velocities of 6,700 feet per second. After many partial successes, he launched a rocket that reached a height of 486 feet and had an ejection velocity of just under 8,000 feet per second.

Goddard realized that he could not afford to continue his research on his own. He wanted to begin his experiments with liquid fuels, and he knew that the effort would be costly. He wrote a paper to describe his rocket theory, the mathematics that supported it, and his expectations for further development. He forwarded his paper entitled "A Method of Reaching Extreme Altitudes" to several scientific institutions to promote interest in his endeavors.

The Smithsonian Institution, whose stated propose is the increase of knowledge, was one of the institutions to which he sent his paper. In his letter to the Smithsonian, he wrote, "For a number of years, I have been at work on a method of raising recording apparatus to altitudes exceeding the limit of sounding balloons.... I have reached the limit of the work I can do singlehanded, both because of the expense and also because further work will require more than one man's time."[188] Goddard and the Smithsonian scientists knew that it would be useful for meteorologists to have additional knowledge of the atmosphere hundreds of miles from the earth's surface.

The Smithsonian Institution decided to support Goddard's projects. Goddard provided the status of his development effort to the Smithsonian on a regular basis. In one of his communications, he mentioned the potential usefulness of rockets in wartime. When the United States declared war in 1917, Dr. Abbott of the Smithsonian passed on his suggestions to the U.S. Army Signal Corps.

Goddard left his teaching position at Clark University and began working on a rocket to be used by the U.S. Infantry against enemy tanks. A successful demonstration was conducted in the fall of 1918 at the Aberdeen Proving Grounds in Maryland. It appeared that this weapon, the forerunner of the World War II bazooka, would be put into immediate production. However, with the signing of the armistice on November 11, 1918, the U.S. Army suspended their interest in rockets for over twenty years.

Goddard returned to Clark University and evolved his designs for nose cones, combustion chambers, and nozzles; he also investigated liquid fuels. He realized early that liquid hydrogen and liquid oxygen would be an optimal fuel. However, liquid hydrogen was very difficult to manage, so he searched for a substitute. He chose gasoline since it was inexpensive and relatively dependable. Handling liquid oxygen was also problematical since its boiling point is 298 degrees below zero Fahrenheit, and it had to be kept under pressure.

Goddard conducted tests of his liquid fuel rockets at a farm owned by a family friend. He first launched a liquid-fuel rocket flight on March 16, 1926. The rocket reached a height four times its length and a speed of sixty miles an hour while traveling a distance of 220 feet. He had to redesign the original rocket because the combustion chamber burned through due to the intense heat. Use of sheet steel was a short-term solution to the problem. He experimented with increasingly large rockets, and he added a thermometer and a barometer as well as a small camera to record the instrument readings.

In July 1929, Goddard had his most successful flight so far. The rocket gained an altitude of ninety feet and traveled 171 feet in its eighteen and one-half seconds of flight. As Goddard and his associates picked up the reusable pieces of the rocket, the crash site was visited by an ambulance, several police cars, and cars with signs marked "Press." They had received a report of an airplane crash. This incident gave the rocket experiments bad publicity. The Smithsonian Institution supported Goddard by explaining that he was attempting to collect weather information at high altitudes. Commonwealth officials would not allow any more experimental rocket flights to be conducted in Massachusetts, however.

Goddard and his assistants looked for a more compatible location to resume rocket testing. They considered the amount of rainfall, topological factors, and general climate conditions and chose Roswell, New Mexico for future tests. In addition to the favorable climate, the area around Roswell was sparsely settled and met their criterion of having few neighbors to become alarmed by the noise of their experiments.

The first major test at the Roswell site was in December 1930. The purpose was to determine if compressed nitrogen gas from an outside tank could be used, when routed through tubes to the fuel and oxidizer tanks, to force gasoline and liquid oxygen into the combustion chambers. In this successful flight, the rocket reached a speed of 500 miles per hour and an altitude of two thousand feet and traveled 1,000 feet from the launch tower.

Goddard experienced continuing problems with the burning through of the narrow opening between the combustion chamber and the nozzle. He tried different metals but finally concluded that the walls of the combustion chamber needed cooling. He solved this problem by using curtain cooling. He evolved a design in which gasoline was sprayed on the inner wall of the combustion chamber prior to its ignition.

In effect, he placed a layer of burning gas around the inside of the combustion chamber that, because it was cooler than the burning gasoline and oxygen in the center of the chamber, resulted in the necessary cooling. In future tests, the problem of rocket engines burning through was reduced considerably. He also experimented with placing parachutes in the nose cone to lessen damage to the rockets as they returned to earth.

On April 19, 1932, Goddard conducted his first test of a rocket equipped with a gyroscope to control the guidance vanes of the rocket. These adjustable vanes were used to keep the rocket on a vertical course longer than had been possible previously. Also, the gyroscope was used to release the parachute as the rocket approached its maximum altitude. The Guggenheim Foundation, which supported Goddard's research when the need for funds exceeded the amount provided by the Smithsonian Institution, was unable to provide support for the years 1933 and 1934. Goddard returned to Worcester and resumed teaching at Clark University. Resumption of the support from the Smithsonian Institution allowed Goddard to continue his design efforts.

The most significant development during Goddard's time back in Worcester was a combustion chamber in which atmospheric air was used as the oxidizer. Obviously, this would not work for a high altitude rocket, but it worked for a rocket that traveled horizontally at low altitudes. This type of rocket could be much lighter than a high altitude rocket since it would not have to carry a tank of liquid oxygen.

Goddard used a funnel as the air intake at the front of the rocket motor. The air passed by a shutter-type intake valve on its way to the combustion chamber. The air came in while the shutters were open, the shutters closed, and combustion occurred, providing the thrust. Then the shutter opened and the process was repeated over again. This concept was used by the Germans on their V-1 rocket of World War II. The air resonance noise of the shutter opening and closing was the unusual sound that gave the "buzz-bomb" its name.

The Guggenheim Foundation resumed its support of Goddard's work in the fall of 1934. By this point, Goddard had concluded that the current design was too complex, and that it must be simplified to increase reliability. He wanted to eliminate the need for nitrogen gas and its associated tank and to use centrifugal pumps to force liquid oxygen and gasoline into the combustion chambers. The size of the tanks and their weight was the main difficulty. Goddard and his associates worked until 1940 to reduce the size and weight of the tanks and pumps.

By 1937, German scientists were performing rocket experiments at a large, liquid-propellant facility at Peenemunde. The Nazi government provided ample financial backing; they had an operational V-2 rocket by 1943.

In May 1940, Harry Guggenheim of the Guggenheim Foundation called a meeting of representatives of the armed forces that provided Goddard an opportunity to present his work and to promote the potential of liquid-propellant rockets in time of war. The Army representative stated that the next war, which had already started in Europe, "will be won by trench mortars." The only interest expressed by Army Air Corps and Navy authorities was for a rocket motor to assist short runway take-off of heavily loaded aircraft.

This joint Army Air Corps and Navy project was the first one assigned to Goddard to aid the war effort. Out of this work came the JATO unit, the jet-assisted take-off device that used solid fuel. His next assignment was to develop a rocket motor with variable thrust that could be controlled by a pilot. This engine design was successful; a version of it was used later on the X-2 and the X-15 experimental aircraft. His last assignment was the development of a small liquid oxygen- and gasoline-powered rocket for use in a guided missile.

Goddard laid out the principles underlying rocket flight, and all modern rockets evolved from concepts developed by him; unfortunately, the United States did not take advantage of his work. Documentation of many of Goddard's early rocket designs was provided upon request. Some of it was technical literature available from the Smithsonian Institution. German rocket scientists, including Werner Von Braun, acknowledged openly that their work was based on Goddard's earlier development.

Robert Goddard is example of an individual whose early academic work was not notable, but, once he had a firm goal in mind, he applied himself to achieve that goal. He was motivated to add to his chosen body of knowledge, even though he received little recognition for his efforts.

CHAPTER 5

ENERGETIC ENDURERS

"We can do whatever we wish to do provided our wish is strong enough.... What do you most want to do? That's what I have to keep asking myself, in the face of difficulties."

Katherine Mansfield

The highly motivated endurers described in this chapter were determined individuals who persevered despite being confronted with challenges that would have been insurmountable to most of us. They overcame the obstacles and were highly productive members of society.

Paul Wittgenstein was a concert pianist acquiring an international reputation prior to World War I. He was drafted into the Austrian Army and lost an arm fighting on the Western Front. He decided to continue with his career despite his handicap. He commissioned many piano concertos for the left hand and went on successful concert tours. Ravel's Piano Concerto No. 4, which Wittgenstein commissioned, became one of the best-known concertos for one hand.

Stephen Hawking, British theoretical physicist who studied the cosmos and "black holes," made major contributions to his field while suffering from amyotrophic lateral sclerosis (ALS), "Lou Gehrig's Disease." Many sufferers of this disease die within two years of its diagnosis. Dr. Hawking was extremely productive despite having been diagnosed with ALS at the age of twenty-one.

Carl Brashear set a goal for himself early in his U.S. Navy career—to become the first African-American master diver. He lost his left leg in a shipboard accident and was in the process of being invalided out of the Navy. He presented his case to a review board that allowed him to remain on active duty and gave him the opportunity to work toward becoming a master diver. He reached his goal, despite considerable opposition.

Christy Brown was born with cerebral palsy. Most of his achievements were accomplished using his left leg and foot, the only strong muscles that he had. His mother worked with him from an early age to make the most of his life despite his disability. He overcame his handicap to write five books.

Jean-Dominique Bauby was the Editor-in-Chief of an international women's fashion magazine when he suffered a massive stroke. For three weeks, doctors weren't sure whether he would live. When he came out of his coma, the only muscle that he could move was the one that controlled his left eyelid. To ensure his friends that he wasn't a complete vegetable, he wrote them a letter with the help of an amanuensis. He then wrote a book by blinking his left eyelid.

These men endured despite immense roadblocks in their paths. They had the necessary energy and were sufficiently motivated to persevere in attaining their goals.

PAUL WITTGENSTEIN (1887-1961) One-armed Concert Pianist

"It [learning to play the piano with one hand] was like attempting to scale a mountain. If you can't climb up from one side, you try another."[189]

Paul Wittgenstein

Paul Wittgenstein was a highly regarded concert pianist prior to World War I. While serving in the Austrian army, he was severely wounded in the right arm, which had to be amputated. For most musicians, loss of an arm would have been a career-ending event. Wittgenstein, however, surveyed the music that could be played with one hand and practiced seven hours a day to learn how to play it.

In *The Music Review*, E. Fred Flindell comments on this accomplishment:

> Wittgenstein amazed the post-war generation. In the years following the war, a period of bizarre turmoil and stunting cynicism, Wittgenstein not only attained world-wide fame, his example fostered a unique image in the minds of scholars, concert-goers, and musicians alike. Neither his family, his wealth, his heroic war record, nor his musical talent could alone account for or carve out such an achievement. His was simply a boundless idealism, one embodying devotion, endurance, and temerity in the service of music.[190]

Paul Wittgenstein, who was born on November 5, 1897 in Vienna, Austria, was the seventh of eight children of Karl and Leopoldine Kalmus Wittgenstein. Karl Wittgenstein immigrated to America at the age of eighteen but returned to Vienna two years later. Eventually, he owned several steel factories and became known as the "Iron King" of Austria. Leopoldine Wittgenstein, the daughter of a wealthy merchant, played arrangements for four hands on the organ and piano with young Paul as his skill on the keyboard developed. Paul's younger brother, Ludwig, became a renowned philosopher.

The Wittgenstein family was wealthy. Paintings of Gustav Klimt and of masters of the Munich and Vienna schools hung on the walls of their home, where they frequently entertained Brahms, Mahler, and Clara Schumann. Paul was fortunate to have the opportunity to play piano duets with Richard Strauss. Bruno Walter and Pablo Casals also performed in the Wittgenstein home. In addition, Karl Wittgenstein provided financial support to Schöenberg.

Young Wittgenstein took piano lessons from the highly regarded teacher, Malvine Brée. Wittgenstein had an incredible memory for music and was a facile sight-reader. His exposure to masters of music in his home elevated his interest in music. He was not concerned about his own limitations in comparison with them. Next he took lessons from Theodor Leschetizky and the blind Austrian composer, Josef Labor. They helped him search for his own musical identity.

Wittgenstein's friend, Trevor Harvey, said about him at this time, "By all accounts in his early days he built up an astonishing left-hand technique, but when I knew him the nervous intensity that he developed led him often to play insensitively and loudly, and not always with great accuracy."[191] He referred to himself as the "Saitenknicker," the mighty key smasher.

In December 1913, Wittgenstein made his debut as a concert pianist at the Grosser Musikverein Saal in Vienna. Three months later, he gave a solo performance with the Vienna Symphony Verein. In August 1914, he was called to active duty as a second lieutenant in the Austrian Army. He was severely wounded in action leading a reconnaissance patrol near Zamosc, Poland.

In his novel about Wittgenstein, *The Crown Prince*, John Barchilon describes what happened when Wittgenstein's patrol was hit by an artillery shell:

> The ground opened up and hurled them in the air, spinning and twisting. Paul saw earth, fire, and sky. Arms, legs, and black dirt swirled around him, and then he began the endless journey back to earth. He fell and fell and fell, landing on something soft. Where were his legs? His arms, hands, where were they? Where was his foot? He heard nothing. Just silence. Black, black nothing. Was this death?[192]

Wittgenstein was taken to an army hospital at Krasnostov, where his right arm was amputated. He was taken prisoner by the Russian Army at the hospital and moved to hospitals in Minsk, in Orel, and in Omsk, Siberia, where he had access to a piano. In November 1915, through efforts of the International Red Cross, he was sent from Siberia to Sweden, where he participated in a prisoner exchange sponsored by the Pope.

In March 1916, Wittgenstein was promoted to first lieutenant and retired on a medical disability pension. Leopoldine Wittgenstein received a letter from his commanding officer, Colonel Rettich of the Imperial Royal Cavalry:

> I wish to express my sincere sympathy with you in connection with the severe wounding of your son. You may be proud of him, because owing to the information obtained by his patrol, the efforts of the Russians to attack us at Famorz were frustrated. He has rendered outstanding services, and I sincerely hope he will get official recognition later on.[193]

In May 1916, Wittgenstein was awarded the Military Cross Class III and the War Decoration Class III. Five months later, he was awarded the Military Cross Class II by the Grand Duke of Mecklenburg. From the summer of 1917 until August 1918, by his own request, he served as a first lieutenant on the Italian front as an aide to General von Hurt and to General von Schiesser.

From the time of his return to Vienna until he volunteered for the Italian front, Wittgenstein practiced compositions for the left hand. He performed in five recitals, in which he played Labor's *Concertpiece for Piano and Orchestra, Sonata in E Flat for Piano and Violin,* and *Piano Quartet in C minor.* In September 1918, he returned to Vienna and the concert stage.

Leschetizky had died in 1915. Wittgenstein did not look for another teacher; he practiced seven hours a day, establishing his own regimen. Initially, he tired easily and had to rest frequently. From 1918 to 1921, Wittgenstein searched libraries, museums, and second-hand retail music shops for compositions for the left hand. He liked Brahms's arrangement of Bach's *Chaconne,* as well as Godowsky's *Suite for the Left Hand Alone,* the *Fugue upon Bach,* and the *Intermezzo and Etude Macabre.* He also admired *Studies for the Left Hand* by Reger, *Etudes for the Left Hand* by Saint-Saëns, and Scriabin's *Prelude and Nocturne for the Left Hand,* which the composer wrote after developing tendonitis in his right hand.

One of the earliest one-armed pianists was the Hungarian Count Geza Zichy, who began playing the piano at the age of five; he decided to be a concert pianist after losing his right arm in a hunting accident in 1864, when he was fifteen. His concert in Berlin in May 1915 was the first known public performance of a one-armed pianist. Count Zichy's friend, Franz Liszt, transcribed a song for him, and Emil Sauer wrote *Etude* for him. Wittgenstein did not like the works that Count Zichy composed for himself.

Wittgenstein wrote his own arrangements of piano compositions and operas using the transcription devices of Liszt and of Godowsky. He also commissioned composers to create new works for the left hand. Wittgenstein observed: "Since it is no particular attainment of mine, I think I may honestly say that I am (perhaps) the pianist for whom the greatest number of special compositions have been written."[194] In 1931, he accepted a teaching position at the New Vienna Conservatory, where he was known for his energy and his idealism.

Wittgenstein didn't hesitate to make extensive changes to other composer's works that he had commissioned, similar to his modifications to Brahms's transcription of Bach's *Chaconne*. He made changes to the compositions of Hindemith and Korngold, as well as to Britten's *Diversions on a Theme*, Prokofiev's *Concerto No. 4*, and *Parergon to the Domestic Symphony* by Richard Strauss. They were twentieth-century composers, and Wittgenstein's style was that of the nineteenth century.

Wittgenstein's impresario, George Kugel, asked Ravel if he would compose a piano concerto for the left hand. He willingly undertook the project. Initially, Ravel and Wittgenstein did not agree on the finished work. Wittgenstein objected to Ravel's inclusion of jazz rhythms in his composition; however, the differences were resolved. Ravel's *Concerto in D for Left Hand* became one of the most frequently played works for one hand.

Wittgenstein continued to perform on the concert stage. One of his students in the 1930s recalled the first time she had heard him play: "I was about twelve years old when I heard Paul Wittgenstein perform for the first time. I was sitting with my father in our subscription seats in the rear of the Weiner Musikverein Saal. After the concert, my father asked me if I had noticed anything unusual about the pianist. I had not. He told me that the pianist had only played with his left hand. I could not believe it."[195]

In November 1934, Wittgenstein performed the Ravel

Concerto for the Left Hand and Orchestra with the Boston Symphony. The music critic of the New York *Herald-Tribune* reported:

> Doubtless the greatest tribute one could pay to Paul Wittgenstein, the famous one-armed pianist, is a simple statement of the fact that after the first few moments wondering how the devil he accomplished it, one almost forgot that one was listening to a player whose right sleeve hung empty at his side. One found oneself engrossed by the sensitiveness of the artist's phrasing, the extent to which his incredible technique was subordinated to the delivery of the musical thought.[196]

Wittgenstein taught at the New Vienna Conservatory until he immigrated to the United States in December 1938. From 1938 until 1943, he taught at the Ralph Wolfe Conservatory in New Rochelle, an affiliate of the Mannes Music School; from 1940 until 1945 he was a Professor of Piano at Manhattanville College of the Sacred Heart. He became a U.S. citizen in 1946. In 1957, Wittgenstein published *School for the Left Hand.* In 1958, he received an honorary Doctor of Music degree from the Philadelphia Musical Academy.

In *The Music Review*, E. Fred Flindell discusses the difficulty of Wittgenstein's playing the piano with one hand:

> The following remark gives us an insight into his particular dilemma. "It takes double talent and energy for a left hand pianist to convey the impression of a musician with two arms." Through personal arrangements and commissions, he established his own repertoire. When performing a corpus of works, he was consistently able to convey the impression of pos-

> sessing two hands This challenge, he con-
> fessed, was an enormous stimulus to his ambi-
> tion. It was, he conceded, the greatest satisfac-
> tion in his life to succeed in doing with one
> hand something that others did with two.[197]

In a June 1967 interview with Leonard Castle, Wittgenstein described some of the piano technique that he used in concerts. He did not use the middle or harp pedal on the piano. He used two fingers on one key for increased volume, and difficult leaps over the keys could be avoided by half pedaling that simulated the two-handed technique. His skill was enhanced by the speed with which he used his left hand and his precise control.

On March 3, 1961, Paul Wittgenstein died in Manhasset, New York. In *The Music Review*, E. Fred Flindell wrote what might be considered an epitaph:

> It is, however, astonishing how many works
> [over forty] the artist took an active part in
> commissioning, determining, and performing.
> Few knew that Wittgenstein spent years help-
> ing others as President of the Society against
> Poverty, or of his countless anonymous and
> gracious deeds of assistance.... Perhaps his
> nineteenth-century ideas and bearing were at
> times anachronistic, even quixotic. Still, his
> endeavor and influence, his courage and skill
> will remain legendary for generations to
> come.[198]

STEPHEN HAWKING (1942-   ) Cosmologist and Researcher of "Black Holes"

"It is the most persistent and greatest adventure in human history, this search to understand the universe, how it works and where it came from. It is difficult to imagine that a handful of residents of a small planet circulating an insignificant star in a small galaxy have as their aim a complete understanding of the entire universe, a small speck of creation truly believing it is capable of understanding the whole"[199]

Murray Gell-Mann

As an undergraduate, Stephen Hawking was an undistinguished student. He was not highly motivated; he studied an average of one hour a day. In 1963, at the age of twenty-one, Hawking was told that he had amyotrophic lateral sclerosis (ALS), which is known as motor neuron disease in Britain and Lou Gehrig's disease in the United States. ALS attacks the nerves of the spinal cord and the portion of the brain that controls voluntary motor functions of the muscles. The nerve cells degenerate causing muscles to atrophy throughout the body, resulting in paralysis. Memory and the ability to think are not affected.

ALS, which worsens in stages, forces the patient to deal with a series of progressively limiting plateaus. Hawking has made incredible contributions to science by ignoring his ailment, to the extent of his ability. He has probably done more than any scientist to expand our understanding of the origin and nature of the universe, and his theoretical work on "black holes" was innovative. He is known for his popular book, *A Brief History of Time*, a runaway best seller.

Stephen Hawking was born in Oxford, England on January 8, 1942, the three-hundredth anniversary of the death of the Italian scientist, Galileo. Hawking's parents, Frank and Isobel Hawking, lived in the northern London suburb of

Highgate but moved to Oxford just before Stephen's birth. London was being bombed by the German Luftwaffe during World War II; however, the Germans had agreed not to bomb Cambridge and Oxford universities if the Royal Air Force would not bomb Göttingen and Heidelberg universities. Frank and Isobel had attended Oxford.

After World War II, Frank Hawking was appointed Division Head of Parasitology at the National Institute of Medical Research. He was away frequently, sometimes on trips to Africa to do medical research. In effect, Isobel raised the children. Frank wrote several novels that were never published, and Isobel, a member of the Labour Party, was active in the nuclear disarmament movement.

The Hawking family lived in Highgate until 1950, when they moved to St. Albans. Young Stephen attended the St. Albans private school, an abbey school with an excellent academic reputation. He was regarded as a bright student who ranked slightly above average in the top class, but he was not much of an athlete. He and his friends played board games for which Stephen devised the rules, and a classmate designed the boards and the movable pieces.

Hawking wanted to major in either physics or mathematics in college, but his father insisted that his son take chemistry so that he could follow him in a medical career. In the spring of 1958, Hawking and his classmates built a computer that they named LUCE, Logical Uniselector Computing Engine, from parts of an old telephone exchange. They had more difficulty with the practical aspects, e.g., soldering, than the design challenges.

Hawking won a scholarship to University College, Oxford University, his parents' alma mater. Oxford was changing at the time. A classmate of Hawking noted that when their class arrived at Oxford, everybody wanted to row, and nobody wore jeans. When they graduated, hardly anybody wanted to row, and everybody wore jeans.

Hawking observed: "The prevailing attitude at Oxford at

the time was anti-work. You were supposed either to be brilliant without effort or to accept your limitations and get a fourth-class degree. To work hard to get a better class of degree was regarded as the mark of a grey man, the worst epithet in the Oxford vocabulary."[200] As a member of the former group, he spent a considerable amount of time drinking with his classmates. Hawking took up rowing to alleviate boredom. Because he didn't weigh much, wasn't muscular, and had a loud, clear voice, he became a coxswain.

When he completed his undergraduate studies at Oxford, Hawking took the final examinations upon which admission to graduate school were based. The finals were difficult, and he hadn't seriously prepared for them. His results placed him on the borderline between a First and a Second, which required an interview with a board of examiners to decide where he should be placed.

Hawking needed a first-class honors degree to be admitted to graduate school at Cambridge University to study cosmology with Dr. Fred Hoyle, the foremost British astronomer of his time. The senior examiner asked Hawking about his plans for the future. He responded, "If I get a first, I will go to Cambridge. If I receive a second, I will remain at Oxford. So I expect that you will give me a first."[201] The board of examiners complied.

In October 1962, when Hawking began his graduate studies at Cambridge, he could choose between two areas of research, elementary particles—the study of small particles, or cosmology—the study of large objects. Cosmology is the study of the origin, evolution, and destiny of the universe.

In Hawking's opinion, "I thought that elementary particles were less attractive, because, although they were finding lots of new particles, there was no proper theory of elementary particles. All they could do was arrange the particles in families, like in botany. In cosmology, on the other hand, there was a well-defined theory—Einstein's general theory of relativity."[202]

Instead of studying under Fred Hoyle, he was assigned to Dennis Sciama, an unknown to Hawking. Hawking was discouraged by this until he realized that Hoyle, who traveled abroad frequently, would not have been as good a mentor as Sciama, a respected scientist who conscientiously guided him in his research. Hawking's first term did not go well; he was not as strong in mathematics as he needed to be.

Hawking also had a personal problem with which to contend. He began to have difficulty tying his shoelaces, he bumped into walls and furniture, and, on a few occasions, he fell. Also, he experienced slurred speech without having a drink to blame it on. When he arrived home for Christmas vacation, his parents, who hadn't seen him for several months, immediately knew that something was wrong. His father thought that he might have contracted a disease in the Middle East during a trip with him over the summer. His parents referred him to a specialist.

At several parties over the holidays, Hawking met and talked with Jane Wilde, the friend of a friend, who attended the local high school. Jane planned to read modern languages at Westfield College in London in the fall. She was attracted to this intellectual and somewhat eccentric character. Their relationship bloomed from their first meeting.

In January, Hawking underwent a battery of medical tests; the diagnosis was amyotrophic lateral sclerosis (ALS). He was faced with decreasing mobility, gradual paralysis, and ultimately death as respiratory muscles lost their functionality or he contracted pneumonia. Many ALS patients do not live two years beyond the diagnosis.

If Hawking had decided to study experimental physics instead of theoretical physics, his career would have been over. He went into a deep depression, locked himself in his room, and listened to music, particularly his favorite composer, Wagner. It was rumored that he drank heavily, but he says that was an exaggeration.

Hawking questioned continuing with his research,

because he might not be around long enough to get his PhD. Literally, he felt that he had nothing to live for. He was not a deeply religious person; nevertheless, he had an experience that helped to put things into perspective: "While I was in hospital, I had seen a boy I vaguely knew die of leukemia in the bed opposite me. It had not been a pretty sight. Clearly there were people who were worse off than me. At least my condition didn't make me feel sick. Whenever I feel inclined to feel sorry for myself, I remember that boy."[203]

Hawking had two recurring dreams in the hospital, one was a dream that he was going to executed. He decided that there were many worthwhile tasks he could do if he were spared from execution. In the second dream, he sacrificed his life to save others. He thought that if he were going to die, he might as well do some good.

Jane visited Stephen upon his return from the hospital and was surprised to find that he had lost the will to live. Their relationship strengthened; she was a major factor in Hawking's turning his life around. His interest in his research was revived. The mathematics and theoretical physics department moved to the Old University Press Building and was called the Department of Applied Mathematics and Theoretical Physics (DAMTP). The working environment was informal. Everyone gathered at 11:00 a.m. for coffee and at 4:00 p.m. for tea.

During his first two years at Cambridge, Hawking's physical condition worsened. He had to use a cane, and, occasionally, he fell. He rejected offers of help in getting around. His speech grew increasingly difficult to understand. He and Jane became engaged. She said, "I wanted to find some purpose to my existence, and I suppose I found it in the idea of looking after him. But we were in love."[204] For Hawking, their engagement gave new direction to his life and gave him something to live for.

Hawking met applied mathematician Roger Penrose at a series of scientific meetings at Kings College in London.

Penrose explained his concept of a singularity occurring at the center of a black hole, a region in space where gravity is so strong that not even light can escape. He showed that the collapse of a star could lead to the formation of a singularity, a mass with zero size and infinite density. One night on the train back to Cambridge from London, Hawking turned to Dennis Sciama and speculated what would happen if Roger's singularity theory were applied to the entire universe.

Penrose had showed that the collapse of a star could cause the formation of a singularity. Hawking conjectured that an important event had begun with the singularity. The event was the reverse of Penrose's collapse, an outward explosion named by Fred Hoyle the "big bang," the origin of the universe. The "big bang" is considered to be the tremendous explosion that began the expansion of the universe fifteen billion years ago.

When Hawking applied Penrose's ideas to the entire universe, he really began to devote himself to his work: "I ... started working hard for the first time in my life. To my surprise, I found I liked it. Maybe it is not really fair to call it work. Someone once said, 'Scientists ... get paid for doing what they enjoy.'"[205] This effort became the final chapter of Hawking's dissertation, "Properties of the Expanding Universe," the work for which he was awarded a PhD by Cambridge University.

Now that he had his PhD, Hawking looked for a post with a salary so that he and Jane could get married. He applied for a theoretical physics fellowship at Caius College, Cambridge University. He was awarded the fellowship, and he and Jane were married in July 1965. Eventually, they bought a small house near the DAMTP where he worked. Jane continued with her studies and graduated in the summer of 1966.

Hawking's condition continued to decline. He now needed crutches to walk, and his ability to speak worsened. His father prescribed a program of steroids and vitamins, which Hawking took until his father's death in 1986. He had a difficult time getting around their house, but he refused offers of help. His strong-willed nature presented a challenge for Jane. She said, "Some would call his attitude determination, some obstinacy. I've called it both at one time or another. I suppose that's what keeps him going."[206]

When asked whether he ever became depressed over his condition, Hawking replied, "Not normally, I have managed to do what I wanted to do despite it, and that gives a feeling of achievement."[207] He maintained a positive outlook, and he was generally cheerful. He didn't waste time worrying about his health.

The Hawkings' first child, Robert, was born in 1967. They were very happy over this new addition; however, it placed an additional burden on Jane, who added child care to home maintenance and care for a seriously disabled husband.

Hawking's approach to his work was largely intuitive—he had a feel for the correctness of an idea. He described his modus operandi:

> I work very much on intuition, thinking that, well, a certain idea ought to be right. Then I try to prove it. Sometimes I find I'm wrong. Sometimes I find that the original idea was wrong, but that leads to new ideas. I find it a great help to discuss my ideas with other people. Even if they don't contribute anything, just having to explain it to someone else helps me sort it out for myself.[208]

At the end of the 1960s, Jane and their friends convinced Hawking that he should be in a wheelchair. He didn't let this change bother him; in fact, he admitted that it enabled him to get around better. His approach to life didn't change. Jane said, "Stephen doesn't make any concessions to his illness, and I don't make any concessions to him."[209]

Hawking recalls when his first black hole breakthrough

occurred. Just after their second child, Lucy, was born in November 1970, he was thinking about black holes while getting ready for bed one evening. As he remembers it: "My disability makes this a rather slow process, so I had plenty of time. Suddenly, I realized that many of the techniques that Penrose and I had developed to prove singularities could be applied to black holes."[210]

Over a six-year period, Hawking coauthored *The Large Scale Structure of Spacetime* with George Ellis. In March 1974, Hawking became a Fellow of the Royal Society at the age of thirty-two. Then, he was invited to spend a year at Caltech in Pasadena. He had a productive year there, and the family enjoyed living in California and sightseeing around the West.

After they returned to Cambridge, the Hawking family moved into a larger house owned by the College. Arrangements were made for one of Hawking's students to live with them to help Jane take care of her husband. The arrangement worked well but Hawking observed that it was difficult for a student to be in awe of his professor after he has helped him to the bathroom.

Hawking continued to collect prizes, six major awards in two years: the Eddington Medal from the Royal Astronomical Society, the Pius XI Medal awarded by the Pontifical Academy of Science in the Vatican, the Hopkins Prize, the Dannie Heineman Prize, the Maxwell Prize, and the Hughes Medal of the Royal Society, which cited "his remarkable results in his work on black holes." As Jane observed the awards and prizes she became more disillusioned with their life, particularly her part in that life. She enrolled in a PhD program in medieval languages with emphasis on Spanish and Portuguese poetry.

Hawking and Jane had another source of resentment that was never resolved. Jane was raised as a Christian and was a very religious person. Hawking, on the other hand, couldn't relate faith to his concept of the universe. In his opinion, "We are such insignificant creatures on a minor planet of a very average star in the suburbs of one of a hundred thousand million galaxies. So it is difficult to believe in a God that would care about us or even notice our existence."[211]

Jane and her husband were at opposite poles on the subject of religion. Hawking didn't attempt to help Jane deal with her concerns about their differences about religion. She said, "I pronounce my view that there are different ways of approaching it [religion], and the mathematical way is only one way, and he just smiles."[212]

In 1978, Hawking was awarded the Albert Einstein Award by the Lewis and Rose Strauss Memorial Fund. During the following year, Hawking coauthored *General Relativity: An Einstein Centenary Survey* with Werner Israel. Hawking was appointed Lucasian Professor at Cambridge University in 1979, 310 years after Isaac Newton was given the same honor. In the spring of 1979, the Hawkings' third child, Timothy, was born. Also, Jane completed work on her PhD and found personal satisfaction in her teaching job.

At about this time, an interviewer asked Hawking again about his disability. He responded: "I think I'm happier now than I was before I started. Before the illness set in, I was very bored with life. I drank a fair amount, I guess, didn't do any work. It really was a rather pointless existence. When one's expectations are reduced to zero, one really appreciates everything that one does have."[213] Later, he observed that if a person is physically disabled, he or she cannot afford to be psychologically disabled.

As Hawking's disability moved to lower plateaus, he needed increased medical care. He looked for additional sources of income, since the cost of this care was expensive. He could move to a university in the United States that would pay him a significantly larger salary. However, the Hawkings liked living in Cambridge, and the DAMTP was one of the elite departments of theoretical physics in the world.

Cambridge University Press hoped that Hawkings latest

book, *The Very Early Universe,* would sell better than his previous one, *Superspace and Supergravity*, which even scientists had difficulty understanding. Simon Mitton of the University Press suggested to Hawking that he write a popular book about cosmology. The Press had success previously publishing popular science books by Arthur Eddington and Fred Hoyle.

Hawking was a tough negotiator, and Mitton didn't think that the University Press could afford the amount of advance that was demanded, £10,000. The initial sample of a section of the book that Hawking provided was much too technical. In particular, it contained too many equations. Mitton told him that every equation would reduce sales significantly.

Just prior to signing with Cambridge University Press, Hawking was told that Bantam Books was interested in his popular book about cosmology. Ultimately, Bantam offered an advance of $250,000 for the United States and Canada. Bantam's editors also suggested that the technical content of the manuscript should be reduced.

By Christmas 1984, the first draft of the manuscript was finished. Bantam began to promote the book: "Hawking is on the cutting edge of what we know about the cosmos. This whole business of the unified field theory, the conjunction of relativity with quantum mechanics, is comparable to the search for the Holy Grail."[214]

In 1985, Hawking spent the summer in Geneva, Switzerland at CERN, the European Center for Nuclear Research, where he continued his research and made corrections to the manuscript of his book. Jane visited friends in Germany. One night in early August, Hawking's nurse checked on him in the middle of the night and found that he was having difficulty breathing. He was making a gurgling sound and was turning purple. He was rushed to the Cantonal Hospital in Geneva and placed in intensive care on a ventilator.

Hawking had suffered a blockage in the windpipe and had

contracted pneumonia. When Jane arrived at the hospital, her husband was on a life-support machine but was not in critical condition. Because he was unable to breathe through his mouth or nose, doctors recommended a tracheostomy. A cut would be made in his windpipe and a breathing device would be implanted. However, Hawking would never be able to speak again. It was a difficult decision for Jane to make, but, without the operation, her husband would have little hope of survival.

Additional nursing care, which they could not afford, was required upon their return to Cambridge. Help came from an American foundation that provided £50,000 a year to defray the cost of the increased care. A California computer technologist, Walt Woltosz, gave Hawking a program called Equalizer, which provided a menu of 3,000 words from which to construct sentences. The sentences were sent to a voice-synthesizer that spoke for him with an American accent. Hawking's life was transformed by this technology.

In early spring of 1988, Hawking's popular book about cosmology, *A Brief History of Time: From the Big Bang to Black Holes,* was released. Within a few weeks, this book about equating relativity theory with quantum mechanics was at the top of the best-seller list, where it stayed. Stephen Hawking fan clubs were formed and Hawking T-shirts went on the market. Sales of the book exceeded everyone's estimates, particularly Bantam's. A reviewer compared its success with the cult success of the 1970s, *Zen and the Art of Motorcycle Maintenance.*

More than any previous accomplishment, *A Brief History of Time* made Stephen Hawking a household name. A documentary, "Master of the Universe" won a Royal Television Society award, and ABC presented a profile of Hawking on its 20 / 20 program. Earlier, Commander of the British Empire (CBE) honors had been conferred upon Hawking, and, in 1989, he was made a Companion of Honor by the Queen.

Hawking's literary success put additional strain on his

marriage. In 1990, after twenty-five years of marriage, Hawking and Jane separated. The Cambridge community was stunned by the news. Jane had been accompanying her husband less frequently on his trips and had been spending more time on her own interests. Religious differences certainly contributed to their marital problems. Hawking had drifted toward atheism, and his latest scientific inquiries had left him without any notion of God whatsoever.

Hawking moved out of their home and into an apartment with his nurse, Elaine Mason. In recent years, Elaine had accompanied Hawking on all of his travels, and they had grown closer than employer / employee. Their relationship was complicated by the fact that Elaine's husband, David Mason, was the computer scientist who had fitted Hawking's personal computer to his wheelchair.

Hawking's list of achievements is impressive, particularly when his handicap is considered. However, we can wonder whether his accomplishments would have been as great if he hadn't had been diagnosed with ALS at the age of twenty-one. Hawking, a strong-willed individual who was obviously highly motivated, always maintained his sense of humor; his upbeat outlook on life contributed significantly to his success. He observed, "One has to be grown up enough to realize that life is not fair. You have to do the best you can in the situation you are in."[215]

Hawking gives us all something to think about in the conclusion of his book, *A Brief History of Time*:

> However, if we do discover a complete theory, it should be in time understandable in broad principle by everyone, not just a few scientists. Then we shall all, philosophers, scientists, and just ordinary people, be able to take part in the discussion of the question of why it is that we and the universe exist. If we find an answer to that, it would be the ultimate triumph of

human reason—for then we would know the mind of God.[216]

CARL BRASHEAR (1931-   ) U.S. Navy Master Diver and Amputee.

"The Navy diver is not a fighting man.
He is a salvage expert.
If it's lost underwater, he finds it.
If it's sunk, he brings it up.
If it's in the way, he moves it.

If he's lucky, he dies two hundred feet beneath the waves,
Because that's the closest he will ever come to being a hero.

No one in their right mind would ever want the job.
Or so they say."[217]

The Diver's Creed

Carl Brashear set a goal for himself at a young age and had sufficient motivation to achieve that goal despite having to overcome both racial discrimination and a major physical injury. Paul Stillwell of the U.S. Naval Institute summarizes Brashear's achievements:

> To become the first black master diver in the Navy, Carl Brashear used a rare combination of grit, determination, and persistence, because the obstacles in his path were formidable. His race was a handicap, as were his origin on a sharecropper's farm in rural Kentucky and the modest education he received there. But these were not his greatest challenges. He was held back by an even greater factor: in 1966, his left leg was amputated just below the knee because he was badly injured on a salvage operation.
>
> After the amputation, the Navy sought to retire

Brashear from active duty, but he refused to submit to the decision. Instead, he secretly returned to diving and produced evidence that he could excel, despite his injury. Then, in 1974, he qualified as a master diver, a difficult feat under any circumstances and something no black man had accomplished before. By the time of his retirement, he had achieved the highest rate for Navy enlisted personnel, master chief petty officer. In addition, he had become a celebrity through his response to manifold challenges and thereby had become a real inspiration to others.[218]

Carl Brashear was born on a farm in Tonieville, Kentucky in January 1931, the sixth of nine children of McDonald and Gonzella Brashear. McDonald Brashear was a hard-working sharecropper with a third-grade education. Young Carl helped his father work the farm and attended a one-room, segregated school through the eighth grade. His mother, who had completed nine years of school, augmented at home the education that her son received in the schoolroom.

At the age of fourteen, Brashear decided that he wanted to be a military man, possibly a soldier. He was influenced by a brother-in-law in the Army. When he was seventeen, he went to the U.S. Army recruiting office to enlist. However, everyone yelled at him, making him so nervous that he failed the entrance examination. He was supposed to return to retake the exam, but he went to the U.S. Navy recruiting office instead. The Navy chief petty officer treated him well, so he enlisted in the Navy.

In February 1948, Brashear reported to the Great Lakes Naval Training Center for basic training and was assigned to an integrated company. He encountered no racial prejudice in boot camp; however, after he completed his training, steward was the only assignment available to him. He was assigned as steward to an air squadron in Key West. The Naval Base in Key West was segregated at the time; recreational opportunities for African-American personnel were limited.

At Key West, Brashear met chief boatswain's mate Guy Johnson, who steered him toward a major turning point in his career. Chief Johnson arranged for Brashear to leave the steward branch and to work for him as a beachmaster, beaching seaplanes from the Gulf of Mexico. Brashear strongly preferred his new assignment to his old one. His duties as a beachmaster required him to get along with people, to respect others, and to work with little supervision. Chief Johnson taught him basic seamanship, gave him guidance on being good sailor, and introduced him to the qualities of leadership.

While stationed at Key West, Brashear decided that he wanted to be a diver. A buoy needed repair, and a self-propelled seaplane wrecking derrick, a YSD, was brought out to repair it. A diver with a face mask and shallow-water diving apparatus went down to make the necessary repairs. Brashear watched the diver work and realized that diving was what he wanted to do.

Brashear requested diving duty on his first two shipboard assignments, on the escort aircraft carriers *USS Palau* (CVE-122) and *USS Tripoli* (CVE-64). He was assigned to the sail locker, with boatswain's mate's duties splicing wire and sewing canvas. He learned about fueling rigs and anchoring and mooring methods.

While Brashear was stationed on the *Tripoli*, a TBM Avenger torpedo bomber rolled off the jettison ramp, and a deep-sea diver went down to attach wires to pull the plane out of the water. Brashear watched the diver go down and come up. He was sufficiently impressed to set a goal for himself to become a deep-sea diver. He requested diving school periodically until he was admitted in 1954.

Brashear joined the boxing team on the *Tripoli* and won many bouts. He met Sugar Ray Robinson, who taught him how to throw jabs and to keep his hands up. Sugar Ray showed him how to be a better defensive boxer. Brashear was good enough to fight for the light-heavyweight championship of the East Coast, but he lost that fight.

Brashear made boatswain's mate third class on the *Tripoli* and gained experience with paravane gear used for minesweeping and with the operations of a tank landing ship (LST). He was responsible for a division of men and learned about leadership and supervision. He had done well, but he realized that further education would increase his opportunities for advancement.

In 1952, Brashear married Juneta Wilcoxson, who was a friend of his sisters in Elizabethtown, Kentucky. She had completed beauty school and was a cosmetologist. They had four children: Shazanta, DaWayne, Philip, and Patrick.

Brashear was promoted to boatswain's mate second class in 1953. While at that rate, he won "sailor-of-the-year" honors and was called "Mr. Navy."

Brashear's next assignment was in Bayonne, New Jersey at diving school, which involved hard work and psychological stress. When he reported for duty, the training officer thought he was reporting in as a cook or steward. When he found out that Brashear was there as a student, he told him, "Well, I don't know how the rest of the students are going to accept you. As a matter of fact, I don't even think you will make it through the school. We haven't had a colored guy come through here before."[219]

When classes started, Brashear found notes on his bunk: "We're going to drown you today, nigger! We don't want any nigger divers."[220] Brashear was ready to quit, but boatswain's mate first class Rutherford, on the staff of the diving school, talked him out of it.

Over a beer at the Dungaree Bar, Rutherford said, "I hear you're going to quit." Brashear admitted that he planned to leave the school. Rutherford told him, "I can't whip you, but I'll fight you every day if you quit. Those notes aren't hurting you. No one is doing a thing to you. Show them you're a better man than they are."[221] Rutherford's pep talk was the only encouragement that Brashear received. One person's upbeat advice was enough to keep Brashear on his chosen career path.

The first week of diving school was orientation; physics courses were taught in the second week. Diving medicine and diving physics were followed by four weeks of pure diving, which included introduction to hydraulics and underwater tools as well as underwater welding and cutting. The course included two weeks of demolition and several weeks of salvage operations, which involved becoming familiar with beach gear and learning how to make splices.

Brashear worked hard in the sixteen-week-long diving school and didn't fail any exams. The school was stressful; the instructors continually challenged the students. Teamwork was emphasized. When working underwater, divers rely on their teammates working alongside them and, obviously, rely heavily on support personnel topside. Seventeen out of thirty-two that started with the class graduated. Brashear graduated sixteenth out of seventeen; he was pleased that he wasn't the anchor man—the last in the class.

In March 1955, Brashear was assigned to a salvage ship, USS Opportune (ARS-41), which had eighteen divers out of a crew of over 100. The Opportune participated in many salvage jobs, including raising a gas barge in Charleston, South Carolina; recovering an antisubmarine plane that had sunk in the Virginia Capes; and pulling a cargo ship off the beach in Argentia, Newfoundland. His experiences on the Opportune increased his understanding of teamwork and the importance of knowing other team members' capabilities in diving. He was promoted to boatswain's mate first class while in Argentia.

Brashear's next duty station was Quonset Point (Rhode Island) Naval Air Station, where, as leading petty officer, he was in charge of the boat house. One of his assignments was retrieving aircraft that had crashed in Narragansett Bay. A collateral duty was to escort President Eisenhower's boat, the *Barbara Ann*, from Delaware to Newport, where Ike played golf. The escort craft was a 104-foot crash boat with a crew of thirteen and two 20-millimeter guns mounted on the wings of the bridge. Brashear also escorted the *Barbara Ann* on pleasure cruises.

After Quonset Point, Brashear was assigned to a ship repair facility in Guam. From an auxiliary ocean tug, divers worked underwater on destroyers and did demolition work. They used 60,000 pounds of explosives to blast out a channel at Merizo for a fuel barge to gain access to a LORAN (long-range aid to navigation) station.

Brashear enrolled in United States Armed Forces Institute (USAFI) courses and passed his general educational development (GED) examination, the high-school equivalency test, in 1960. A high school diploma wasn't required for the first phase of diving school, but it was for later phases, such as mixed-gas diving.

Brashear's next assignment was the *USS Nereus*, home-ported in San Diego, California, where he made chief petty officer and was assigned to first-class diver school in Washington, D.C. First-class diver school was demanding, with courses in medicine, decompression, physics, treatments, mathematics, and mixing gases to the proper ratio. Brashear flunked out. Most salvage divers who failed first-class school left as a second-class diver.

Brashear was astounded to hear that he was leaving as a non-diver. After seven years of diving experience, he had reached the low point in his career. He wrangled a set of orders to the fleet training center in Hawaii, which he knew had a second-class diver school. Lieutenant (junior grade) Billie Delanoy, whom Brashear knew from a previous assignment, was in charge of that school. Delanoy knew that his old shipmate should be a diver and enrolled him in the school, which was not difficult for Brashear. He passed it easily and reverted to a level that he had mastered previously.

While in Hawaii, Brashear dove to inspect the hull of the *USS Arizona* (BB-39), which had been sunk by the Japanese at Pearl Harbor. The amount of list had to be determined before they could proceed with the work to build a memorial in the harbor. Using plumb lines, they determined that the *Arizona* had two degrees of list. It gave him an eerie feeling diving around a hull that interred 1,100 shipmates who had not survived the Japanese attack.

At the fleet training center in Hawaii, Brashear received temporary additional duty (TAD) to report to Joint Task Force Eight as a diver supporting nuclear testing during Operation Dominic in 1962. Thor intermediate-range ballistic missiles (IRBMs) with 20- or 30-megaton warheads were tested on Johnston Island. Brashear was skipper of a large self-propelled harbor tug (YTB-262) and was also a diver.

After his TAD, Brashear received orders to report to the submarine rescue ship *USS Coucal*. Lieutenant George Stenke, inventor of the Stenke hood, was the skipper of the *Coucal*. The Stenke hood was used to make a buoyant ascent from a sunken submarine, allowing one to breathe until reaching the surface. Another rescue device is the McCann submarine rescue chamber, which was used to bring up thirty-three men from the *USS Squalus* (SS-192) in 1939.

After studying math for two years, in 1963 Brashear got a second opportunity to attend first-class diving school in Washington, D.C. He thought that he would go through fourteen weeks of training with the class of thirty salvage divers, learning about diving medicine, diving physics, mixing gases, and emergency procedures. However, the training officer made him go through twenty-six weeks of class as though he had never been a salvage diver. He graduated third out of the seventeen who completed the course.

After serving a year on the fleet ocean tug *USS Shakori* (ATF-162), Brashear was assigned to the salvage ship *USS Hoist* (ARS-40), where he could train to become a master diver. The *Hoist* participated in the search for a nuclear bomb that had been dropped into the sea off Palomares, Spain when a B-52 bomber and a refueling plane had collided in midair. After a search of two and a half months, the bomb was found by the deep-diving research vessel *Alvin* six miles off the coast in 2,600 feet of water. Brashear rigged a spider, a three-legged contraption with grapnel hooks, to the bomb to bring it to the surface.

A mechanized landing craft (LCM-8) was moored alongside the *Hoist* to receive the bomb. Brashear was bringing the bomb up with the capstan to place it in a crate when a line parted, causing the landing craft to break loose. He saw what had happened and ran to push one of his men out of the way of the line. A pipe tied to the mooring pulled loose, sailed across the deck, and struck Brashear's left leg just below the knee, virtually severing it. The bomb fell back into 2,600 feet of water.

The *Hoist* had no doctor and no morphine and was six and a half miles from the cruiser *USS Albany* and the nearest doctor. Corpsman placed two tourniquets on Brashear's leg, but, because his leg was so muscular, the bleeding couldn't be stopped. He was placed on board a helicopter to be transported to the hospital at Torrejon Air Force Base in Spain. The helicopter didn't have enough fuel to make it to Torrejon, so it landed at a dilapidated airport in Spain, where a light plane took him to Torrejon.

Brashear had lost so much blood that he went into shock at 9:00 p.m. By the time he reached Torrejon, he had hardly any heartbeat or pulse. The doctor thought that Brashear was going to die; however, he regained consciousness after they had given him eighteen pints of blood. He was told that they would try to save his leg, but that it would be three inches shorter than his right leg. Unfortunately, his leg became infected, and gangrene set in. The doctor asked him if he wanted to be shipped back to the United States for treatment. He agreed and was transported to the Portsmouth (Virginia) Naval Hospital.

In Portsmouth, Brashear was told that his rehabilitation would take three years. He decided that he couldn't wait that long to get on with his life, so he asked the doctor to amputate. The doctor said that amputation was the easy way out. He explained that it was more of a medical challenge to fix the injured leg. Brashear told them that he planned to go back to diving; they thought that he shouldn't even consider it. The leg was amputated; in July 1966, another inch and a half of his leg had to be trimmed from his stump.

Brashear had read of an Air Force pilot with no legs who flew fighter aircraft. Possibly that was Douglas Bader, a Royal Air Force ace in World War II. He also read that a prosthesis could be designed to support any amount of weight. He was sent to a prosthesis center in Philadelphia to be fitted. He worked around the hospital and refused to have people wait on him. Brashear told the doctor that once he was fitted for an artificial leg, he was going to return the crutch and never use it again. They told him that he couldn't do it. After he was fitted with an artificial leg; he never used crutches again.

Brashear returned to the Portsmouth Naval Hospital and visited Chief Warrant Officer Clair Axtell, who was in charge of the nearby diving school. He told Axtell, whom he knew from salvage diving school, that he had to dive. He needed to get some pictures to prove that he could dive. Axtell reminded Brashear that if anything happened to him, his own career would be over; nevertheless, he obtained a photographer and gave him a chance. Brashear dove in a deep-sea rig, in shallow-water equipment, and with scuba gear while the photographer documented his activities. He returned for a second set of dives and another set of pictures.

Brashear's medical board was convened at the naval hospital, where Rear Admiral Joseph Yon, Medical Corps, talked with him about returning to diving. Brashear took the initiative to endorse his own orders, "FFT (for further transfer) to the second-class diving school," and reported to the school. A lieutenant commander from the Bureau of Medicine and

Surgery (BuMed) called Brashear and asked how he had been admitted to the diving school. Brashear replied, "Orders, sir," which caused considerable confusion.

Brashear had ignored the first physical evaluation board; now they told him to report to a second one. He had sent all of his diving photographs along with the findings of the medical board to BuMed. They concluded that if he could dive in Virginia, he could do it again. They invited him to spend a week with a captain and a commander at the deep-sea diving school in Washington, D.C. BuMed sent observers to evaluate his performance.

At the end of the week, Captain Jacks, policy control, called Brashear in and told him, "Most of the people in your position want to get a medical disability, get out of the Navy, and do the least they can and draw as much pay as they can. And then you're asking for full duty. I don't know to handle it. Suppose you would be diving and tear your leg off." Brashear said, "Well, Captain, it wouldn't bleed."[222] Captain Jacks told him to get out of his office and get back to work.

Brashear reported to diving school in Virginia. Axtell had moved on to a new assignment and Chief Warrant Officer Raymond Duell had replaced him. Brashear dove every day for a year, including weekends. He led calisthenics every morning and ran every day. Occasionally, he would return from a run and find a puddle of blood from his stump in the artificial leg. Instead of going to sick bay, he soaked his stump in a bucket of warm salt water. At the end of the year, Duell wrote a very favorable letter, and Brashear returned to duty with full diving assignments—the first time in naval history for an amputee.

Brashear received orders to the boat house at the Norfolk Naval Station, where he was a division officer in charge of the divers. Their principal duties were search and rescue and recovery of downed aircraft. They picked up helicopters and jet aircraft that had crashed and assisted civilian divers at the Norfolk Naval Shipyard.

At various times, Brashear considered becoming a warrant officer or a limited duty officer, one who had come up from the enlisted rates. However, a master diver must be a chief petty officer, a senior chief petty officer, or a master chief petty officer, and Brashear's goal was still to be the first African-American master diver in the Navy.

In 1970, Brashear went from the Norfolk Naval Air Station boat house to saturation diving school at the Experimental Diving Unit in Washington, D.C. Saturation diving involves going to deep depths and staying down for long periods of time. Upon graduation from saturation diving school, he stayed on to attend master diving school. A master diver is proficient in all phases of diving, submarine rescue, and salvage; it is the highest position in naval diving.

Evaluation is done by master divers, ex-master divers, and the commanding officer and the executive officer of the master diving school. Emphasis is placed on emergency procedures. Considerable pressure is placed on participants, and many attempts are made to rattle them. At times, participants are given an incorrect order; they are expected to know better than to obey it. Self-confidence is a necessity. Master divers have to know how to treat all types of diving injuries. Four out of six in the class made master diver, including Brashear. Grades weren't given, just pass or fail evaluations.

Brashear had been in competition with chief petty officer Davis to become the first African-American master diver. When he lost his leg, Davis told him that he had lost the contest, and that he, Davis, would be the first of their race to make it. But Brashear did make it, about two years before Davis became a master diver. The commanding officer of the master diving school called Brashear into his office and told him, "If there was a mark that we'd give, you made the highest mark of any man that ever came through this school to be evaluated for master. You did not make a mistake. We vote you master."[223]

Brashear was assigned to the submarine tender *USS*

Hunley (AS-31) in Charleston, South Carolina. He was a division officer on the *Hunley*, which was a tender for nuclear submarines, both the fast attack type and "boomers" with missiles. Divers who went down when reactors were critical used film badges to continually check radiation levels. They had to make security checks, looking for foreign objects attached to the hull.

Brashear's next duty was on the salvage ship *USS Recovery* (ARS-43). He preferred salvage work to duty on a tender because the jobs were less repetitive. *Recovery* divers evaluated the feasibility of raising a ship that had sunk off Newport News in 1918 and salvaged a helicopter off the coast of Florida. They also dove into a flooded engine room on the *USS Saratoga* (CVA-60). *Recovery* was happy ship; Brashear contributed to this environment by being fair, by leading by example, and by following a policy of admitting an error when one was made. Men respected him.

Brashear's next assignment was the Naval Safety Center in Norfolk, where he worked for Rear Admiral Robert Dunn. Dunn was impressed; every time his master diver would go out on an assignment, someone would send a bravo zulu message, meaning well done, upon his return. During this assignment, Brashear headed a team that conducted a field change on the Mark I dive system, including modifications to the breathing mechanism and the bail-out bottle connection. Naval Sea Systems Command approved the changes, which saved the government thousands of dollars.

Brashear represented the Safety Center in investigating diving accidents, determining the cause, and making recommendations to prevent future accidents. He also conducted safety presentations and wrote and answered "safety grams." While at the Center, he was mentioned in newspapers and magazines and received television coverage. Robert Manning in the Office of the Navy's Chief of Information (Chinfo) suggested making a short movie about Brashear; a four-and-a-half minute film was made for TV.

Manning suggested that Brashear should be a candidate for the "Come Back" program about people who have been injured or stumbled in their career and made a comeback. That year a thirty-minute documentary was made about Brashear as well as Rosemary Clooney, Freddie Fender, Neil Sadaka, and Bill Veeck.

Brashear's final tour of duty in the Navy was reassignment to the *USS Recovery*. The commanding officer of the *Recovery* had requested him. Brashear considered it a feather in his cap to finish his Navy career on the *Recovery*.

Brashear retired in April 1979. His retirement ceremony was planned for the *USS Hoist*, the ship on which he had lost his leg. However, the *Hoist* was too small to accommodate everyone, so his ceremony was moved to the gymnasium at the Little Creek Amphibious Base. The gymnasium was filled; two television stations covered the event.

Brashear had the drive to reach his goal in the Navy despite racist opposition and a physical disability and had a rewarding career. As with many successful people, Brashear always radiated the "can do" spirit. His life is an inspiration to us.

CHRISTY BROWN (1932-1981) Overcame Cerebral Palsy to Write Five Books

"Apart from any literary value, and the surpassing interest that Christy Brown's portrait of a Dublin family gives us, this work [*My Left Foot*] seems to me of universal importance. Seldom, except in the great story of Helen Keller and Annie Sullivan, has a crippled, blind, or deaf person been so gifted that he has been able to lift the curtain that hangs around the lives of so many of our less fortunate brothers and sisters and let us see within.

Never, I think, has one read a life so completely different from the normal which has been written with such craftsmanship that one can actually feel what the writer felt himself. For me, the whole experience has been an extraordinary revelation, and a proof of the amazing power of the spirit of the man who overcame the impossible and, perhaps most of all, of the utmost need of the human soul to escape from every sort of prison."[224]

Robert Collis, Foreword, *My Left Foot*

Christy Brown had a severe case of athetosis due to an abnormal birth. In athetosis, the middle part of the brain is affected, causing abnormal writhing when any attempt is made to accomplish coordinated movements. The only muscles that Christy could control were those in the left leg and left foot. He could not speak until he began therapy at the age of seventeen. He overcame his ailment to write an autobiography, *My Left Foot*, two novels, *Down All the Days* and *Shadow on Summer*, and two books of poems, *Come Softly to My Wake* and *Background Music*. In achieving success, he was aided by the perseverance of his remarkable mother who worked with him from his early years to overcome his handicap.

Christy was born in Rotunda Hospital, Dublin, Ireland on June 5, 1932. He was the tenth of twenty-two children, four of whom did not survive infancy. His birth was a difficult one, and both he and his mother almost died. He was four months old when his mother began to suspect that he had a physical ailment; his head always fell backwards while he was being fed. She noticed that her son's hands were always clenched, and that he had a difficult time gripping the nipple of the bottle with his jaws. At the age of six months he had to be surrounded by pillows to sit upright.

When he was a year old, Christy's parents made the rounds of the clinics and hospitals in the area searching for a doctor who could help their son. The doctors were all very negative; they said that his case was hopeless, and that nothing could be done for him. Furthermore, they diagnosed him as mentally retarded, which his mother did not believe.

Mrs. Brown refused to merely feed and wash Christy and then put him in the back room. He was her child, and she was determined to treat Christy as a full-fledged member of the family. Christy was saved because his mother's love helped him overcome as many of his obstacles as he could. She had five other children at home to care for; nevertheless, she spent as much time with Christy as she could. While Mr. Brown, a bricklayer, was at work, Mrs. Brown ensured that the other children treated Christy as an equal member of the family.

At the age of five, Christy showed the first indication of activity. His sister Mona and his brother Paddy were writing on a piece of slate with a bright yellow piece of chalk. Christy reached over and took the chalk out of his sister's hand—with his left foot. He scribbled on the slate. All other activity in the room stopped. Mona looked at him with wide eyes. His father leaned forward in his chair, looking tense.

Mrs. Brown enter the room, observed the tension, walked over to Christy, and said that she would show him what to do with the chalk. She made an "A" on the slate and told him to copy it. He tried, but he wasn't successful on the first and second attempts. On the third attempt, he began to write the "A," but the chalk broke. Mrs. Brown placed her hand on his shoulder to encourage him. He completed the "A" on the fourth attempt. Tears flowed down Mrs. Brown's cheek. Mr. Brown reached down and hoisted his son upon his shoulders. Writing the letter "A" was the beginning for Christy in leading a productive life.

Mrs. Brown taught Christy the entire alphabet. His next projects were to write his initials, "C. B.," and then his full name. Christy's eldest sister, Lily, was a great help to the family. She did the cooking and looked after the other children while her mother worked with Christy. Christy surprised his mother one day by calling her over to watch him write a word on the slate. He spelled out "M-O-T-H-E-R." She was quiet for some time and then turned, placed her hand on her son's shoulder, and smiled broadly.

When Christy was seven, his brothers took him along when they played in the streets. They pulled him in an old dilapidated two-wheeled go-cart that they called the "chariot." All of the neighborhood children accepted Christy; in fact, they treated him with a youthful version of deference and respect. Christy participated in hide-and-seek and blind-man's-buff, two of the most popular games. One day Christy went with his brothers to the canal, where they swam. After watching his brothers swim, Christy grunted to them that he wanted to swim too. They put his brother Jim's swimming suit on Christy, folding it and pinning it because it was too big. Then they put Christy in the canal; he floated, kicked his left leg, and thoroughly enjoyed himself.

When he was ten, Christy's go-cart broke, and this time it was not repairable. Suddenly, Christy was cut off from his brothers' activities. He was devastated. It was obvious to the family that Christy was depressed. Mrs. Brown had saved enough money to buy the go-cart's replacement, a wheelchair with a padded seat and rubber tires. However, Christy had changed. He no longer liked going out and seeing the strange looks that outsiders gave him. Increasingly, he stayed at home.

At Christmas, Christy received a set of lead soldiers, and his brother Paddy was given a box of paints. Paddy thought that the paints were a sissy gift, but Christy was fascinated by the bright colors and suggested that they trade gifts. Paddy was happy with the set of lead soldiers. Christy began to paint regularly; he had found a reason to be happy again.

When Christy was eleven, his mother became very ill giving birth to the Brown family's twenty-second and last child. She was in the hospital for an extended period, and the family, particularly Christy, missed her. One evening there was a knock on the door, and Mr. Brown opened the door to a slender, eighteen-year-old girl, who was the prettiest girl that Christy had ever seen. She introduced herself as Katriona Delahunt, a social worker from the hospital. Mrs. Brown had told her about Christy. Katriona asked Christy to write a note to his mother, so that she would know that everything was all right at home. Christy wrote: "Dear Mom. Don't worry. All okay. Lots of grub. Get well soon. Christy."[225]

Katriona came into Christy's life at a time when he needed a boost from outside of his own family and neighborhood. He needed someone to make him realize that he could rise above his handicap and perhaps accomplish more than his brothers, who were beginning to settle into jobs. She brought him many new paints, paintbrushes, and drawing books. Christy still couldn't talk, but he and Katriona managed to communicate; he looked forward to her visits.

Just before Christmas, Christy noticed the announcement of a Christmas painting competition for children from twelve to sixteen. He had just turned twelve, and he wanted to enter the competition. Katriona and his mother encouraged him to enter the contest. One day a *Sunday Independent* reporter and photographer knocked on the door. Katriona had told them that one of the entries in the painting competition was painted by a young boy using his left foot. They wanted to verify what they had been told.

The next copy of the *Sunday Independent* contained a

photograph of Christy's painting and announced that he had won the competition. His mother congratulated him and told him never to stop trying. Katriona stopped by to congratulate him; she took his hand in hers and kissed him on the forehead. Christy thought that he was in heaven. However, painting had become something that he liked to do; it was no longer something that he loved to do. Christy's new interest was writing. One of his early themes was the American Wild West. Others were boy-meets-girl stories and detective stories.

One day, the inevitable happened; Katriona was wearing an engagement ring when she visited. She showed the diamond ring to Mrs. Brown and to Christy. She told Christy not to frown and that she would still come to see him after she was married. Mrs. Brown took Christy to the wedding in his wheelchair. He was introduced to Katriona's husband, Mr. Maguire. Christy thought that he looked like a kind man, but he was jealous.

On one of her visits, Katriona asked Christy if he had ever thought about visiting the shrine at Lourdes, which Catholics consider to be the site of miraculous cures. He said that he had, but he didn't know how he would pay for the trip. The Lourdes Committee, the organizers of the pilgrimage, contributed £10, and an elderly aunt contributed £5 toward the £34 cost of the trip. Katriona invited her friends to play bridge for money, and they made up the difference.

The flight to Lourdes was the first time that Christy had gone anywhere without a member of his family. He saw many people on this trip who were in worse shape than he was. In his words:

> As I saw all those people each with his or her own suffering, a new light began to dawn on me. I was rather bewildered; I had not imagined there could be so much suffering in the world. I had been like rather like a snail shut away in his own narrow shell and that was

> only now beginning to see the great crowded world that lay beyond.
>
> Not only were only were those people afflicted, but, to my surprise, their handicaps were actually worse than my own! Up to then, I had not thought I was seeing with my eyes and really feeling with my heart the plight of others whose burdens were so great as to make mine seem nothing in comparison.[226]

As their van pulled into the town of Lourdes, Christy saw the beautiful Basilica and Rosary Square. He was impressed by the long, thin spire topped by a gold cross. He could hear a choir singing a hymn in the chapel. The square was crowded with people. The next morning they were taken to the healing baths, where Christy was stripped of his clothing by two Frenchmen and lowered into the water. After he went under a second time, the men lifted him out, recited prayers in French, and gave him a small cross to kiss. He felt reborn.

In the afternoon, Christy was taken to the Grotto. The road to the Shrine was crowded with people of virtually every nationality. A marble statue of Mary in a blue robe looked down on them from a niche carved out of the rock. He prayed fervently that he might be cured. That night, Christy participated in a torch-light procession through Lourdes from the Basilica to the Shrine. Thousands of pilgrims gathered in Rosary Square. The facade of the Basilica was illuminated. Thousands of candles were lit, and everyone sang *Ave Maria*. He considered it to be the most beautiful moment of his life.

Christy had been depressed about his condition before he went to Lourdes, and within a short time after he arrived back in Ireland, his depression returned. He tried to be patient and resigned to suffering like the pilgrims at Lourdes, mindful of the reward that awaited them in heaven. However, Christy concluded that he was too human and not meek enough to be like them. He wanted to accomplish more in this world before he thought about the next.

Christy summarized his visit to Lourdes:

> Lourdes had left a lasting impression on my mind. I saw that far from being alone and isolated as I thought myself to be, I was merely one of a brotherhood of suffering that stretched over the whole globe. I remember the courage and perseverance that shone in the faces of the afflicted people who came from all parts of the world to hope and to pray at the feet of the Virgin in the Grotto.
>
> There I had seen the story of my own life reflected in the eyes of those I had prayed with, those men and women who spoke different tongues and who live according to different ideals, but who were now made all brothers and sisters, all part of one family by right of a common heritage of pain. No one thought of anyone else as a "foreigner" in that holy little village; all the barriers that separate single persons and whole nations from one another were broken down and burned away by that common need for understanding and communication which we all felt and which suffering alone could have inspired.[227]

Back home in Dublin, Christy received a visit from Dr. Robert Collis, who ran a clinic in Dublin for the treatment of cerebral palsy. He asked Christy if he would be willing to undergo a new treatment for his ailment. When Dr. Collis looked at him, Christy felt that the doctor's penetrating eyes were looking into him. He said, "Christy, there is a new treatment for cerebral palsy—the thing that is wrong with you. I believe you can be cured—but only if you are willing to try hard enough with us. I can't help you if you don't try to help yourself. You must want to get better before anything can be done for you. Will you try if I help?" Christy couldn't talk, but Dr. Collis read the answer in his eyes and said, "Right. We'll start tomorrow."[228]

The next day, Dr. Louis Warnants came to the Browns' house to examine Christy. He was a young man with a military bearing who radiated confidence. He planned a preliminary set of physical exercises for Christy. After a few visits, it was apparent that the kitchen was too small to use for exercising and for the examinations. Mrs. Brown said that they would use their back yard, in which vegetables refused to grow, to build a small house for Christy.

Mrs. Brown had been given an estimate of £50 to build the little house. She couldn't afford that much, but she managed to scrape together £20, enough for a start. However, neither her husband nor her bricklayer sons were willing to begin the project. She ordered 100 concrete blocks, four bags of cement, and two bags of mortar. The bricklayers of the family still refused to build the room. Mrs. Brown told them that she would do it herself and laid the first row of blocks. When her husband and her older sons came home from work, they informed her that she had neglected to build a foundation, and that the blocks were not level. Then they took over the job and completed it.

It looked like a vault with windows, a fireplace, and a chimney; the addition of furniture made it look more livable. Although its initial purpose was an exercise room, over time it became a living room and study with shelves for books. It was a boon to Christy, since he now had a place to paint and write without interruption.

In January 1949, Dr. Collis told Christy that he wanted him to be examined in London by his sister-in-law, Eirene Collis, a highly regarded specialist in cerebral palsy. Dr. Warnants met Christy and Mrs. Brown and took them to

Middlesex Hospital. Mrs. Collis's examination at the hospital would determine how comprehensive a rehabilitation program should be planned.

Mrs. Collis and an assistant, Mr. Gallagher, who put Christy at ease with their casualness, examined him. Mrs. Collis told him, "You can be cured if you are prepared to do lots of really hard work over the next few years. But—first you must make a big sacrifice. Nothing good is ever obtained without one, and yours is—you must resolve never to use your left foot again."[229]

Christy was very apprehensive, but he agreed. Mrs. Collis's reasoning was that although using his left foot gave Christy's mind a way to express itself, it placed considerable strain on the rest of his body; the condition of his crippled muscles was worsening. The treatment would be done at Dr. Collis's clinic in Dublin, and Christy would be provided with transportation between his home and the clinic.

Christy's first visit to the clinic was terrifying. All of the other patients were young children, three years old and younger. At seventeen, he was by far the oldest one there for treatment. At Lourdes, he had seen many older people with disabilities and a few children. Seeing large numbers of severely handicapped children overwhelmed him.

Christy's experiences at the clinic helped him to take a larger view of things and to stop feeling sorry for himself. One of the staff members, Sheila, was particularly helpful to him. She suggested that he do productive things that he liked doing, such as writing. She told him: "The good God gave you an excellent brain and an artistic streak. He also gave you a physical handicap.... Your present struggle against your athetosis is inevitable.... Remember your mother, too, without whose good sense you might easily have turned into a most objectionable young man always talking about 'what might have been.'"[230]

At home one day, Christy saw his twelve-year-old brother, Eamonn, struggling with a composition assignment.

Christy saw an opportunity; he offered to help Eamonn with his compositions if he would help him write his life story. Christy had not read widely. Charles Dickens novels had been his principal reading experience. His first attempts at writing produced a labored text loaded with many-syllable words. Instead of calling himself a cripple, he was an "unfortunate item of mortality." His questionable choice of a title was *The Reminiscences of a Mental Defective*.

Christy asked Dr. Collis to read the manuscript and to give him suggestions for improvement. Dr. Collis had two literary brothers, John Stewart and Maurice Collis. He told Christy that his writing was awful, mainly because its style was fifty years out of date. Dr. Collis looked up while reading the manuscript and told Christy that he had written at least one sentence that was outstanding, and it indicated to him that he could write if only he knew how. Dr. Collis gave him two books by Sean O'Faolain and a book of L. A. G. Strong's short stories and suggested that he work to improve his writing style. He suggested that Christy begin again on his autobiography.

Dr. Collis's advice to Christy was:

> There are two first principles attached to writing any sort of story. First you must have a story to tell and, secondly, you must tell it in such a way that the person reading it can live in it himself. Now let me give you some concrete points: Whenever you can, use a short word rather than a long one. You have painted pictures with a brush, try and do the same thing with a pen. Practice it. Describe the room here: your queer chair, the picture on the smudged wall here, the broken mirror, the books—the colored photograph....[231]

At the clinic, Christy was taught how to relax his muscles.

Staff personnel also helped him to improve his ability to speak, beginning with learning how to breathe properly. He began to grunt less and to speak more, enunciating more clearly. Christy understood the importance of self-confidence and of being less self-conscious in learning to speak well. He respected the staff members at the clinic and had a high regard for the treatment they provided. He realized that their care was based on a feeling of pride, not pity.

Christy began writing the second version of his life story, using his thirteen-year-old brother, Francis, as scribe. Francis was not merely a scribe; he offered suggestions for improvement to Christy. Version two was clearer and more orderly than his first attempt; however, Dr. Collis thought that it was still too "literary." Christy's writing was still too pretentious and overly dramatic. Also, he was using too many clichés.

Dr. Collis suggested that Christy continue his education before he wrote version three. He suggested a tutor. Katriona Maguire helped Dr. Collis to find Mr. Guthrie, a master in a large national school in the area. Twice a week, Christy learned about the philosophy of Bertrand Russell, the poetry of Yeats, mathematics, geometry, Latin, history, Shakespeare, and Shaw.

One day, Christy attempted to dictate to Francis, but the words just wouldn't come. He told Francis to leave and ripped the sock off of his left foot and began to write. His frustration level dropped, and he could write freely. The doctor from the clinic came in and saw him writing with his left foot. The doctor said that he had wondered how long Christy could hold out from using it. He understood that dictating wasn't enough and said that he wouldn't tell Eirene Collis. However, he advised Christy only to use his left foot when he had to.

Dr. Collis planned a benefit for cerebral palsy in Dublin. He had met Burl Ives at the Chest Hospital in London, where Ives gave a concert for the patients. Dr. Collis invited Ives to Dublin for the cerebral palsy benefit in Aberdeen Hall at the Gresham Hotel sponsored by the Ireland-American Society.

John Huston, the movie director, was the president of the Society. The benefit was well publicized, and over 500 people crowded into the ballroom at the hotel. The Brown family was chauffeured to and from the benefit in a limousine owned by a friend.

Burl Ives began the benefit by singing "The Blue-tailed Fly," "Mr. Frog Went A'Courting," and "The House Where Grandmother Dwells." The entire audience joined Ives in the singing. After Ives's concert, the president of the Ireland-American Society announced that Dr. Collis would address the audience representing the Cerebral Palsy Association. Dr. Collis didn't make a speech, and he didn't make an appeal. He said that he would read the first chapter of Christy Brown's autobiography, written with his left foot, which would give them an insider's view of cerebral palsy.

When Dr. Collis began reading, the room was noisy, but it soon became absolutely quiet. Everyone was listening. Someone in the front row was crying, and Christy's mother's eyes moistened. Complete silence reigned when Dr. Collis stopped reading. When he reached down and helped Christy to his feet, the entire ballroom broke out into loud applause. A large bouquet of roses was given to Mrs. Brown, whose face glowed with pride. Christy was happy as he listened to Burl Ives conclude the program with "She Moved Through the Fair."

In the late 1970s, Mary Carr took care of Christy. They fell in love and were married. They lived together until Christy died in 1981. In 1988, the movie, *My Left Foot*, based on Christy's life story premièred starring Daniel Day Lewis. The screenplay was written by Shane Connaughton and Jim Sheridan, who also directed. The producer was Noel Pearson, and music was composed by Elmer Bernstein.

JEAN-DOMINIQUE BAUBY (1952-1997) Wrote a Book by Blinking His Left Eyelid

"Through the frayed curtain at my window, a wan glow announces the break of day. My heels hurt, my head weighs a ton, and something like a giant invisible diving bell holds my whole body prisoner. My room emerges slowly from the gloom. I linger over every item: photos of loved ones, my children's drawings, posters, the little tin cyclist sent by a friend the day before the Paris—Roubais bike race, and the IV pole hanging over the bed where I have been confined these past six months, like a hermit crab dug into his rock.... My diving bell becomes less oppressive, and my mind takes flight like a butterfly. There is so much to do. You can wander off in space or in time, set out for Tierra del Fuego or for King Midas's court...."[232]

Jean-Dominique Bauby, *The Diving Bell and the Butterfly*

Jean-Dominique Bauby, Editor-in-Chief of the French fashion magazine *Elle*, was known for his wit and joy of life. At the age of forty-three, the career journalist enjoyed life in the fast lane in Paris until he had a massive stroke that left him paralyzed. The diagnosis was "locked-in syndrome," in which the brain stem—the link between the brain and the spinal cord, and therefore the body—has been destroyed by a stroke, or "cerebro-vascular accident."

Bauby was totally dependent on hospital personnel and machines for all of his bodily functions. His brain was fully functional after coming out of a three-week-long coma and a few weeks of being groggy and sleepy. However, the only muscle he could control was his left eyelid. Blinking this eyelid was his only means of communicating with the outside world. He made the maximum use of this way of communicating with those around him.

Bauby's stroke occurred on December 8, 1995, a gray day

on which Paris was recovering from a transport strike. He had an appointment that day to test drive BMW's latest automobile that the importer had provided along with a driver. Bauby recalled listening to "A Day in the Life" by the Beatles as they crossed the Bois de Boulogne. He was dropped off at his office after making arrangements to be picked up at 3:00 p.m. to go to his mother's house, twenty-five miles outside of the city, to pick up his son, Théophile, and then to return to Paris early in the evening.

Bauby's workday was typical. He defended the magazine from the subject of one of its articles containing obvious errors that should have been caught by proofreaders. The staff luncheon in the executive dining room provided the "chief" an opportunity to keep in touch with his staff and to deliver the full range of messages from criticisms to compliments. Bauby recalled that the main course of his last decent meal was beef, and that his last drink was water.

Bauby did not get away from the office until after 4:00 p.m., causing him and the driver to get caught in heavy traffic. The BMW moved along smoothly until they bogged down in traffic crossing the Pont de Suresnes. They passed by the racecourse at Saint-Cloud and the Raymond-Poincaré Hospital at Garches. After an hour and a half, they arrived at his mother's place, where Théophile was sitting on his backpack near the gate, waiting for them.

While Bauby remembered everything clearly up to this point, things began to appear blurry to him. He climbed into the driver's seat to drive the car back to Paris. He began to perspire, and he seemed to be functioning in slow motion. He passed another car and began to see double. He pulled over at the next intersection, had difficulty standing up, and collapsed on the rear seat. Beginning to lose consciousness, Bauby asked his son to run back to the village to the house of his sister-in-law, Diane, who was a nurse. When she saw him, Diane realized that they had to get him to a clinic as soon as possible. The closest one was ten miles away.

The driver took off at high speed, passing every vehicle on the road. Bauby, who by this time felt like he was on LSD, wanted to tell the driver to slow down but realized that no sounds were coming out of his mouth. His head wobbled around on his shoulders, out of control. The staff at the clinic ran about frantically, while Bauby was thinking that they would not be on time for the play they had planned to see that evening. He decided that they would have to go tomorrow night instead and then sank into a deep coma.

Bauby came out of the coma twenty days later in room 119 at Berck-sur-Mer Naval Hospital on the French channel coast. When he came to, the hospital's ophthalmologist was sewing his right eyelid shut with a needle and thread. While Bauby worried that the left eyelid was going to sewn shut too, the ophthalmologist called out: "Six months." This doctor, who did not know the meaning of the term "bedside manner," either did not see or chose to ignore Bauby's fluttering left eyelid. Later, Bauby was told that his right eyelid was no longer providing a protective cover for the eye and might cause an ulcerated cornea if it were not closed.

Bauby's breathing was aided by a respirator, and his nourishment was provided by a gastric tube. He was unable to swallow the excess saliva that filled his mouth. His day began with the duty nurse pulling back the curtain around his bed, checking the intravenous feed and tracheostomy, and turning on the television set so he could watch the morning news.

Bauby made a point of not looking in the mirror. On the one occasion that he did, he saw an "unknown face." He observed, "Reflected in the glass I saw the head of a man who seemed to have emerged from a vat of formaldehyde. His mouth was twisted, his nose damaged, his hair tousled, his gaze full of fear. One eye was sewn shut, the other goggled like the doomed eye of Cain. For a moment I stared at that dilated pupil until I realized it was only mine."[233]

Eventually the hospital staff decided that Bauby was ready for an outing in a wheelchair. They dressed him in his street clothes, explaining that the effort was worth it because it was good for the morale. Many hospital staff members came to watch the preparations for this milestone.

In twenty weeks following his stroke, Bauby lost sixty-six pounds. He had started on a diet the week before his cerebro-vascular accident. He wished that he could say the diet was successful beyond his wildest dreams.

Bauby looked forward to his weekly bath. However, other activities called up contradictory emotions: "One day, for example I can find it amusing, in my forty-fifth year, to have my bottom wiped and swaddled like a newborn's. I even derive a guilty pleasure from this total lapse into infancy. But the next day, the same procedure seems to me to be unbearably sad, and a tear rolls down my cheek."[234]

Bauby was indebted to his speech therapist, Sandrine, who devised the system he used to communicate. He gave various winks and nods to ask to have the TV turned on, to close the door, or to have his head shifted on the pillow. He decided that the hospital staff was divided into two factions, one that would not think of leaving his room until they had determined what he was trying to say, and another who, not understanding what he wanted, pretended that they did not see his attempts to communicate. One member of the second group turned off the Bordeau-Munich soccer game at half-time, while ignoring his distress signals.

On Fathers' Day, Bauby had a visit from his two children. While their mother wheeled Bauby down the hall in the hospital, Théophile used a tissue to remove the excess saliva from the side of his father's mouth, and Celeste hugged his head as she planted many kisses on his forehead, while repeating, "You're my dad, you're my dad." Later, she would tell him about her experiences with her pony. Their visits gave him a feeling of ambivalence. He thoroughly enjoyed seeing their youthful energy and listening to their laughter. On the other hand, he realized that these visits were not ideal entertainment for his eight-year-old daughter and his ten-year-old son.

Initially, Bauby communicated by blinking his left eyelid once for "yes" and twice for "no." Eventually, his "guardian angel," Sandrine the speech therapist, devised a way of communicating using letters of the alphabet arranged from the most frequently used in the French language to the least used: E S A R I N T U L O M D P C F B V H G J Q Z Y X K W. Sandrine would go through this alphabet until she came to the letter that he wanted, and he would blink his left eyelid.

Obviously, infinite patience was required with this method of making his intentions known. Sandrine could finish some words and even some sentences herself, but some of those with whom he attempted to communicate would make Bauby blink out every letter. He was amazed that some people could not supply the "nable" that "intermi" and "abomi" need to exist. With this mode of communication, at least he could play the game "hangman" with his children.

Bauby's friends and associates were saddened to hear that he was "a complete vegetable." He wanted to do something to show them that "my IQ was still higher than a turnip's." He decided to send out a monthly letter. In June 1996, his first letter, addressed to sixty people, began with:

> On June 8 it will be six months since my new life began. Your letters are accumulating on the dresser, your drawings on the wall, and since I cannot hope to answer each one of you, I have decided to issue these samizdat bulletins to report on my life, my progress, and my hopes. At first I refused to believe that anything serious had happened. In my semiconscious state following the coma, I thought I would shortly be back in my Paris stomping grounds, with just a couple of canes to help me along.[235]

Editors at Robert Laffont, S.A., a French publisher that Bauby had worked with previously, were so impressed with the letter that they proposed that he write a book describing his condition. Claude Mendibil of Laffont patiently worked with Bauby to write the book. Writing with a ballpoint pen, the young woman filled a large notebook. When a friend of Bauby's told her about his past, "my quick temper, my love of books, my immoderate taste for food, my red convertible." Claude, who had only known Bauby for two weeks, said, "I didn't realize you were like that."[236]

Laboriously, the 137-page book, *Le Scaphandre et le Papillon (The Diving Bell and the Butterfly)*, was prepared using about 200,000 blinks of his eyelid. The book's first printing of 25,000 copies sold out quickly, and 146,000 copies were in print in France a week after the publication date. An English-language translation was commissioned and Vintage Books, a division of Random House, was contracted to print the book in the United States.

On March 7, 1997, Bauby died, seventy-two hours after completing his book, which he subtitled *A Memoir of Life in Death*. The week after his death, "Bouillon de Culture," the highest rated television show on cultural affairs in France, aired a program about Bauby and his book. The documentary was produced by Jean-Jacques Beineix, the French filmmaker who also produced the popular documentary "Diva."

After his stroke, Bauby had nagging memories of having reread *The Count of Monte Christo* by Alexander Dumas and having made plans to write a modern version of the book. One of the characters in the book, Noirtier de Villefort, Dumas describes as a profoundly handicapped living mummy who was three-quarters of the way to the grave. Noirtier, who is confined to a wheelchair, can only communicate by blinking an eye: one blink meant yes, and two blinks meant no. The irony of the situation was overwhelming to Bauby. In his words, "To foil the decrees of fate, I am now planning a vast saga in which the key witness in not a paralytic but a runner.

You never know. Perhaps it will work."[237]

A New York *Times* staff writer observed about Bauby, "In the depths of darkest adversity, some men and women are able to reach into the recesses of their characters and find astonishing reserves of strength and courage."[238] Bauby concludes his book by asking, "Does the cosmos contain keys for opening up my diving bell? A subway line with no terminus? A currency strong enough to buy my freedom back? We must keep looking. I'll be off now."[239]

EPILOGUE

"Man is still responsible. He must turn the alloy of modern experience into the steel and mastery of character. His success lies not with the stars but with himself. He must carry on the fight of self-correction and discipline. He must fight mediocrity as sin and live against the imperative of life's highest ideal."

Frank Curtis Williams, D.D.

The twenty-five individuals whose lives are described in this book have displayed a high degree of motivation that drove them to attain their goals and to achieve their purpose in life. Although self-motivation is probably the most important single factor in achieving success, receiving support from relatives, teachers, and mentors is also important.

Frederick Delius's talented wife, Jelka, gave up her career as an artist to help him with his career. Also, when he became incapacitated, the support of Eric Fenby allowed him to continue to compose. Helen Keller would not have been nearly as successful as she was without the assistance of Anne Sullivan. Vincent Van Gogh could not have continued to paint without the financial and moral support of his brother, Theo. Christy Brown overcame cerebral palsy to write and to become a productive individual because of the early and ongoing support of his mother. Jean-Dominique Bauby could not have written a book after his massive stroke without the help of Claude Mendibil, who patiently converted his eyeblinks into words and sentences and ultimately into a book.

In our everyday lives, we encounter obstacles that appear to be insurmountable. Some individuals work two jobs to support a family and still find time to take courses to advance in their chosen career. Many young women are wives and mothers while working at a full-time job. Examples of motivation are all around us. The lives of relatives, friends, acquaintances, and neighbors serve as examples for us. If they can do it, so can we.

We should avoid arriving in the future and looking back and thinking of what might have been. If we are at the fork in the road now in making a decision, let us hope that we have the drive to measure up to our potential and to do what we know we can do.

Just being highly motivated isn't enough; that motivation should be productive and lead to achievement. Abraham Maslow addresses this point in discussing inspiration in *Motivation and Personality:*

> Inspirations are a dime a dozen. The difference between the inspiration and the final product, for example, Tolstoy's *War and Peace,* is an awful lot of hard work, an awful lot of discipline, and an awful lot of training ... the virtues which go with the secondary kind of creativeness, the creativeness which results in the actual products, in the great paintings, the great novels, in the bridges, the new inventions, and so on, rest heavily on other virtues — stubbornness, patience, and hard work and so on, as they do upon the creativeness of personality.[240]

The goal of this book is to convey the importance of the human quality of motivation in achieving our potential. With motivation, many obstacles can be overcome and much can be accomplished. Without it, potential goes unfulfilled, and achievements will either be delayed or not accomplished at all.

NOTES

Prologue

   1 Harris, Victoria. "What's Happening." Brighton-Pittsford (New York) *Post* 20 Jan. 1997. Quotation cited by Linda Quinlan.

   2 Goble, Frank G. *The Third Force: The Psychology of Abraham Maslow.* (New York: Grossman, 1970) 52, 150-151.

   3 Goble, Frank G. *The Third Force: The Psychology of Abraham Maslow.* (New York: Grossman, 1970) 154.

   4 Wlodkowski, Raymond J. *Motivation in Education.* (N.p.: National Education Association of the United States, 1982) 5.

   5 Maslow, Abraham H. *Motivation and Personality.* (New York: Harper & Row, 1970) 46.

   6 Stanley, Bessie Anderson. *Elbert Hubbard's Scrapbook.* Ed. Elbert Hubbard. (New York: Wm. H. Wise, 1923) 56. Mrs. Arthur J. Stanley's definition of success won first prize in a contest conducted by *Brown Book* Magazine in 1904.

Chapter 1

   7 Lubbock, Constance A. *The Herschel Chronicle: The Life-Story of William Herschel and His Sister Caroline Herschel.* (New York: Macmillan, 1933) 81, 82.

   8 Sidgwick, J. B. *William Herschel.* (London: Faber and Faber, 1953) 73.

   9 Holden, Edward S. *Sir William Herschel: His Life and Works.* (New York: Charles Scribner's Sons, 1881) 56.

   10 Bowen, Catherine Drinker Bowen. *Yankee from Olympus: Justice Holmes and His Family.* (Boston: Little, Brown, 1945) 65.

   11 Bowen, Catherine Drinker Bowen. *Yankee from Olympus: Justice Holmes and His Family.* (Boston: Little, Brown, 1945) 16-17.

   12 Sullivan, Wilson. *New England Men of Letters.* (New York: Macmillan, 1972) 230.

13 Sullivan, Wilson. *New England Men of Letters*. (New York: Macmillan, 1972) 228.

14 Bowen, Catherine Drinker Bowen. *Yankee from Olympus: Justice Holmes and His Family*. (Boston: Little, Brown, 1945) 56.

15 Sullivan, Wilson. *New England Men of Letters*. (New York: Macmillan, 1972) 231.

16 Sullivan, Wilson. *New England Men of Letters*. (New York: Macmillan, 1972) 232.

17 Bowen, Catherine Drinker Bowen. *Yankee from Olympus: Justice Holmes and His Family*. (Boston: Little, Brown, 1945) 67.

18 Bowen, Catherine Drinker Bowen. *Yankee from Olympus: Justice Holmes and His Family*. (Boston: Little, Brown, 1945) 72.

19 Sullivan, Wilson. *New England Men of Letters*. (New York: Macmillan, 1972) 235.

20 Benét, Laura. *Famous New England Authors*. (New York: Dodd, Mead, 1970) 47.

21 Sullivan, Wilson. *New England Men of Letters*. (New York: Macmillan, 1972) 238.

22 Sullivan, Wilson. *New England Men of Letters*. (New York: Macmillan, 1972) 238.

23 Dianin, Serge. *Borodin*. (London, Oxford UP, 1963) 16.

24 Dianin, Serge. *Borodin*. (London, Oxford UP, 1963) 20.

25 Dianin, Serge. *Borodin*. (London, Oxford UP, 1963) 33.

26 Dianin, Serge. *Borodin*. (London, Oxford UP, 1963) 34.

27 Dianin, Serge. *Borodin*. (London, Oxford UP, 1963) 42.

28 Abraham, Gerald E. H. *Borodin: The Composer and His Music*. (London: William Reeves, 1927) 20, 23.

29 Dianin, Serge. *Borodin*. (London, Oxford UP, 1963) 45.

30 Dianin, Serge. *Borodin*. (London, Oxford UP, 1963) 68.

31 Dianin, Serge. *Borodin*. (London, Oxford UP, 1963) 77.

32 Dianin, Serge. *Borodin*. (London, Oxford UP, 1963) 83.

33 Dianin, Serge. *Borodin*. (London, Oxford UP, 1963) 136.

34 Dianin, Serge. *Borodin*. (London, Oxford UP, 1963) 152.

35 Abraham, Gerald E. H. *Borodin: The Composer and His Music*. (London: William Reeves, 1927) 19.

36 Laffitte, Sophie. *Chekhov: 1860-1904*. (New York: Charles Scribner's Sons, 1973) 74.

37 Laffitte, Sophie. *Chekhov: 1860-1904*. (New York: Charles Scribner's Sons, 1973) 13.

38 Untermeyer, Louis. *Makers of the Modern World*. (New York: Simon & Schuster, 1955) 294.

39 Laffitte, Sophie. *Chekhov: 1860-1904*. (New York: Charles Scribner's Sons, 1973) 16.

40 Toumanova, Princess Nina Andronikova. *Anton Chekhov: The Voice of Twilight Russia*. (New York: Columbia UP, 1937) 44.

41 Untermeyer, Louis. *Makers of the Modern World*. (New York: Simon & Schuster, 1955) 297.

42 Laffitte, Sophie. *Chekhov: 1860-1904*. (New York: Charles Scribner's Sons, 1973) 7, 8.

43 Untermeyer, Louis. *Makers of the Modern World*. (New York: Simon & Schuster, 1955) 298.

44 Untermeyer, Louis. *Makers of the Modern World*. (New York: Simon & Schuster, 1955) 299.

45 Toumanova, Princess Nina Andronikova. *Anton Chekhov: The Voice of Twilight Russia*. (New York: Columbia UP, 1937) 117.

46 Toumanova, Princess Nina Andronikova. *Anton Chekhov: The Voice of Twilight Russia*. (New York: Columbia UP, 1937) 180, 181.

47 Laffitte, Sophie. *Chekhov: 1860-1904*. (New York: Charles Scribner's Sons, 1973) 233.

48 Untermeyer, Louis. *Makers of the Modern World*. (New York: Simon & Schuster, 1955) 300.

49 Laffitte, Sophie. *Chekhov: 1860-1904*. (New York: Charles Scribner's Sons, 1973) 239.

50 Laffitte, Sophie. Chekhov: 1860-1904. (New York: Charles Scribner's Sons, 1973) 215.

51 Gelderman, Carol. *Louis Auchincloss: A Writer's Life*.

(New York: Crown, 1993) 1.

52 Parsell, David B. *Louis Auchincloss*. (Boston: Twayne, 1988) 3, 4.

53 Gelderman, Carol. *Louis Auchincloss: A Writer's Life*. (New York: Crown, 1993) 36.

54 Gelderman, Carol. *Louis Auchincloss: A Writer's Life*. (New York: Crown, 1993) 62.

55 Gelderman, Carol. *Louis Auchincloss: A Writer's Life*. (New York: Crown, 1993) 83.

56 Auchincloss, Louis. *A Writer's Capital*. (Boston: Houghton Mifflin, 1979) 99.

57 Gelderman, Carol. *Louis Auchincloss: A Writer's Life*. (New York: Crown, 1993) 110.

58 Auchincloss, Louis. *A Writer's Capital*. (Boston: Houghton Mifflin, 1979) 125, 126.

59 Gelderman, Carol. *Louis Auchincloss: A Writer's Life*. (New York: Crown, 1993) 170.

Chapter 2

60 Warlock, Peter (Philip Heseltine). *Frederick Delius*. (New York: Oxford UP, 1952) 23.

61 Warlock, Peter (Philip Heseltine). *Frederick Delius*. (New York: Oxford UP, 1952) 9.

62 Jahoda, Gloria. *The Road to Samarkand: Frederick Delius and His Music*. (New York: Charles Scribner's Sons, 1969) 147.

63 Jahoda, Gloria. *The Road to Samarkand: Frederick Delius and His Music*. (New York: Charles Scribner's Sons, 1969) 124.

64 Warlock, Peter (Philip Heseltine). *Frederick Delius*. (New York: Oxford UP, 1952) 21.

65 Warlock, Peter (Philip Heseltine). *Frederick Delius*. (New York: Oxford UP, 1952) 145.

66 Jahoda, Gloria. *The Road to Samarkand: Frederick Delius and His Music*. (New York: Charles Scribner's Sons, 1969) 224.

67 Warlock, Peter (Philip Heseltine). Frederick Delius. (New York: Oxford UP, 1952) 194, 195.

68 Warlock, Peter (Philip Heseltine). *Frederick Delius*. (New York: Oxford UP, 1952) 149.

69 Gould, Jean. *A Good Fight: The Story of F.D.R's Conquest of Polio*. (New York: Dodd, Mead, 1960) 117.

70 Gould, Jean. *A Good Fight: The Story of F.D.R's Conquest of Polio*. (New York: Dodd, Mead, 1960) 69, 70.

71 Gould, Jean. *A Good Fight: The Story of F.D.R's Conquest of Polio*. (New York: Dodd, Mead, 1960) 116.

72 Gould, Jean. *A Good Fight: The Story of F.D.R's Conquest of Polio*. (New York: Dodd, Mead, 1960) 121.

73 Gould, Jean. *A Good Fight: The Story of F.D.R's Conquest of Polio*. (New York: Dodd, Mead, 1960) 123, 124.

74 Gould, Jean. *A Good Fight: The Story of F.D.R's Conquest of Polio*. (New York: Dodd, Mead, 1960) 140.

75 Gould, Jean. *A Good Fight: The Story of F.D.R's Conquest of Polio*. (New York: Dodd, Mead, 1960) 160.

76 Gould, Jean. *A Good Fight: The Story of F.D.R's Conquest of Polio*. (New York: Dodd, Mead, 1960) 178.

77 Burns, James McGregor. *Roosevelt: The Lion and the Fox*. (New York: Harcourt, Brace, 1956) 101.

78 Gould, Jean. *A Good Fight: The Story of F.D.R's Conquest of Polio*. (New York: Dodd, Mead, 1960) 198.

79 Gould, Jean. *A Good Fight: The Story of F.D.R's Conquest of Polio*. (New York: Dodd, Mead, 1960) 226.

80 Whitman, Alden. "Triumph out of Tragedy." (New York *Times* 2 Jun. 1968) 76.

81 Keller, Helen. *The Story of My Life*. (New York: Airmont Books, 1965) 187.

82 Whitman, Alden. "Triumph out of Tragedy." (New York *Times* 2 Jun. 1968) 76.

83 Whitman, Alden. "Triumph out of Tragedy." (New York *Times* 2 Jun. 1968) 76.

84 Whitman, Alden. "Triumph out of Tragedy." (New York *Times* 2 Jun. 1968) 76.

85 Franz, Joe B. *Gail Borden: Dairyman to a Nation.* (Norman: U of Oklahoma P, 1951) 200.

86 Franz, Joe B. *Gail Borden: Dairyman to a Nation.* (Norman: U of Oklahoma P, 1951) 189.

87 Franz, Joe B. *Gail Borden: Dairyman to a Nation.* (Norman: U of Oklahoma P, 1951) 198.

88 Franz, Joe B. *Gail Borden: Dairyman to a Nation.* (Norman: U of Oklahoma P, 1951) 211.

89 Franz, Joe B. *Gail Borden: Dairyman to a Nation.* (Norman: U of Oklahoma P, 1951) 228.

90 Franz, Joe B. *Gail Borden: Dairyman to a Nation.* (Norman: U of Oklahoma P, 1951) 239.

91 Baker, Nina Brown. *Texas Yankee: The Story of Gail Borden.* (New York: Harcourt, Brace, 1955) 59.

92 Prichard, Peter S. *The Making of McPaper: The Inside Story of USA Today.* (New York: St. Martin's, 1987) 334, 335.

93 Prichard, Peter S. *The Making of McPaper: The Inside Story of USA Today.* (New York: St. Martin's, 1987) 26.

94 Prichard, Peter S. *The Making of McPaper: The Inside Story of USA Today.* (New York: St. Martin's, 1987) 291.

95 Neuharth, Al. *Confessions of an S. O. B.* (New York: Doubleday, 1989) 166, 167.

96 Prichard, Peter S. *The Making of McPaper: The Inside Story of USA Today.* (New York: St. Martin's, 1987) 378.

97 Neuharth, Al. *Confessions of an S. O. B.* (New York: Doubleday, 1989) 104.

Chapter 3

98 Castle, Barbara. *Sylvia and Christabel Pankhurst.* (New York: Penguin, 1987) 110.

99 Mitchell, David. *The Fighting Pankhursts: A Study in Tenacity.* (New York: Macmillan, 1967) 19.

100 Castle, Barbara. *Sylvia and Christabel Pankhurst.*

(New York: Penguin, 1987) 47.

101 Castle, Barbara. *Sylvia and Christabel Pankhurst.*
(New York: Penguin, 1987) 49.

102 Castle, Barbara. *Sylvia and Christabel Pankhurst.*
(New York: Penguin, 1987) 51.

103 Castle, Barbara. *Sylvia and Christabel Pankhurst.*
(New York: Penguin, 1987) 52.

104 Castle, Barbara. *Sylvia and Christabel Pankhurst.*
(New York: Penguin, 1987) 53.

105 Castle, Barbara. *Sylvia and Christabel Pankhurst.*
(New York: Penguin, 1987) 59, 60.

106 Castle, Barbara. *Sylvia and Christabel Pankhurst.*
(New York: Penguin, 1987) 72, 73.

107 Castle, Barbara. *Sylvia and Christabel Pankhurst.*
(New York: Penguin, 1987) 102.

108 Castle, Barbara. *Sylvia and Christabel Pankhurst.*
(New York: Penguin, 1987) 109, 110.

109 Castle, Barbara. *Sylvia and Christabel Pankhurst.*
(New York: Penguin, 1987) 133.

110 Castle, Barbara. *Sylvia and Christabel Pankhurst.*
(New York: Penguin, 1987) 138.

111 Castle, Barbara. *Sylvia and Christabel Pankhurst.*
(New York: Penguin, 1987) 147.

112 Castle, Barbara. *Sylvia and Christabel Pankhurst.*
(New York: Penguin, 1987) 109.

113 Peck, Mary Gray. *Carrie Chapman Catt: A Biography.*
(New York: H. W. Wilson, 1944) 65.

114 Reynolds, Moira Davison. "Carrie Chapman Catt"
*Women Champions of Human Rights: Eleven U.S.
Leaders of the Twentieth Century.* (London: McFarland,
1991) 90.

115 Reynolds, Moira Davison. "Carrie Chapman Catt"
*Women Champions of Human Rights: Eleven U.S.
Leaders of the Twentieth Century.* (London: McFarland,
1991) 91.

116 Reynolds, Moira Davison. "Carrie Chapman Catt"

Women Champions of Human Rights: Eleven U.S. Leaders of the Twentieth Century. (London: McFarland, 1991) 96.

117 Irwin, Inez Hayes. *The Story of Alice Paul and the National Woman's Party.* (Fairfax, VA: Denlinger's, 1977) 15, 16.

118 Fry, Amelia R. "Alice Paul." *The Influence of Quaker Women on American History: Biographical Studies.* (Lewiston: Edwin Mellen, 1986) 384, 385.

119 Lunardini, Christine A. *From Equal Suffrage to Equal Rights: Alice Paul and the National Woman's Party, 1910-1928.* (New York: New York UP, 1986) 133, 134.

120 Gray, Charlotte. *Mother Teresa: Her Mission To Serve God By Caring For the Poor.* (Milwaukee: Gareth Stevens, 1988) 53.

121 Egan, Eileen. *Such a Vision of the Street: Mother Teresa—The Spirit and the Work.* (Garden City, NY: Doubleday, 1985) 25.

122 Gray, Charlotte. *Mother Teresa: Her Mission To Serve God By Caring For the Poor.* (Milwaukee: Gareth Stevens, 1988) 10.

123 Gray, Charlotte. *Mother Teresa: Her Mission To Serve God By Caring For the Poor.* (Milwaukee: Gareth Stevens, 1988) 20.

124 Clucas, Joan Graff. *Mother Teresa.* (New York: Chelsea House, 1988) 49.

125 Clucas, Joan Graff. *Mother Teresa.* (New York: Chelsea House, 1988) 50.

126 Clucas, Joan Graff. *Mother Teresa.* (New York: Chelsea House, 1988) 51.

127 Clucas, Joan Graff. *Mother Teresa.* (New York: Chelsea House, 1988) 55.

128 Gray, Charlotte. *Mother Teresa: Her Mission To Serve God By Caring For the Poor.* (Milwaukee: Gareth Stevens, 1988) 43.

129 Hoobler, Dorothy and Thomas. *Nelson and Winnie*

Mandela. (New York: Franklin Watts, 1987) 78.

130 Hoobler, Dorothy and Thomas. *Nelson and Winnie Mandela*. (New York: Franklin Watts, 1987) 26.

131 Hoobler, Dorothy and Thomas. *Nelson and Winnie Mandela*. (New York: Franklin Watts, 1987) 37.

132 Vail, John. *Nelson and Winnie Mandela*. (New York: Chelsea House, 1989) 35.

133 Hoobler, Dorothy and Thomas. *Nelson and Winnie Mandela*. (New York: Franklin Watts, 1987) 52.

134 Hoobler, Dorothy and Thomas. *Nelson and Winnie Mandela*. (New York: Franklin Watts, 1987) 60.

135 Hoobler, Dorothy and Thomas. *Nelson and Winnie Mandela*. (New York: Franklin Watts, 1987) 69.

136 Hoobler, Dorothy and Thomas. *Nelson and Winnie Mandela*. (New York: Franklin Watts, 1987) 69.

137 Hoobler, Dorothy and Thomas. *Nelson and Winnie Mandela*. (New York: Franklin Watts, 1987) 71, 72.

138 Hoobler, Dorothy and Thomas. *Nelson and Winnie Mandela*. (New York: Franklin Watts, 1987) 74.

139 Hoobler, Dorothy and Thomas. *Nelson and Winnie Mandela*. (New York: Franklin Watts, 1987) 77.

140 Vail, John. *Nelson and Winnie Mandela*. (New York: Chelsea House, 1989) 69.

141 Hoobler, Dorothy and Thomas. *Nelson and Winnie Mandela*. (New York: Franklin Watts, 1987) 92.

142 Vail, John. *Nelson and Winnie Mandela*. (New York: Chelsea House, 1989) 99.

143 Hoobler, Dorothy and Thomas. *Nelson and Winnie Mandela*. (New York: Franklin Watts, 1987) 110.

144 Hoobler, Dorothy and Thomas. *Nelson and Winnie Mandela*. (New York: Franklin Watts, 1987) 111.

145 Hoobler, Dorothy and Thomas. *Nelson and Winnie Mandela*. (New York: Franklin Watts, 1987) 111, 112.

146 Hoobler, Dorothy and Thomas. *Nelson and Winnie Mandela*. (New York: Franklin Watts, 1987) 112.

147 Mandela, Nelson. *Long Walk To Freedom*. (Boston:

Little, Brown, 1994) 493.

148 Hoobler, Dorothy and Thomas. *Nelson and Winnie Mandela.* (New York: Franklin Watts, 1987) 537, 538.

149 Mandela, Nelson. *Long Walk To Freedom.* (Boston: Little, Brown, 1994) 541.

150 Mandela, Nelson. *Long Walk To Freedom.* (Boston: Little, Brown, 1994) 544.

Chapter 4

151 Untermeyer, Louis. *Makers of the Modern World.* (New York: Simon & Schuster, 1955) 59.

152 Untermeyer, Louis. *Makers of the Modern World.* (New York: Simon & Schuster, 1955) 48.

153 Untermeyer, Louis. *Makers of the Modern World.* (New York: Simon & Schuster, 1955) 49.

154 Untermeyer, Louis. *Makers of the Modern World.* (New York: Simon & Schuster, 1955) 53.

155 Allen, Gay Wilson. *Melville and His World.* (New York: Viking, 1971) 106.

156 Untermeyer, Louis. *Makers of the Modern World.* (New York: Simon & Schuster, 1955) 58.

157 Untermeyer, Louis. *Makers of the Modern World.* (New York: Simon & Schuster, 1955) 58.

158 Untermeyer, Louis. *Makers of the Modern World.* (New York: Simon & Schuster, 1955) 55.

159 Untermeyer, Louis. *Makers of the Modern World.* (New York: Simon & Schuster, 1955) 55.

160 Allen, Gay Wilson. *Melville and His World.* (New York: Viking, 1971) 130.

161 Untermeyer, Louis. *Makers of the Modern World.* (New York: Simon & Schuster, 1955) 133.

162 Ferlazzo, Paul J. *Emily Dickinson.* (Boston: Twayne, 1975)142.

163 Untermeyer, Louis. *Makers of the Modern World.* (New York: Simon & Schuster, 1955) 137, 138.

164 Olsen, Victoria. *Emily Dickinson.* (New York:

Chelsea House, 1990) 51.

165 Ferlazzo, Paul J. *Emily Dickinson*. (Boston: Twayne, 1975) 69, 70.

166 Ferlazzo, Paul J. *Emily Dickinson*. (Boston: Twayne, 1975) 62.

167 Olsen, Victoria. *Emily Dickinson*. (New York: Chelsea House, 1990) 68.

168 Untermeyer, Louis. *Makers of the Modern World*. (New York: Simon & Schuster, 1955) 134, 135.

169 Olsen, Victoria. *Emily Dickinson*. (New York: Chelsea House, 1990) 74.

170 Olsen, Victoria. *Emily Dickinson*. (New York: Chelsea House, 1990) 67.

171 Dickenson, Donna. *Emily Dickinson*. (Dover, NH: Berg, 1985) 106.

172 Olsen, Victoria. *Emily Dickinson*. (New York: Chelsea House, 1990) 91.

173 Olsen, Victoria. *Emily Dickinson*. (New York: Chelsea House, 1990) 95.

174 Olsen, Victoria. *Emily Dickinson*. (New York: Chelsea House, 1990) 99, 100.

175 Longsworth, Polly. *Emily Dickinson: Her Letter to the World*. (New York: Thomas Y. Crowell, 1965) viii.

176 Hulsker, Jan. *Vincent and Theo Van Gogh: A Dual Biography*. (Ann Arbor: Fuller, 1990) 420, 421.

177 Untermeyer, Louis. *Makers of the Modern World*. (New York: Simon & Schuster, 1955) 228, 237.

178 Untermeyer, Louis. *Makers of the Modern World*. (New York: Simon & Schuster, 1955) 237.

179 Honour, Alan. *Tormented Genius: The Struggles of Vincent Van Gogh*. (New York: William Morrow, 1967) 123.

180 Hulsker, Jan. *Vincent and Theo Van Gogh: A Dual Biography*. (Ann Arbor: Fuller, 1990) 440.

181 Honour, Alan. *Tormented Genius: The Struggles of Vincent Van Gogh*. (New York: William Morrow, 1967)

149.

182 Sichel, Pierre. *Modigliani: A Biography*. New York: (E. P. Dutton, 1967) 552.

183 Sichel, Pierre. *Modigliani: A Biography*. New York: (E. P. Dutton, 1967) 98.

184 Sichel, Pierre. *Modigliani: A Biography*. New York: (E. P. Dutton, 1967) 236.

185 Sichel, Pierre. *Modigliani: A Biography*. New York: (E. P. Dutton, 1967) 513.

186 Sichel, Pierre. *Modigliani: A Biography*. New York: (E. P. Dutton, 1967) 551.

187 Coil, Suzanne M. *Robert Hutchings Goddard: Pioneer of Rocketry and Space Flight*. (New York: Facts On File, 1992) 12.

188 Lehman, Milton. *This High Man: The Life of Robert H. Goddard*. (New York: Farrar, Straus, 1963) 78.

Chapter 5

189 Flindell, E. Fred. "Paul Wittgenstein (1887-1961): Patron and Pianist." *The Music Review*. xxxii (1971): 114.

190 Flindell, E. Fred. "Paul Wittgenstein (1887-1961): Patron and Pianist." *The Music Review*. xxxii (1971), 113.

191 Flindell, E. Fred. "Paul Wittgenstein (1887-1961): Patron and Pianist." *The Music Review*. xxxii (1971), 111.

192 Barchilon, John. *The Crown Prince*. (New York: Norton, 1984) 256.

193 Rettich, Alfred. (Colonel of the 6th Regiment, Imperial Royal Cavalry). Letter from Headquarters of the Imperial Royal Cavalry to Leopoldine Wittgenstein. 11 Nov. 1914.

194 Flindell, E. Fred. "Paul Wittgenstein (1887-1961): Patron and Pianist." *The Music Review*. xxxii (1971), 114.

195 Atterman, Erna Otten. Letter to Paul Wittgenstein.

20 Jun. 1967. Mrs. Atterman was a student
of Wittgenstein in the 1930s.

196 Flindell, E. Fred. "Paul Wittgenstein (1887-1961):
Patron and Pianist." *The Music Review*. xxxii (1971),
117.

197 Flindell, E. Fred. "Paul Wittgenstein (1887-1961):
Patron and Pianist." *The Music Review*. xxxii (1971),
113.

198 Flindell, E. Fred. "Paul Wittgenstein (1887-1961):
Patron and Pianist." *The Music Review*. xxxii (1971),
124.

199 Ferguson, Kitty. *Stephen Hawking: Quest for a Theory
of the Universe*. (New York: Franklin Watts, 1991) 30.

200 Hawking, Stephen W. *Black Holes and Baby Universes
and Other Essays*. (New York: Bantam, 1993) 14.

201 Boslough, John. *Stephen Hawking's Universe*.
(New York: Avon, 1985) 13.

202 White, Michael and John Gribben. *Stephen Hawking:
A Life In Science*. (Minneapolis: Dutton, 1992) 57, 58.

203 Hawking, Stephen W. *Black Holes and Baby Universes
and Other Essays*. (New York: Bantam, 1993) 22.

204 White, Michael and John Gribben. *Stephen Hawking:
A Life In Science*. (Minneapolis: Dutton, 1992) 70.

205 White, Michael and John Gribben. *Stephen Hawking:
A Life In Science*. (Minneapolis: Dutton, 1992) 72.

206 White, Michael and John Gribben. *Stephen Hawking:
A Life In Science*. (Minneapolis: Dutton, 1992) 98.

207 White, Michael and John Gribben. *Stephen Hawking:
A Life In Science*. (Minneapolis: Dutton, 1992) 192.

208 White, Michael and John Gribben. *Stephen Hawking:
A Life In Science*. (Minneapolis: Dutton, 1992) 104.

209 Boslough, John. *Stephen Hawking's Universe*.
(New York: Avon, 1985) 16, 17.

210 White, Michael and John Gribben. *Stephen Hawking:
A Life In Science*. (Minneapolis: Dutton, 1992) 122.

211 White, Michael and John Gribben. *Stephen Hawking:*

A Life In Science. (Minneapolis: Dutton, 1992) 166.

212 White, Michael and John Gribben. *Stephen Hawking: A Life In Science*. (Minneapolis: Dutton, 1992) 170.

213 White, Michael and John Gribben. *Stephen Hawking: A Life In Science*. (Minneapolis: Dutton, 1992) 192.

214 White, Michael and John Gribben. *Stephen Hawking: A Life In Science*. (Minneapolis: Dutton, 1992) 231.

215 White, Michael and John Gribben. *Stephen Hawking: A Life In Science*. (Minneapolis: Dutton, 1992) 293.

216 White, Michael and John Gribben. *Stephen Hawking: A Life In Science*. (Minneapolis: Dutton, 1992) 167.

217 Robbins, David. *Men of Honor*. (New York: Onyx, 2000) 11.

218 Stillwell, Paul. *The Reminiscences of Master Chief Carl M. Brashear, U.S. Navy (Retired)*. (Annapolis: U.S Naval Institute, 1998) Preface.

219 Stillwell, Paul. *The Reminiscences of Master Chief Carl M. Brashear, U.S. Navy (Retired)*. (Annapolis: U.S Naval Institute, 1998) 23.

220 Stillwell, Paul. *The Reminiscences of Master Chief Carl M. Brashear, U.S. Navy (Retired)*. (Annapolis: U.S Naval Institute, 1998) 23.

221 Stillwell, Paul. *The Reminiscences of Master Chief Carl M. Brashear, U.S. Navy (Retired)*. (Annapolis: U.S Naval Institute, 1998) 23.

222 Stillwell, Paul. *The Reminiscences of Master Chief Carl M. Brashear, U.S. Navy (Retired)*. (Annapolis: U.S Naval Institute, 1998) 90.

223 Stillwell, Paul. *The Reminiscences of Master Chief Carl M. Brashear, U.S. Navy (Retired)*. (Annapolis: U.S Naval Institute, 1998) 114.

224 Brown, Christy. *My Left Foot*. (New York: Simon and Schuster, 1955) xii, xiii.

225 Brown, Christy. *My Left Foot*. (New York: Simon and Schuster, 1955) 59.

226 Brown, Christy. *My Left Foot*. (New York: Simon and

Schuster, 1955) 94, 95.

227 Brown, Christy. *My Left Foot*. (New York: Simon and Schuster, 1955) 102.

228 Brown, Christy. *My Left Foot*. (New York: Simon and Schuster, 1955) 105.

229 Brown, Christy. *My Left Foot*. (New York: Simon and Schuster, 1955) 123.

230 Brown, Christy. *My Left Foot*. (New York: Simon and Schuster, 1955) 149.

231 Brown, Christy. *My Left Foot*. (New York: Simon and Schuster, 1955) 150.

232 Bauby, Jean-Dominique. *The Diving Bell and the Butterfly*. (New York: Vintage, 1997) 3, 5.

233 Bauby, Jean-Dominique. *The Diving Bell and the Butterfly*. (New York: Vintage, 1997) 24, 25.

234 Bauby, Jean-Dominique. *The Diving Bell and the Butterfly*. (New York: Vintage, 1997) 16, 17.

235 Bauby, Jean-Dominique. *The Diving Bell and the Butterfly*. (New York: Vintage, 1997) 81.

236 Bauby, Jean-Dominique. *The Diving Bell and the Butterfly*. (New York: Vintage, 1997) 86.

237 Bauby, Jean-Dominique. *The Diving Bell and the Butterfly*. (New York: Vintage, 1997) 48.

238 "French author dies; he wrote book by blinking." (From the New York *Times*) Rochester *Democrat and Chronicle* 16 Mar. 1997. 18A

239 Bauby, Jean-Dominique. *The Diving Bell and the Butterfly*. (New York: Vintage, 1997) 131, 132.

Epilogue

240 Goble, Frank G. *The Third Force: The Psychology of Abraham Maslow*. (New York: Grossman, 1970) 27.

BIBLIOGRAPHY

Abraham, Gerald E. H. *Borodin: The Composer and His Music.* London: William Reeves, 1927.

Allen, Gay Wilson. *Melville and His World.* New York: Viking, 1971.

Armitage, Angus. *William Herschel: The Pioneer of a New Era in Astronomy.* New York: Doubleday, 1963.

Arvin, Newton. *Herman Melville.* New York: Sloane, 1950.

Atterman, Erna Otten. Letter to Paul Wittgenstein. 20 Jun. 1967.

Auchincloss, Louis. *A Writer's Capital.* Boston: Houghton Mifflin, 1979.

Baker, Nina Brown. *Texas Yankee: The Story of Gail Borden.* New York: Harcourt, Brace, 1955.

Baker, Theodore. *Baker's Biographical Dictionary of Musicians, 6th Ed.* New York: Schirmer, 1978.

Barchilon, John. *The Crown Prince.* New York: Norton, 1984.

Barker, Dudley. "Mrs. Emmeline Pankhurst." *Prominent Edwardians.* New York: Atheneum, 1969.

Bauby, Jean-Dominique. *The Diving Bell and the Butterfly.* New York: Vintage, 1997.

Benét, Laura. *Famous American Poets.* New York: Dodd, Mead, 1961.

Bonafoux, Pascal. *Van Gogh: The Passionate Eye.* New York: Harry N. Abrams, n.d.

Boslough, John. *Stephen Hawking's Universe.* New York: Avon, 1985.

Bowen, Catherine Drinker. *Yankee from Olympus: Justice Holmes and His Family.* Boston: Little, Brown, 1945.

Brooks, Van Wyck. *Helen Keller: Sketch for a Portrait.* New York: E. P. Dutton, 1956.

Brown, Christy. *My Left Foot.* New York: Simon & Schuster, 1955.

Burns, James McGregor. *Roosevelt: The Lion and the Fox.* New York: Harcourt, Brace, 1956.

Castle, Barbara. *Sylvia and Christabel Pankhurst*.
New York: Penguin, 1987.

Chase, Richard. *Herman Melville*. New York: Macmillan,
1949.

Chasins, Abraham. *Speaking of Pianists*. New York:
Alfred A. Knopf, 1958.

Chawla, Navin. *Mother Teresa*. Rockport, MA: Element,
1996.

Clerke, Agnes M. *The Herschels and Modern Astronomy*.
London: Cassell, 1895.

Clucas, Joan Graff. *Mother Teresa*. New York:
Chelsea House, 1988.

Coil, Suzanne M. *Robert Hutchings Goddard: Pioneer of
Rocketry and Space Flight*. New York: Facts On File,
1992.

Comfort, Harold W. *Gail Borden and His Heritage Since
1857*. New York: Newcomen Society of North America,
1953.

Connaughton, Shane, and Jim Sheridan. *My Left Foot*
(Screenplay). London: Faber and Faber, 1989.

Crawford, Deborah. *The King's Astronomer:
William Herschel*. New York: Julian Messner, 1968.

Crumley, Bruce. "A Triumph of the Spirit." *Time*.
24 Mar 1997: 90.

Dale, Maud. *Modigliani*. New York: Alfred A. Knopf, 1929.

De Leeuw, Ronald, ed. *The Letters of Vincent Van Gogh*.
New York: Penguin, 1997.

Dewey, Anne Perkins. *Robert Goddard: Space Pioneer*.
Boston: Little, Brown, 1962.

Dianin, Serge. *Borodin*. London: Oxford UP, 1963.

Dickenson, Donna. *Emily Dickinson*. Dover, NH: Berg,
1985.

Egan, Eileen. *Such a Vision of the Street: Mother Teresa—
The Spirit and the Work*. Garden City, NY: Doubleday,
1985.

Ferguson, Kitty. *Stephen Hawking: Quest for a Theory of the Universe*. New York: Franklin Watts, 1991.

Ferlazzo, Paul J. *Emily Dickinson*. Boston: Twayne, 1975.

Flindell, E. Fred. "Paul Wittgenstein (1887-1961): Patron and Pianist." *The Music Review*. xxxii (1971), 107-124.

Fowler, Robert Booth. *Carrie Catt: Feminist Politician*. Boston: Northeastern UP, 1986.

Franz, Joe B. *Gail Borden: Dairyman to a Nation*. Norman: U of Oklahoma P, 1951.

Fry, Amelia R. "Alice Paul." *The Influence of Quaker Women on American History: Biographical Studies*. Lewiston: Edwin Mellen, 1986.

Gelderman, Carol. *Louis Auchincloss: A Writer's Life*. New York: Crown, 1993.

Georges-Michel, Michel. *From Renoir to Picasso*. Boston: Houghton Mifflin, 1957.

Goddard, Robert H. *Rocket Development*. New York: Prentice-Hall, 1948.

Goldring, Douglas. *Artist Quarter*. London: Faber and Faber, 1944.

Gould, Jean. *A Good Fight: The Story of F.D.R's Conquest of Polio*. New York: Dodd, Mead, 1960.

Gray, Charlotte. *Mother Teresa: Her Mission to Serve God by Caring for the Poor*. Milwaukee: Gareth Stevens, 1988.

Groves, George. *Dictionary of Music and Musicians, 5th Ed.* London: Macmillan, 1954.

Gunther, John. *Roosevelt in Retrospect: A Profile in History*. New York: Harper, 1950.

Hanson, Lawrence and Elizabeth. *Passionate Pilgrim: The Life of Vincent Van Gogh*. New York: Random House, 1955.

Hardwick, Elizabeth. *Herman Melville*. New York: Viking, 2000.

Harris, Victoria. "What's Happening." Brighton-Pittsford

(New York) *Post* 20 Jan. 1997.

Harvey, Trevor. "Paul Wittgenstein: A Personal Reminiscence." *The Gramophone.* xxxix (1961), 2.

Hawking, Stephen W. *Black Holes and Baby Universes and Other Essays.* New York: Bantam, 1993.

—. *A Brief History of Time: From the Big Bang to Black Holes.* New York: Bantam, 1988.

Hendrickson, Walter B., Jr. *Handbook for Space Travelers.* New York: Bobbs-Merrill, 1959.

Holden, Edward S. *Sir William Herschel: His Life and Works.* New York: Charles Scribner's Sons, 1881.

Honour, Alan. *Tormented Genius: The Struggles of Vincent Van Gogh.* New York: William Morrow, 1967.

Hoobler, Dorothy and Thomas. *Nelson and Winnie Mandela.* New York: Franklin Watts, 1987.

Hoskin, Michael A. *William Herschel and the Construction of the Heavens.* New York: Norton, 1963.

Howard, Leon. *Herman Melville.* Minneapolis: U of Minnesota P, 1961.

Hubbard, Elbert. *Elbert Hubbard's Scrap Book.* East Aurora, NY: Roycrofters, 1923.

Hulsker, Jan. *Vincent and Theo Van Gogh: A Dual Biography.* Ann Arbor: Fuller, 1990.

Irwin, Inez Hayes. *The Story of Alice Paul and the National Woman's Party.* Fairfax, VA: Denlinger's, 1977.

Jahoda, Gloria. *The Road to Samarkand: Frederick Delius and His Music.* New York: Charles Scribner's Sons, 1969.

Keller, Helen. *The Story of My Life.* New York: Airmont Books, 1965.

Laffitte, Sophie. *Chekhov 1860-1904.* New York: Charles Scribner's Sons, 1971.

Lawrence, Mortimer W. *The Rockets' Red Glare.* New York: Coward-McCann, 1960.

Lehman, Milton. *This High Man: The Life of Robert H.*

Goddard. New York: Farrar, Straus, 1963.

Le Joly, Edward. *Mother Teresa of Calcutta: A Biography.* San Francisco: Harper & Row, 1983.

Longsworth, Polly. *Emily Dickinson: Her Letter to the World.* New York: Thomas Y. Crowell, 1965.

Lubbock, Constance A. *The Herschel Chronicle: The Life-Story of William Herschel and His Sister Caroline Herschel.* New York: Macmillan, 1933.

Lunardini, Christine A. *From Equal Suffrage to Equal Rights: Alice Paul and the National Woman's Party, 1910-1928.* New York: New York UP, 1986.

Mandela, Nelson. *Long Walk To Freedom.* Boston: Little, Brown, 1994.

—. *The Struggle Is My Life.* New York: Pathfinder, 1986.

Meier-Graefe, Julius. *Vincent Van Gogh.* New York: Harcourt, Brace, 1933.

Meredith, Martin. *Nelson Mandela: A Biography.* New York: St. Martin's, 1997.

Mitchell, David. *The Fighting Pankhursts: A Study in Tenacity.* New York: Macmillan, 1967.

Modigliani, Jeanne. *Modigliani: Man and Myth.* New York: Orion, 1958.

Mumford, Lewis. *Herman Melville.* New York: Harcourt, Brace, 1929.

My Left Foot. Videocassette. Miramax Film, 1989. 103 min.

Neuharth, Al. *Confessions of an S. O. B.* New York: Doubleday, 1989.

Olsen, Victoria. *Emily Dickinson.* New York: Chelsea House, 1990.

Palmer, Christopher. *Delius: Portrait of a Cosmopolitan.* London: Duckworth, 1976.

Pankhurst, E. Sylvia. *The Life of Emmeline Pankhurst: The Suffragette Struggle for Women's Citizenship.* Boston: Houghton Mifflin, 1936.

Parsell, David B. *Louis Auchincloss.* Boston: Twayne, 1988.

Peck, Mary Gray. *Carrie Chapman Catt: A Biography*.
New York: H. W. Wilson, 1944.

Prichard, Peter S. *The Making of McPaper: The Inside Story of USA Today*. New York: St. Martin's, 1987.

Reinfeld, Fred. *The Great Dissenters: Guardians of Their Country's Laws and Liberties*. New York:
Thomas Y. Crowell, 1959.

Rettich, Alfred. Letter to Leopoldine Wittgenstein.
11 Nov. 1914.

Reynolds, Moira Davison. "Carrie Chapman Catt." *Women Champions of Human Rights: Eleven U.S. Leaders of the Twentieth Century*. London: McFarland, 1991.

Robbins, David. *Men of Honor*. New York: Onyx, 2000.

Robertson-Lorant, Laurie. *Melville: A Biography*. New York:
Clarkson Potter, 1996.

Rollins, Jr., Alfred B. *Roosevelt and Howe*. New York:
Knopf, 1962.

Scholes, Percy Alfred. *The Oxford Companion to Music, 10th Ed*. New York: Oxford UP, 1970.

Sebba, Anne. *Mother Teresa: Beyond the Image*. New York:
Doubleday, 1997.

Sherwood, Robert E. *Roosevelt and Hopkins: An Intimate History*. New York: Harper, 1948.

Sichel, Pierre. *Modigliani: A Biography*. New York:
E. P. Dutton, 1967.

Sidgwick, John Benson. *William Herschel, Explorer of the Heavens*. London: Faber and Faber, 1953.

Sime, James. *William Herschel and His Work*. New York:
Charles Scribner's Sons, 1900.

Small, Miriam Rossiter. *Oliver Wendell Holmes*. New York:
Twayne, 1962.

Stefoff, Rebecca. *Nelson Mandela: A Voice Set Free*.
New York: Fawcett Columbine, 1990.

Stillwell, Paul. *The Reminiscences of Master Chief Carl M. Brashear, U.S. Navy (Retired)*. Annapolis: U.S. Naval

Institute, 1998.

Stone, Geoffrey. *Melville*. New York: Sheed and Ward, 1949.

Stone, Irving. *Dear Theo*. Boston: Houghton Mifflin, 1937.

—. *Lust for Life*. New York: Grosset, Dunlap, 1934.

Sullivan, Wilson. *New England Men of Letters*. New York: Macmillan, 1972.

Sweetman. David. *Van Gogh: His Life and His Art*. New York: Crown, 1990.

Thoughts On the Business of Life. New York: Forbes, 1968.

Tilton, Eleanor M. *Amiable Autocrat: A Biography of Dr. Oliver Wendell Holmes*. New York: Henry Schuman, 1947.

Toumanova, Princess Nina Andronikova. *Anton Chekhov: The Voice of Twilight Russia*. New York: Columbia UP, 1937.

Untermeyer, Louis. *Makers of the Modern World*. New York: Simon & Schuster, 1955.

Vail, John. *Nelson and Winnie Mandela*. New York: Chelsea House, 1989.

Waite, Helen Elmira. *Valiant Companions: Helen Keller and Anne Sullivan Macy*. Philadelphia: Macrae Smith, 1959.

Warlock, Peter (Philip Heseltine). *Frederick Delius*. New York: Oxford UP, 1952.

White, Michael and John Gribben. *Stephen Hawking: A Life In Science*. Minneapolis: Dutton, 1992.

Whitman, Alden. "Triumph out of Tragedy." *New York Times* 2 Jun. 1968: 1, 76.

Wight, Frederick S. *Van Gogh*. New York: Beechurst, 1954.

INDEX